Mr. and Mrs. Charles Dickens

Entertain at Home

By the same Author

The Hostess Cookery Book (Angus & Robertson)

Pressure Cooking for the Modern Home (Whitcombe & Tombs)

Pressure Cookery (Odhams)

Time Saving Cooking (Odhams)

Traditional English Cooking (Angus & Robertson)

Food, Flowers and Wine (Odhams)

The Floral Art Book of Reference (Pergamon Press)

Mr. and Mrs. Charles Dickens

Entertain at Home

By HELEN COX

With *Dickens on Food* Selected by

STUART McHUGH

A GREAT GRANDDAUGHTER OF CHARLES DICKENS

PERGAMON GENERAL BOOKS

First edition 1970

Library of Congress Catalog Card No. 71–125985

Printed in Great Britain by A. Wheaton & Co., Exeter

08 007108 2

Occasions

The Menus

List of Illustrations

Mr. and Mrs. Charles Dickens

Entertain at Home

An Invitation into the Past

THE BOOK

It is a life of Mr. and Mrs. Charles Dickens told in a series of parties, or "Occasions", given in their own homes. With each is given the lists of distinguished guests, a Victorian Menu taken from Kate Dickens's book *What Shall We Have for Dinner?* and a matching one for use today. Recipes for carrying out both types of Menu follow each "Occasion". We begin with the first dinner party of their married life in 1836 and end with the completion of the book in 1852.

THE PLAN

This is a quartet theme, with a repetition of four pages right through to the end. The first page of the quartet gives the date of the party (sometimes approximately), the home at which it was given, the guests present, and the life story. The second and third pages are devoted to matching Menus and recipes and the fourth is an extract from Dickens's own works, chosen by his great granddaughter, Mrs. Stuart McHugh.

THE GUESTS

From the early days of the *Sketches* on to the novels and mounting fame, Dickens attracted to his circle men who themselves were destined for greatness. It was astonishing to find, during my researches, that the guest lists were made up almost exclusively of men who even today are remembered in the spheres of letters, art, medicine, philanthropy, theatre and politics.

Imagine the stimulating conversations that must have graced those dinners! So many brilliant minds sharpening their wits one upon the other. Perhaps some day, as science moves on to further wonders, we shall be able to rescue those Dickens *conversaziones* and listen to them on our radios! Roll on that day.

THE MENUS

Kate Dickens's book, *What Shall We Have For Dinner?* (brought to my notice by Mrs. McHugh), is mainly Menus, hundreds of them, all classified according to the numbers of guests. In the Victorian days, Menus were worked out in that way—the larger the party, the longer the Menu. Thus we have very short ones for 2–3 persons and prodigious ones, up to fourteen courses, for 18–20 persons.

THE RECIPES

Kate gave us very few recipes to accompany her Menus. Perhaps she thought that our cooks would know what to do with the rest. She would never have envisaged a time when an elegant hostess would do her own cooking. A little flower-arranging or needlework perhaps, but cooking, *never!* Why should she bother anyway, when servants could be had for a wage of £6 per year and a good cook for £20.

To make up for the omission, all the recipes for both Victorian and modern Menus have been included. All Kate's are there as well, together with a few typically Victorian ones, but the majority are for use today.

THE RECIPE INDEX

As all the recipes belong to their Menus and are not separated out into chapters, their existence depends entirely on the Index. This is fully classified so that any recipe may be found easily and quickly.

DICKENS ON FOOD

The fourth page of each quartet has been devoted to writings on food from Charles Dickens's own works together with the illustrations. Mrs. McHugh has chosen the passages and also supplied us with the charming and interesting pictures. Some are of family treasures that only she possesses. She has also plied me with extracts from the books of reminiscences written by Dickens's two elder children, Charley (her grandfather) and Mamie. Charley's book was called *Reminiscences of My Father* and Mamie's, *My Father as I Recall Him*. I was particularly glad to be able to use these, as they were irrefutable testimonies to Dickens as a compassionate family man. In spite of the tremendous demands made on his time and mind by his great creative powers and his philanthropic commitments, he was always deeply concerned for the well-being, happiness and progress of his family.

HELEN COX

Family Notes

The extracts on the subject of Food which I have edited are taken from twenty two of the books written by my Great grandfather, Charles Dickens in the hope that they may whet the appetite of readers to seek a larger portion from a feast of words.

During the benign Edwardian years my own childhood was steeped in Dickensiana and skilled reading aloud made the characters in his books utterly real, quotations Household Words.

My maternal Grandfather Charley and his sister Mamie both died in the year 1896, before I was born but in my Mother's (Beatrice Dickens) six sisters I was surrounded by warm hearted Aunts of diverse characters. The birth of the eldest, Mary Angela caused Charles Dickens to affirm that he was now "ancient and venerable" and he was called Venables by the grandchildren who followed. Aunt Mary as a baby announced herself as Miss Dickens which sounded like Me Ditty and became M'Kitty by which name she was known to the family. Of my one Dickens Uncle, Charley III I knew nothing except his feelings on the subject of a boiled egg which, he said "Is the watery horror of my heart". My own attitude to boiled eggs is entirely the same!

Among relations remembered from those far off days is my Mother's Godmother, Great great Aunty Georgina Hogarth, wrapped in fleecy shawls topped by frilly caps and looking exactly like John Tenniels illustrations of the Sheep in Alice through the Looking Glass. I still have the gold cross with our initials entwined which she gave me (see Picture). Great Aunt Kitty (Mrs Perugini) was most elegant yet slightly formidable. Great Uncle Henry (Sir Henry Fielding Dickens K.C.) as "Pupsey" and Great Aunt Marie as "Mumsey" were outside my sphere until later in my life.

We all loved Little Granny, a tiny woman, broken by the death of her husband Charley, love of his life since childhood. Her silver table napkin ring, engraved with her name Bessie and their wedding date 1861 (see Picture) I use every day.

The older I grow the more I find an absorbing interest in the life, times, and writings of my Great Grandfather and it is joy to even in a small way:

"Keep his Memory Green"

Ivy Cecil Stuart McHugh

Charles Dickens at age 27

The Bride and Bridegroom

Furnival's Inn, Early May 1836

CATHERINE and Charles Dickens were married on April 2nd, 1836 at the Chelsea Church of St. Luke's and afterwards spent a short honeymoon in the Kent village of Chalk.

Their best man was Thomas Beard, a young man Dickens had met when, in 1832, they were both reporters in the Gallery of the House of Commons. Beard was at that time on the staff of the *Morning Chronicle* and when Dickens, with the help of his Uncle Barrow, applied for the job of reporter there, Tom put in a good word for him, describing him as "the fastest and most accurate man in the Gallery". Dickens got the job.

At the time of his wedding, Dickens was 24 and already recognized as a writer of merit. His penetrating and entertaining *Sketches by Boz* were being eagerly read and had attracted the attention of editors and publishers. John Macrone, a young publisher of 3, St. James Square, had produced the *Sketches* in book form and it was the fee of £150 for the Edition that enabled Dickens to set a date for his wedding. The offer from Chapman & Hall (see p. 46) that launched the first great novel, bringing in a further £14 per month, was another incentive.

After the honeymoon they set up house in rooms at Furnival's Inn, Holborn. Dickens had been living there in bleak and sparsely furnished quarters known as the "three-pair-back", but for his bride he moved to rooms more suited to the exalted state of matrimony. Here Catherine, always called Kate, gave her first dinner parties and no doubt began to compile the menus and recipes that were to lead to the publication of her book, *What Shall We Have For Dinner?*

One of the first of the established literary set to offer friendship to the rising young writer was William Harrison Ainsworth, whose name still ranks with the famous in literature. He wrote thirty-nine novels. *Rookwood* appeared in 1843 and *The Tower of London* in 1840. He was said to be handsome, well dressed and much admired by the ladies! He had entertained Dickens several times at Kensal Lodge near the village of Willesden, so it was natural that the favour should be returned. Very soon after the wedding, he was invited to dine at Furnival's Inn and with him came John Macrone. The publication of a second series of *Sketches* was being contemplated, so no doubt the conversation dwelt on this project, with Ainsworth, seven years older than Dickens, giving mature advice.

A KATE DICKENS MENU	A MODERN MENU
(2–3 persons)	(4 or more people)
Fried Sole with Shrimp Sauce	*Fried Sole with Shrimp Sauce*
Haricot Mutton	*Savoury Lamb Casserole with Potatoes*
Mashed and Brown Potatoes	*Green Vegetable. Candied Carrots*
Tartlets	*Omelette Soufflé*
Omelette (p. 60)	*Biscuits and Cheeses*

Fried Sole
Serves 4

3 tablesp. oil, butter or margarine
4 fillets of sole
1 beaten egg with 1 tablesp. water
1 level teasp. salt and a little pepper
Crisp breadcrumbs
Parsley and lemon wedges

(1) Heat fat in frying-pan.
(2) Skin fillets, wash, then dry with kitchen paper.
(3) Put egg and water on a plate and add the seasoning. Dip fillets first in flour, then in the egg, then in the breadcrumbs.
(4) When fat is quite still with a faint white haze rising (about 375°F), fry fillets on both sides until a light golden brown.
(5) Serve on heated dish, garnished with parsley and lemon.

Shrimp Sauce. To ½ pint white sauce add 1 good teasp. tomato purée from a tube, 1 teasp. sugar, 1 tablesp. anchovy sauce and 4–6 oz. cooked prepared shrimps.

Savoury Lamb Casserole with Potatoes
Serves 4

4 or more lamb chump chops
1 level tablesp. butter or oil
2 peeled chopped onions
1½ level tablesp. flour
½ lb. peeled tomatoes
¼ pint (½ cup) water
1 chicken cube
2 teasp. sugar and salt and pepper to taste
8 sliced stuffed olives
Whole large potatoes

(1) Preheat oven to 300° or No. 2½.
(2) Trim a little fat from chops and snip edges to prevent curling.
(3) Sear either by grilling or frying. Grilling saves time and fat.
(4) Melt butter or oil. Add onions and fry for 2 minutes. Add flour and fry for another 2 minutes.
(5) Add all the other ingredients, except the potatoes and bring to the boil.
(6) If you are using a dual-purpose casserole, add chops. If not, put chops in ordinary casserole and pour gravy over.
(7) Arrange the potatoes on top. Cover with lid and bake for about 2 hours.

Candied Carrots
Serves 4

1 lb. carrots
2 tablesp. golden syrup
2 level tablesp. butter
Chopped mint

(1) If carrots are small, leave whole, otherwise slice in halves lengthwise. Boil in salted water until tender.
(2) In a pan melt the butter and syrup together.
(3) Add carrots and cook, turning frequently for about 10 minutes.
(4) Serve sprinkled with chopped mint.

Haricot Mutton (Victorian Recipe)
Serves 4

2 lb. scrag end of mutton
2 tablesp. butter
2 level tablesp. flour
1½ pints stock (or water with 2 pale
    meat cubes)
2 large onions
3 carrots and 3 turnips
Bouquet garni
Salt and pepper

(1) Trim some of the fat from the chops.
(2) Melt fat in large pan and add vegetables. Fry for a few minutes. Add flour and stir in.
(3) Add chops and sear for a few minutes.
(4) Add stock, bouquet garni and plenty of salt and pepper.
(5) Cover with lid and simmer gently for about 3 hours. Remove bouquet garni before serving.

Note. Lamb will need only about 1½–2 hours.

Omelette Soufflé
Serves 4

4 eggs, separated
2 level tablesp. sugar
2 level tablesp. flour
¼ teasp. salt
Jam
Whipped cream, with or without
    brandy

(1) Preheat oven to 350° or No. 4.
(2) Put pieces of butter or margarine papers on bottom of two 8-inch cake pans.
(3) Separate whites and yolks of eggs. To the yolks add the sugar and beat until smooth. Stir in the flour.
(4) Add salt to egg whites and whisk until very stiff. Fold into the mixture.
(5) Pour half mixture into each pan and bake for about 12 minutes.
(6) When cooked, turn out, put together with jam.

Serve with cream. If whipped with brandy, add 1 teasp. sugar and 1 or 2 tablesp. brandy to ¼ pint heavy cream.

Wedding Food

Dombey and Son

AFTER the death of his first wife and then of his son Paul, Mr. Dombey marries the icily cold beauty, Edith Skewton.

On the morning of the wedding there is a great stir and bustle in Mr. Dombey's house among the women; not one of whom has had a wink of sleep since four o'clock. Gorgeous are Mr. Dombey's new blue coat, fawn coloured pantaloons and lilac waistcoat and a whisper goes round that Mr. Dombey's hair is curled. In the Bride's dark house in Brook Street the pastry cook is hard at work and the hired, very tall young footmen are busy looking on. One of them already smells of sherry and his speech is hazy.

After the ceremony, the Bride enters the dark brown dining room composed, erect, resplendent and majestic, a glow upon her proud cheek, a flashing in her eyes. The pasty cook has done his duty like a man and a rich breakfast is set forth. When the company have breakfasted, the bloom of champagne is on every cheek.

The servants have been breakfasting too. Champagne has grown too common among them to be mentioned, and roast fowls, raised pies, and lobster salad have become mere drugs. The very tall young footman has recovered his spirits but his comrade's eye stares at objects without taking cognizance thereof. There is a general redness in the faces of the women and the whole party has become very frolicsome. Mr. Dombey's cook who generally takes the lead in society has said it is impossible to settle down after this and why not go to a play? The housemaid is turning hysterical when she and all the rest are roused by the intelligence that the Bride is going away and hurry upstairs to witness her departure.

Left alone Mrs. Skewton feels a little giddy from her strong emotions and falls asleep. Giddiness prevails below stairs too. The very tall young footman appears to have his head glued to the table in the pantry and cannot be detached from it. The Butler has a singing in his ears and a large wheel going round and round in his head. Everyone conceives that it ought to be at the earliest ten o'clock at night, whereas it is not yet three in the afternoon.

In the brown dining room, the hatchments look down on crumbs, dirty plates, spillings of wine, half thawed ice, stale discoloured heeltaps, scraps of lobster, drumsticks of fowls, and pensive jellies gradually resolving themselves into a luke warm gummy soup. The marriage is by this time, almost as denuded of its show and garnish as is the wedding breakfast.

A Musical Evening

Furnival's Inn, July 23rd, 1836

DICKENS had a strong affinity with the theatre and at the age of 20 made a serious attempt to be accepted as an actor. He wrote for an audition to Bartley, the stage manager at Covent Garden, and in his letter said that he believed he had a strong perception of character and oddity and a natural power of reproducing in his own person what he observed in others.

Poor Charles. On the day of his audition he was ill with a bad cold and inflamed and swollen face. He expected the setback to be only temporary, but by the time another audition was possible the success of his *Sketches* told him that his true vocation lay in writing.

As events proved, he would have become as successful in the theatre as in everything else he touched, but the world is richer for that swollen face and should give it thanks.

The theatre was not completely ignored. Indeed his fascination for it persisted all through his life and many of his friends were actors, theatre managers and musicians. He kept in touch as much as possible and spent an extraordinary amount of his time in play-writing, producing and acting.

Now, in 1836, his play *The Strange Gentleman* was in rehearsal at the new St. James's Theatre in London and he had just finished writing his operetta *The Village Coquettes*. He decided to try it out on "a few confidential friends, musical and literary" and his invitation to John Macrone reads: "I intend reading my opera and trying the music next Saturday evening at 7 o'clock. Mrs. Dickens desires me to say that if you will with Mrs. Macrone join the friends who wish to hear it she will be most happy to see you."

Among the "friends musical" would be John Hullah who had written the music for the operetta; Dickens's father-in-law, George Hogarth, theatrical and musical critic of the *Morning Chronicle*, and his sister Fanny who had studied at the Royal Academy of Music. On the "literary" side those whose opinions would have been valuable were Macrone, who eventually published the operetta, Tom Beard, Tom Mitton, an old school friend who became Dickens's Agent, and of course Harrison Ainsworth.

As this was an "evening" and not a dinner gathering, Kate would have served a typical Victorian supper.

A VICTORIAN HAND-AROUND SUPPER	MODERN BUFFET SUPPER
Oyster Patties (p. 195)	*Cheese Puff Patties*
Chicken Moulds in Savoury Jelly	*Chicken Moulds in Savoury Jelly*
Assorted Sandwiches	*Ham and Sweetcorn Salad*
Pressed Tongue with Salad	*Buttered Rolls and Crisp Bread*
Maids of Honour (p. 23)	*Jellied Apricot Ring with Fruit Salad*
Jellied Prunes	*Biscuits and Assorted Cheeses*

Cheese Puff Patties   *Makes 24*

1 lb. puff pastry
1½ oz. (2 level tablesp.) butter
½ pint (1 cup) milk
1 level teasp. salt, a little pepper, and ½ teasp. celery or onion salt
2 eggs, separated
4 oz. (1 cup) grated cheese

(1) Preheat oven to 400° or No. 6.
(2) Roll out pastry thinly and line 24 deep patty pans.
(3) Melt butter then add flour. Cook together for about 2 minutes without browning. Add milk gradually, whisking and cooking until thick and smooth.
(4) Stir in cheese and seasonings. Remove from heat and beat in egg yolks.
(5) Beat egg whites until very stiff. Fold into mixture.
(6) Fill lined pans almost full with the mixture. Bake for about 20 minutes.

Chicken Moulds in Savoury Jelly   *Makes about 22*

1 lb. minced cooked chicken
½ lb. minced ham
¼ pint cream or evaporated milk
1 pint packet of aspic jelly
2 tablesp. sherry
About 1 tablesp. chopped parsley
Salt and pepper to taste
Cooked green peas

(1) Dissolve aspic jelly in boiling water, using ¾ pint instead of 1 pint.
(2) Cover bottom of little moulds with peas.
(3) Put 3 tablesp. of the aspic in a cup and add 2 tablesp. water. Pour 1 teasp. of this over peas in each mould. Allow to set.
(4) Combine chicken, ham, cream, parsley, sherry and seasoning. Stir in the rest of the jelly.
(5) Spoon mixture over the set peas and put away until set.
(6) To unmould, dip each for a few seconds into hot water. Place each in a crisp little lettuce heart leaf.

Ham and Sweetcorn Salad   *Serves 10*

1 lb. can of sweetcorn, drained
½ lb. chopped ham
2 tablesp. chopped chives or
   spring onions
2 cups finely chopped celery
2 grated carrots
1 cup grated cheese (optional)
1 teasp. sugar and salt and
   pepper to taste
2 lettuces
Mayonnaise

(1) The salad bowl may be first rubbed with a cut clove of garlic.
(2) Combine all ingredients except lettuce.
(3) Sprinkle with sugar, salt and pepper.
(4) Remove outer leaves of lettuce and tear the tender ones into penny-size pieces. Toss with the rest of the salad.
(5) Serve with the mayonnaise.

Jellied Apricot Ring

1 29-oz. can of apricots in syrup
4 oz. sugar
Grated rind and juice of 1 large
   orange
2 level tablesp. cornflour
2 packets powdered gelatine
   (4 level dessertsp.)
¼ pint evaporated milk or fresh
   cream
2 eggs, separated
May be served with whipped cream
   into which apricot brandy has
   been added. To ¼ pint cream,
   allow 1 tablesp. brandy
See p. 172 for Fruit Salad.

(1) Have a 4-pint ring mould, or 2 smaller ones. Or ordinary jelly moulds could be used.
(2) Drain apricots. Measure syrup and, with orange, make up to 1 pint with water. Add sugar.
(3) Tip into saucepan and heat. Mix cornflour with 3 tablesp. water and stir in. Cook and stir until thick and smooth. Beat in yolks.
(4) Mix gelatine with 3 tablesp. cold water. Add to hot syrup and allow to dissolve. Add apricots, chopped.
(5) Tip in evaporated milk or cream. Put into a large bowl and put away until almost set.
(6) Beat egg whites until very stiff and fold in. Pour into mould and allow to set. Dip into hot water for a few seconds, then turn out. Put Fruit Salad in hollow and around dish.

Jellied Prunes

¾ lb. prunes
4 oz. brown sugar
1½ pints (3 cups) water
2 packets lemon jellies
¼ pint port wine or sherry
   (or extra water)
3 egg whites
½ pint whipped cream, with or
   without brandy

(1) Cook prunes with water and sugar until they are very soft.
(2) Drain liquid and make up to 1½ pints with water. Put into another saucepan and bring to the boil.
(3) Add the jellies and allow to dissolve. Add wine, sherry or water. Put away until beginning to thicken.
(4) Stone and chop prunes.
(5) Beat egg whites until dry and stiff. First stir prunes into half set jelly, then fold in beaten egg whites. Tip into serving dish and allow to set. Top with the cream.

Embarrassing Food

Bashful Young Gentleman from *Sketches of Young Gentlemen*

DICKENS wrote in the conclusion of this little book that his advice to young lady readers was to seek for a young gentleman combining the best qualities of all, the weakness of none and lead him forthwith to the altar.

The young gentleman was fresh-coloured, with as good a promise of light whisker as one might wish to see and possessed of a very velvet-like, soft-looking countenance. On his first appearance in the drawing room above stairs, his face was suffused with a crimson blush, and held the timid retiring look of a man ill at ease with himself. After making a desperate effort to get through the ceremony of introductions, he dived across the room and shrouded himself in some hangings until the eagle eye of the hostess detecting him, on the announcement of dinner, he was requested to pair off with a lively single lady of thirty three.

The young gentleman seated himself at table with evident misgivings and, turning sharp round to pay attention to his loquacious neighbour, overset his bread. There was nothing very bad in this, and if he had had the presence of mind to let it go, and say nothing, nobody but the man who laid the cloth would have been a bit wiser. But in various attempts to prevent its fall, he played with it a little as gentlemen in the streets may be seen to do with their hats on a windy day, and then giving the roll a smart tap in his anxiety, knocked it with great adroitness into a tureen of white soup at some distance to the unspeakable terror of an amiable, bald gentleman who was dispensing the contents.

We thought the bashful young gentleman would have gone off in an apoplectic fit from the violent rush of blood to his face. From this moment, in the phraseology of the "fancy", it was "all up" with him. Several benevolent persons endeavoured to relieve his embarrassment by taking wine with him, but it only augmented his sufferings. After mingling sherry, champagne, hock and moselle together, when he applied the greater part of the mixture externally instead of internally, he was left to the care of the talkative lady, who did not notice the wildness of his eye. He broke a glass or two in the course of the meal and disappeared shortly afterwards; it is inferred that he went away in some confusion, inasmuch as he left the house in another gentleman's coat and the footman's hat.

Holiday Dinner at Elm Lodge

Petersham, Early August 1836

As a rule the summer months saw Dickens and his family in some rented house either in the country, by the seaside or abroad. For the first August of his married life he took a house, Elm Lodge, in Petersham, Surrey, not far from Richmond. Kate was expecting her first child and was not very well so the escape from the dust and stench of Victorian London must have been welcome.

Evidently the peace and pure air of the country had the desired effect and Kate was soon well enough to entertain friends for dinners and week-ends. Two interesting men were one day bidden to dine. One was John Braham, famous tenor of St. James's Theatre, and the other J. P. Harley, stage manager there who with others already mentioned was to become a lifelong friend.

The *Village Coquettes* was again given an airing. Dickens hoped that it would follow *The Strange Gentleman*, now doing very well at St. James's and was anxious to get a decision. Both men were enthusiastic about it. Indeed Harley declared that it was "a sure card; nothing wrong there. Bet you it runs fifty nights." It ran for three months.

Rehearsals began later in the summer but in the early stages were disturbed by the objection of one of the actresses to the words, "well warmed to bed we go", which she thought indelicate. Dickens wrote tartly to Hullah and said, "If the young ladies are especially horrified at the bare notion of anybody's going to bed, I have no objection to substituting 'Around, old stories go . . .'. But you may respectfully signify to Cramers (the producer) that I will see them d——d before I make any further alteration." In the end the young ladies relented and the demned risqué passage remained. The play opened in December.

Six numbers of *Pickwick Papers* had by now been launched and their success brought sufficient credit on the young author to entice from London a man who would normally have expected writers to come a-begging to *him*. He was William Bentley, proprietor of an important literary magazine, *Bentley's Miscellany*. Over another of Kate's dinners at Elm Lodge he made Dickens a most flattering offer. It was to edit the magazine and also to contribute each month the instalments of a new novel. This visit must have paid Bentley handsomely. The novel was *Oliver Twist*.

A KATE DICKENS MENU	A MODERN MENU
(4–5 persons)	(4 or more people)
Carrot Soup (*p.* 115)	*Filled Avocados*
Filleted Sole à la Maître d'Hôtel	*Fried Sole with Maître d'Hôtel Sauce*
Roast Leg of Lamb (p. 19)	*Cold Roast Lamb*
Minced Collops (p. 83)	*Green Salad*
Salad	*Scalloped Potatoes*
Mashed and Brown Potatoes	
Cold Lemon Pudding (p. 152)	*Lemon Chiffon Pie*
	Biscuits and Cheeses
Toasted Cheese (p. 40)	

Filled Avocados   *Serves 6–7*

Allow ½ avocado per person
6 oz. crabmeat
1 medium-sized tomato, peeled
3 teasp. tarragon vinegar
1 teasp. Worcester sauce
1 teasp. sugar and salt and pepper
  to taste
Olives

(1) Combine crabmeat, tomato, vinegar, Worcester sauce, sugar and seasoning.
(2) Peel avocados, cut in halves and remove pits.
(3) Fill hollows with mixture, then garnish with halved stuffed olives, or stoned ripe ones.

Fried Sole with Maître d'Hôtel Sauce
(Kate Dickens's Recipe)   *Serves 6–7*

Recipe for Fried Sole on p. 7.
Maître d'hôtel sauce
8 tablesp. white sauce
4 tablesp. milk
3 oz. maître d'hôtel butter (below)
Note. Use the butter with Mackerel
  as well

(1) Put white sauce into pan with milk and boil 5 minutes.
(2) Stir in the maître d'hôtel butter. Stir quickly over fire until butter has melted, but do not let it boil. This sauce should be made at the time of serving.

Maître d'Hôtel Butter
(Kate Dickens's Recipe)

¼ lb. butter
Juice of 1 lemon
2 tablesp. chopped parsley
Salt and pepper to taste

(1) Put butter on a plate. (A warm plate would help.)
(2) Add lemon, parsley and seasoning. Mix well together and keep in a cool place for use.

Scalloped Potatoes

Serves 6

1½ lb. potatoes
2 oz. (2 tablesp.) butter
2 level tablesp. flour
½ pint milk
3 oz. grated onion if desired
Salt and pepper
A little more butter
Fine dry breadcrumbs

(1) Preheat oven to 350° or No. 4.
(2) Butter a deep ovenware dish.
(3) Peel potatoes and cut into thin slices, not more than ⅛ inch thick.
(4) Put one-third into dish, dot with one-third of the butter, sprinkle with one-third of the flour and a little salt and pepper. If you are using the grated onion, add that too.
(5) Repeat the layers until all ingredients have been used. Pour the milk over. Dot with butter.
(6) Cover with lid and bake for 1½ hours. After 1 hour, remove lid, sprinkle with fine dry breadcrumbs and continue baking until lightly browned.

Lemon Chiffon Pie

Serves 6

Crust
6 oz. (1½ cups) crushed biscuit or cookie crumbs, or Zwieback crumbs
3 oz. (3 rounded tablesp.) butter
1 level tablesp. sugar
½ teasp. vanilla essence

Filling
Grated rind and juice of 2 lemons
8 oz. (1 cup) sugar
1 level tablesp. cornflour
1 packet powdered gelatine
   (1 level tablesp.)
¼ pint (½ cup) cream or evaporated milk
2 eggs, separated
Cream

(1) Crush cookies and add melted butter, sugar and vanilla. Mix well until damp and crumbly. Press into an 8½- or 9-inch pie dish about 1½–2 inches deep. Press firmly and neatly. If edge is difficult to manage, leave it until it gets hard. Put away in refrigerator until firm.
(2) Put grated rind and juice of lemons and sugar into pan with ½ pint (1 cup) water. Heat.
(3) Mix cornflour with 2 tablesp. water and stir in. Cook and stir until thick.
(4) Mix gelatine with 2 tablesp. cold water and add. Allow to dissolve.
(5) Whisk in the yolks. Tip into a bowl and put away until beginning to set.
(6) Beat whites as stiffly as possible. Fold into the half-set jelly. Tip into the lined dish and allow to set.
   Top with whipped cream. It may be laced with brandy.

Kate Dickens at age 24

Fun at Furnival's Inn

Early September 1836

WHEN Kate and Charles returned to London from Petersham, they decided to invite Mary Hogarth, Kate's 16-year-old sister, to stay with them. For Kate, expecting her child in four months, it must have been a comfort to have a member of her family near—not only to keep her company when Charles was working, but also to help with the preparation of the layette.

For Charles, it seems, Mary's presence in the house added extra piquancy to his domestic life. It must have delighted him to find that underneath a demure and angelic exterior there shone a gaiety and wit that matched his own. In later and sadder years he recalled working "among merry banterings" and enjoying a "sympathy more precious than the applause of the whole world". Little did he realize how tragically brief those halcyon days were to be.

Mary's parents, Mr. and Mrs. George Hogarth, brought her that day to Furnival's Inn and stayed for a 5.30 dinner. With them came the youngest girl, Georgina, who, many years ahead, was to figure dramatically in the lives of Charles and Kate.

Dickens had been associated with George Hogarth since 1834 when they were both on the staff of the *Morning Chronicle*. Hogarth had liked the young man and admired the quality of his work and soon had invited him home to meet his family. At that time Charles was recovering from his unsuccessful wooing of Maria Beadnell, so his heart must have been ready to embrace another love. It found it, as we know, in Kate, the eldest of the Hogarth girls. Two years later, at the time of this family dinner, the Hogarths must have been pleased that they had not treated Dickens as the Beadnells had done and placed Kate beyond his reach. Perhaps, too, as the star continued to ascend, there could have been some remorseful nail-biting and gnashing of teeth in the Beadnell camp!

Charles's brother Fred, then 16, was another member of the household, so Charles began very early in his career paying for the bed and board of his and Kate's relations.

A KATE DICKENS MENU	A MODERN MENU
(6–7 persons)	*Chilled Consommé Julienne*
Scotch Broth	
	Roast Lamb
Fresh Herrings	*Onion and Tomato Scallop*
	New Potatoes. Peas
Roast Shoulder of Mutton	
Onion Sauce	
Curried Oysters	*Spanish Cream with Tipsy Jam*
	Fruit and Cheese Platter
Jam Roll Pudding (p. 176)	
Toasted Cheese (p. 40)	

Consommé Julienne, Chilled   *Serves 6–7*

2 pints stock with all fat removed or water plus 3 bouillon cubes, or canned consommé
2 finely chopped onions (5 oz.)
2 large carrots and 2 parsnips cut into match-like sticks
Bouquet garni
Brandy (optional)

(1) Add vegetables and bouquet garni to stock.
(2) Simmer, covered, until vegetables are tender.
(3) Chill in refrigerator.
(4) If desired 2 teasp. brandy may be added to each bowl just before serving.
The soup may also be served hot.

Scotch Broth (Kate Dickens's Recipe)

Set on the fire 4 oz. pearl barley with 3 Scotch pints (or 6 qt.) of salt water. When it boils skim it and add what quantity salt beef or fresh brisket you choose, and a marrow bone or a fowl, with a couple of pounds of either lean mutton and a good quantity of leeks, cabbages or savoys, or you may use turnips, onions and grated carrots. Keep it boiling for at least 4 or 5 hours, but if a fowl be used, let it not be put in until just time enough to bring it to the table when well done, for it must be served up separately.

Roast Lamb, any Joint (Oven or Spit)

Leg, loin or forequarter (this is excellent for 6–7 or more people)
1 tablesp. fat
If baked potatoes are needed, boil them in salted water first for 3–4 minutes. Bake with the meat at the low temperature for about 2–2½ hours.

(1) Preheat oven to 300° or No. 2½–3.
(2) Put meat into baking dish with fat. (Lots more will come from the meat.)
(3) Put meat into oven. Let it cook very slowly and silently for about 3½–4 hours for a 4 lb. or larger joint, and about 3 hours for 2½–3 lb. piece. Baste once after 1 hour. Slow cooking at a low temperature will make the meat succulent and full of flavour. On a spit keep temp. low as well, about 250° or No. 2.

Onion Sauce. Boil 2 peeled sliced onions in a little salted water until tender, flavouring with a bay leaf. In another saucepan melt 2 level tablesp. butter, then add 2 level tablesp. flour. Cook for 2 minutes then add $\frac{1}{4}$ pint milk and $\frac{1}{4}$ pint ($\frac{1}{2}$ cup each) onion liquid. Whisk until smooth and thick. Chopped parsley may be added.

Tomato and Onion Scallop   *Serves 6–7*

1 lb. tomatoes
3 teasp. sugar
$\frac{1}{2}$ lb. onions
$\frac{1}{2}$ teasp. basil
$\frac{1}{2}$ teasp. salt and a little pepper
2 tablesp. butter or margarine
4 oz. (2 cups) soft breadcrumbs

(1) Peel tomatoes. Either hold them on a fork over a gas flame for a few seconds, or pop into boiling water.
(2) Slice and put into deep ovenware dish. Add onions and stir in sugar, seasoning and basil.
(3) Melt butter and mix with breadcrumbs. Arrange on top. Bake for about 1 hour at medium heat.

Spanish Cream with Tipsy Jam   *Serves 6–7*

1 pint milk
1$\frac{1}{2}$ packets gelatine ($\frac{3}{4}$ oz.)
3 oz. (3 rounded tablesp.) sugar
3 eggs, separated
$\frac{1}{4}$ teasp. salt
1 tablesp. lemon juice
1 teasp. vanilla essence
8 tablesp. jam and 4 tablesp. sherry or brandy

(1) Heat milk in saucepan.
(2) Mix gelatine with 2 tablesp. water and stir in. Bring to the boil.
(3) Separate yolks and whites of eggs. Beat yolks with sugar. Add to milk. Again bring to boil. Remove from heat.
(4) Add salt, vanilla and lemon.
(5) Beat egg whites until as stiff as possible. Add to milk, etc. Do not stir too much or beat.
(6) Tip into mould and allow to set. To unmould dip into very hot water for a few seconds and turn out.
(7) Combine jam and sherry or brandy. Serve separately.

Curried Oysters
(or Chilled Oyster Cocktail)   *Serves 6*

18 oysters, bearded and halved
2 level tablesp. butter
2 level tablesp. flour
1 level tablesp. curry powder
2 teasp. lemon juice
1 level teasp. sugar
$\frac{1}{2}$ pint (1 cup) milk
Salt to taste

(1) Make sauce by first melting butter in saucepan, then adding flour and curry powder. Cook together for 2 minutes.
(2) Gradually add milk, whisking and cooking until thick and smooth. Add lemon juice, sugar and salt to taste. Remove from heat. Cover and chill.
(3) Put oysters into stemmed cocktail glasses and add a little sauce to each. Garnish with parsley and tiny wedges of lemon.

Food on Principle

The Posthumous Papers of the Pickwick Club

WHEN Mr. Pickwick was seized for debt and incarcerated in the Fleet Prison, his faithful servant Sam Weller insisted on sharing his fate. Nothing if not loquacious, Sam tells a story of an equally firm determination.

"I takes my determination on principle Sir," said Sam. "Which puts me in mind o' the man as killed his-self on principle. On principle he took dinner at the same place, occupying the best table for three hours and then to a coffee house a few streets off and have a pot o' coffee and four crumpets before bed. One night he took wery ill; sends for the doctor; doctor comes in a green fly with a kind o' Robinson Crusoe set o' steps to let down and be pulled up to perwent the coachman getting down in a Livery coat and not trousers to match.

" 'Wot have you been a eatin' on?' says the doctor. 'Roast weal,' says the patient. 'Wot's the last thing you dewoured?' says the doctor. 'Crumpets,' says the patient. 'I'll send you a box o' pills, and don't you never take no more of 'em.'

" 'Pills?' says the patient. 'No, crumpets,' says the Doctor. 'Wy?' says the patient, starting up in bed. 'I've eat four crumpets ev'ry night for fifteen years on principle. Crumpets is wholesome.' 'Crumpets is not wholesome, Sir,' says the Doctor, wery fierce. 'But so cheap,' says the patient, coming down a little. 'And so wery filling at the price.' 'They'd be dear to you at any price; dear if you wos paid to eat 'em. Four crumpets a night vill do your business in six months.'

" 'Are you sure o' that 'ere Sir?' 'I'll stake my professional reputation on it.' 'How many crumpets at a sitting do you think 'ud kill me off at once?' 'I don't know,' says the Doctor. 'Do you think half a crown's wurth 'ud do it?' 'I think it might.' 'Three shillings' wurth 'ud be sure to do it I s'pose?' 'Certainly,' says the Doctor. 'Wery good,' says the patient. 'Good night.'

"Next morning he gets up, has a fire lit, orders in three shillings' wurth o' crumpets, toasts 'em all, eats 'em all and blows his brains out. In support of his great principle that crumpets wos wholesome, and to show that he wouldn't be put out o' his way for nobody!"

A Victorian At-home Day

Doughty Street, 1836

WITH the birth of their baby on January 6th, the Furnival's Inn rooms became so full of fluttering female relatives and other essential aids to the Victorian confinement that Charles could find no corner in which to write in peace. There was only one solution. He would have to find a larger house. Taking Mary with him, he began a house-hunting spree and a few weeks later accepted a three-year lease for No. 48 Doughty Street, a tall terraced house of twelve rooms.

They moved in at the end of March and a few days later, on April 2nd, celebrated their first wedding anniversary. Probably because of the chaos that inevitably follows a move, the celebration dinner was held, not at their new home, but at an hotel, The Prince of Wales in Leicester Place.

No. 48, built in 1800, was part of a charming Georgian terrace and the street, of the type common in London at that time, was enclosed at each end with a gate. A watchman in livery was permanently on duty and saw that the gates were closed each night. It is now a through road, lined with parking meters, but although surrounded with main bus routes choked with traffic, it is still quiet and gracious and leads into a large leafy square. The house is now a Dickens Museum and home of the Fellowship.

The furniture from Furnival's Inn was far from adequate for the larger house, so for the shopping Charles again asked the help of Mary. Together they went around from shop to shop buying necessities and a few frills and soon the house was adequately furnished and Kate was ready to receive callers.

They came to welcome the newcomers to the neighbourhood and, as was the custom, merely knocked at the door and left cards with the maid. The next move was up to Kate and at a discreet interval she returned the favour. On the cards, apart from name and address, was the date of the monthly at-home day and all who had exchanged calls were free to visit each other on that day if and when they wished.

The card etiquette was strict. If husband tagged along, one card for Mr. and Mrs. or two separate cards for each would suffice. But let husband skip the visit and go about his manly business and another card would have to be left, making one for wife and two for husband. The second husbandly card was, of course, an apology for not being present. Since few husbands ever appeared at at-home days, the silver salvers on the hall tables soon became overflowing with cards and it was not until all the calls were returned that it could be emptied.

A VICTORIAN AT-HOME DAY	MODERN TEA-PARTY
Scones	*Cheese Scones*
Cucumber Sandwiches	*Asparagus Rolls*
Richmond Maids of Honour	*Richmond Maids of Honour*
Gateaux Napolitaine	*Golden Syrup Sponge with Rum Cream Filling*
Curates	*Curates*
Malt or Honey Sultana Cake	

Cheese Scones
Makes about 20

10 oz. (2 cups) S.R. flour
1 level teasp. baking powder
2 level teasp. salt
⅛ teasp. pepper and 1 teasp. sugar
2 oz. (2 tablesp.) butter
1 beaten egg and ¼ pint (½ cup) milk
4 oz. (1 cup) grated tasty cheese

(1) Preheat oven to 450° or No. 8.
(2) Sieve flour, baking powder, salt and pepper. Add sugar.
(3) Rub in the butter until mixture is crumbly. Add cheese.
(4) Combine beaten egg and milk. Save 2 teasp. for final brushing, and add the rest to the dry ingredients.
(5) Mix to a soft, not dry, dough.
(6) Pat out on to a floured board to 1-inch thickness. Cut into shapes.
(7) Place on floured oven tray. Brush tops with the egg and milk. Bake for 10 minutes.

Asparagus Rolls

Thin slices of fresh sandwich loaf, crusts removed
Butter
Mayonnaise
Asparagus tips

(1) Cut each slice in half cornerwise. Spread with butter.
(2) Cut tough ends from tips. Dip in mayonnaise.
(3) Place 1 tip on each piece of bread with the tip on the point. Fold the other 2 points over.

Richmond Maids of Honour
(Almond Darioles)
Makes about 24

1 lb. puff pastry
½ pint (1 cup) milk
2 eggs
2 oz. (2 rounded tablesp.) sugar
½ teasp. vanilla essence
½ teasp. almond essence
3 rounded tablesp. ground almonds
Red currant jelly and whipped cream

(1) Preheat oven to 400° or No. 6.
(2) Roll out pastry rather thinly, and cut into rounds with a 3-inch cutter.
(3) Line deep patty tins. Put a piece of crust in each and bake for 15 minutes. Remove crusts.
(4) Heat milk. Add beaten eggs, sugar, essences and almonds. While still hot, pour into shells.
(5) Bake for another 15 minutes.
(6) When cool, put 1 teasp. jelly and whipped cream on each.

Malt or Honey Sultana Cake

About 2¼ lb.

½ lb. butter or margarine
4 oz. (2 tablesp.) malt or honey
6 oz. (¾ cup) brown sugar
2 tablesp. boiling water
¾ lb. (2⅓ cups) S.R. flour
2 oz. (2 tablesp.) cornflour
½ teasp. salt
3 eggs
¾ lb. sultanas
1 teasp. cocoa and ½ teasp. ground
   cinnamon
½ teasp. each of vanilla, lemon and
   almond essence

(1) Preheat oven to 325° or No. 3. Line an 8-inch deep pan with butter or margarine papers.
(2) Put butter, honey or malt, boiling water and sugar into large mixing bowl. Cream until light and smooth, either with electric mixer or wooden spoon.
(3) Line pan.
(4) Sieve dry ingredients together. Add 1 tablesp. to the creamed mixture.
(5) Add eggs, one at a time, beating well between each addition.
(6) Add dry ingredients, fruit and essences. Mix well.
(7) Tip into pan. Make top even then make a slight depression in the centre. Bake for about 2 hours.

Golden Syrup Sponge

3 eggs
6 oz. (¾ cup) sugar
5 oz. (1 cup) S.R. flour
¼ teasp. salt
1½ oz. (2 level tablesp.) butter
2 oz. (1 level tablesp.) golden syrup
1 tablesp. water
Whipped cream flavoured with
   1 teasp. sugar and 1 tablesp.
   rum or brandy

(1) Preheat oven to 350° or No. 4. Butter sides of two 8-inch sandwich pans and cover bottom with two pieces of butter or margarine papers.
(2) Beat eggs and sugar until light and very thick. A good job for your electric mixer.
(3) Sieve dry ingredients together.
(4) Put butter, syrup and water into small saucepan and heat until butter has melted.
(5) Add flour and melted mixture alternately to egg and sugar. Stir as little as possible. Do not beat or you will break the bubbles.
(6) Pour into pans and bake for 20–25 minutes. To test, press one finger lightly on the cake. If it springs back it is done.
(7) Turn out and when cold fill with the cream. Dust top with icing sugar.

Curates (Eighteenth Century)

Makes 20

Sponge-mix or recipe for
   Queen cakes (p. 88)
20 small sugar cubes
3 tablesp. lemon juice

(1) Preheat oven to 350° or No. 4. Grease 20 patty pans.
(2) Put sugar cubes and lemon on a plate and let them become saturated.
(3) Fill pans two-thirds with cake mixture then put a sugar cube in the centre of each. Bake for 17–20 minutes.

Hypocritical Food

Martin Chuzzlewit

MARTIN is accepted into the home of that oily hypocrite Mr. Pecksniff and at once is shown around. With extra special graciousness he is taken to the "bower" of Pecksniff's two acidulated daughters, Charity and Mercy.

"Those," intoned Mr. Pecksniff, "who seek heartless splendour would seek here in vain, but plants you observe; books and birds." The latter by the by comprised in all one staggering old sparrow without a tail, borrowed from the kitchen. Back in the parlour the two Miss Pecksniffs and Tom Pinch were waiting with hospitable looks. There were two bottles of currant wine—red and white; a dish of sandwiches (very long and very slim) another of apples; another of ship's biscuits (which were always a moist and jovial sort of viand); a plate of oranges cut up small and gritty with powdered sugar and a highly geological home made cake.

"Martin," said Mr. Pecksniff, "between you my dears, Tom Pinch by me. Let us drink to our new inmate. Martin, my dear friend, my love to you; Mr. Pinch if you spare the bottle we shall quarrel," and trying to look as if the wine were not acid and made him wink, Mr. Pecksniff did honour to his own toast and took a Captain's biscuit. Tom Pinch, to assure himself that what he saw was not a dream, ate of everything and in particular the slim sandwiches. He attacked the bottle with such vigour that every time he filled his glass anew Miss Charity could not repress a fixed and stony stare as if her eyes had rested on a ghost. Mr. Pecksniff also became thoughtful at these moments, not to say dejected; but as he knew the vintage, it is very likely that he may have been speculating on the probable condition of Mr. Pinch tomorrow and discussing within himself the best remedies for colic.

The next evening Miss Charity set forth for Martin and Tom Pinch the fragments of yesterday's feast. Two chaotic heaps of last night's pleasure consisting of certain filmy bits of orange, some mummified sandwiches, various disrupted masses of the geological cake and several entire Captain's biscuits and choice liquor was not wanting. The remains of the two bottles of currant wine had been poured together and corked with a curl paper; so that every material was at hand for making quite a heavy night of it.

After the Tragedy—Forster's First Visit

Hampstead, Early June 1837

THE tragedy of May 7th that brought such anguish to the young couple smote them without warning and after a particularly happy evening at the theatre. Mary Hogarth, only 17 and now an even more precious member of the household, had a sudden choking seizure and sent out an anguished cry for help. Charles and Kate rushed to her bedroom and Fred was sent flying for a doctor. But it was no use. In the arms of an incredulous and trembling Charles, the young heart, deprived of air, ceased to beat and Mary was dead.

For Kate, expecting her second child, the shock and grief brought on a miscarriage. For Charles, that man of deep emotions and tenderness, it meant dark depths of sorrow that for many months was so acute that he was unable to continue his work and the following numbers of *Pickwick* and *Oliver Twist* were suspended. Indeed it remained embedded in his mind for the rest of his life and its projection into his novels gave us the deaths of Little Nell and Paul Dombey over which to wring our hearts and weep.

The tragedy had caused sorrow of equal intensity in the Hogarth household and Mrs. Hogarth lay for twenty-four hours insensible to everything around her. Poor Kate, herself ill after her miscarriage, had to give help to everyone, and for this Charles paid her a glowing tribute. "She has borne up through her severe trial like what she is," he said, "a fine-hearted noble-minded girl. . . ." The house was so impregnated with memories and sadness that they decided to escape to new surroundings. Charles rented a house, Collins Farm in Hampstead, for two weeks and here a new friend, John Forster, came to dine. He and Charles had met at the home of Harrison Ainsworth and had instantly taken a liking to each other. He was born in the same year as Dickens and when they met was attracting the same respect as a critic as was Dickens as a writer. Their remarkable friendship stretched right on through their lives, and between Dickens's death in 1870 and his own in 1876 Forster wrote the famous biography.

On that June evening another guest came with Forster. He was the artist Daniel Maclise who had known and loved Kate before her marriage and had been rejected for Charles. He, too, remained a lifelong friend and was a frequent guest at the Dickens' homes. After dinner they both listened with sympathy while Charles in endless reminiscences about Mary, poured out their great sorrow.

A KATE DICKENS MENU	MODERN LUNCHEON MENU
(4–5 persons)	*(4, 6 or more people)*
Asparagus Soup	*Asparagus Soup (Canned or Packet)*
Salmon Curry à la Soyer	*Salmon and Prawn Curry*
Cold Mutton. Minced Collops (p. 83)	*Saffron Rice*
Mashed Potatoes. Salad	*Green Salad or Green Vegetable*
Sweet Omelette (p. 8)	*Pineapple Mousse with Stuffed Peaches*
Broccoli au Gratin à la Soyer	*Grilled Stuffed Mushrooms*
Note. Soyer was a famous French chef whose recipes were very fashionable in Dickens's day.	*or*
	Biscuits and Cheeses

Asparagus Soup (Kate Dickens's Recipe)

Take 2 quarts of good beef or veal broth, put to it 4 onions, 2 or 3 turnips and some sweet herbs, with the whole part of 100 of young asparagus, but if very old or large at the stem, half that quantity will do, and let them all simmer until sufficiently tender to be rubbed through a tammy which is not an easy matter if they be not very young; then strain and season it. Have the boiled tops which have been cut from the stems, and add them to the soup.

Or poach $\frac{1}{2}$ dozen eggs rather hard, have ready 100 of asparagus heads boiled tender, boil 3 quarts of clear gravy soup, put into it for a minute or two a fowl just roasted, then add a few tarragon leaves, season with a little salt, put the eggs and asparagus heads quite hot into the tureen and pour the soup over them; the fowl will be just as good as before for made dishes.

Salmon and Prawn Curry with Saffron Rice   *Serves 5–6*

1 lb. salmon, poached or canned (or tuna fish)
$\frac{1}{2}$ lb. prawns, cooked
2 level tablesp. butter
1 small grated onion
2 level tablesp. flour
2 level teasp. curry powder
$\frac{3}{4}$ pt. (1$\frac{1}{2}$ cups) milk
Salt to taste
1 tablesp. lemon juice
1 teasp. sugar
Saffron rice (see over)

(1) Prepare salmon or tuna and prawns.
(2) Make Curry Sauce. First melt butter, then add onion. Fry without browning for 5 minutes. Prepare rice.
(3) Add flour and curry powder. Cook for 2 minutes.
(4) Gradually add milk. Whisk and cook until thick and smooth. Taste and add salt.
(5) Lastly add lemon juice and sugar.
(6) Flake salmon, or cut into cubes, add with the prawns just before serving. The sauce may be made the day before.

Saffron Rice

¾ lb. long grain rice
2 pints water
1 chicken cube
Salt and pepper
½ teasp. powdered saffron
1 tablesp. butter

(1) Put rice into large pan with water, chicken cube and saffron.
(2) Boil until rice is tender—about 15 minutes. Rice will absorb liquid.
(3) Toss with butter.

Salmon Curry à la Soyer
(Kate Dickens's Recipe)

2 slices of salmon weighing about 1 lb. each, cut into pieces about the size of a walnut. Cut up 2 medium onions and fry with 1 oz. butter, a clove of garlic and 1 teasp. curry powder and ½ teasp. curry paste. Add 1 pint broth, then add salmon and cook ½ an hour. Serve with rice.

Pineapple Mousse with Stuffed Peaches
Serves 5–6

Ingredients as for Jellied Apricot Ring (p. 12), but use pineapple instead of apricots.

Method as for Jellied Apricot Ring but the mixture may be tipped into a serving dish and allowed to set.
This will save the bother of turning out.

Stuffed Peaches

1 29-oz. can of peach halves
1 tablesp. cake crumbs for each half
4 tablesp. sherry
Maraschino cherries

(1) Drain peaches from syrup.
(2) Put cake crumbs in a bowl and mix with 4 tablesp. sherry. The mixture should be damp and crumbly, so add more sherry if necessary.
(3) Fill hollows of peaches with the mixture. Top each with a cherry. Add more sherry to the peach syrup and serve separately. Kirsch may be added to the whipped cream.

Grilled Stuffed Mushrooms

Choose large black mushrooms. Wash well. Fill centres either with 1 teasp. liver pâté, or Parmesan cheese and sprinkle with dry bread-crumbs. Grill until sizzley.

Broccoli Au Gratin

Broccoli
1 small grated onion
½ pint (1 cup) white sauce
3 or more oz. grated Parmesan cheese
Paprika

(1) Boil broccoli in salted water.
(2) When making white sauce add the grated onion and cook until soft. Season well.
(3) Drain broccoli, tip into serving dish. Pour sauce over and sprinkle generously with the cheese. A little paprika pepper makes a pretty finish.

Thieves' Food

Oliver Twist

Vicious Bill Sikes is recovering from his wound in his dismal hideout.

The housebreaker was lying in bed wrapped in his white greatcoat by way of a dressing gown and displaying a set of features in no degree improved by the cadaverous hue of illness and the addition of a soiled nightcap and a stiff black beard of a week's growth. His dog sat at the bedside, uttering a low growl as the Jew Fagin hurried in attended by his two young henchmen, Dawkins—known as the Artful Dodger, and Charley Bates. Sikes got out a few appropriate oaths and tried a little blasphemy. "What evil wind has blowed you here?" asked Sikes. "No evil wind my dear," replied Fagin. "For evil winds blow nobody any good, and I've brought some good things with me. Dodger my dear, open the bundle and give Bill the little trifles that we spent all our money on this morning."

Mr. John Dawkins untied the bundle which was formed of an old tablecloth, and handed out the articles one by one. "Sich a rabbit pie Bill," he exclaimed disclosing to view a huge pasty; "Sich delicate creatures with sich tender limbs Bill that the wery bones melt in your mouth and there's no occasion to pick 'em; half a pound of seven and sixpenny greens, so precious strong that if you was to mix it with biling water, it'll go nigh to blow the lid off the teapot; a pound and a half of moist sugar that the niggers didn't work at all afore it was got to sich a pitch of goodness——oh no! Two half quarter brans; pound of best fresh; piece of double Glo'ster and to wind up with, some of the richest lush you ever lushed!"

The Dodger at the same instant poured out a wineglassful of raw spirits from the bottle he carried which the invalid tossed down his throat without a moment's hesitation.

"Ah," said the Jew, rubbing his hands, "you'll do now Bill."

"I might have been done for twenty times afore you done anything to help you false hearted wagabond," exclaimed Mr. Sikes. "Takes no more notice of me all this mortal time than if I was this 'ere dog. Drive 'im down Charley."

"Smelling the grub like an old lady a going to market," cried Charley Bates as the dog retreated under the table. "I couldn't help leaving you. Upon my honour," said Fagin. "Upon your what?" growled Sikes. "Cut me off a piece of that pie to take the taste out of my mouth, or it'll choke me dead."

Portraits

Doughty Street, October 1837

TODAY our likenesses are mainly recorded by that impartial instrument the camera and whether it lies or not, has itself no personal axe to grind. The first photographs—Daguerre's invention, the daguerreotype—were produced in 1839, but for many years afterwards the preference for drawings and paintings persisted.

At Doughty Street George Cruikshank, Samuel Laurence and Daniel Maclise all did drawings and paintings of Dickens and his wife and the differences in interpretation indicates how completely at the mercy of the artist a sitter could be.

The drawing reproduced on p. 33 was done by Cruikshank in Dickens's study. Cruikshank was already established as a painter, caricaturist and illustrator and, although he illustrated works by other writers and painted some important pictures (one, *The Worship of Bacchus*, hangs in the National Gallery, London), he is chiefly remembered for his remarkable interpretations of many of Dickens's characters. He was twenty years older than Dickens and outlived him by eight.

The portrait by Maclise on p. 49 is considered to be the most accurate likeness.

The description of Dickens's appearance before he grew a moustache was given by his eldest son in his reminiscences: "It was impossible for a painter to quite catch the brightness and alertness of look and manner which distinguished the sitter in so remarkable degree," he said. "Later the beard and moustaches concealed that wonderfully expressive mouth, but in the days of which I speak the face was clean shaven and the firm yet mobile lips, as well as the keen and vivid light in those eloquent eyes assisted in conveying the ever changing expression, grave, gay, humorous or pathetic which were reflected in that singularly handsome face. Those who only knew him in later days have no idea of the delicacy and refinement which were almost as conspicuous as the force and power in the face of Charles Dickens of those days."

Leigh Hunt also gave a description of Dickens's face and said: "In his face was the quickness, keenness and practical power, the ever restless energetic outlook on each several feature which seemed to tell so little of a student or writer of books and so much of a man of action. Light and motion flashed from every part of his face and it has the life and soul in it of fifty human beings."

A KATE DICKENS MENU	*A MODERN MENU*
(4–5 persons)	(4 or more people)
Fried Whitings with Shrimp Sauce	*Crab and Grape Cocktail*
Roast Leg of Mutton with Oysters	*Duck en Casserole with Curaçao Orange Slices. French Beans*
French Beans. Potatoes	*Rice with Peppers*
Partridges	*Pears in Sherry with Coated Bananas*
Apple Pudding	*Biscuits and Cheeses*
Toasted Cheese (p. 40) Watercress	

Fried Whiting with Shrimp Sauce

3 tablesp. oil or butter
1 Whiting per person
A little flour
1 egg
Crisp breadcrumbs
Salt and pepper
Shrimp Sauce (p. 7)

(1) Heat fat in pan until quite still.
(2) Wash and dry fish and remove skin. Put tail into mouth and secure with small skewer.
(3) Dip in flour, then in beaten egg, then in breadcrumbs. Sprinkle with salt and pepper.
(4) Fry in the hot fat until browned. Serve with the Sauce.

Crab and Grape Cocktail   *Serves 4–5*

Lettuce
6 oz. crabmeat
Mayonnaise
Pitted white grapes
Mint or parsley sprigs

(1) Shred a little heart of lettuce finely and mix with mayonnaise. Fill cocktail glasses one-third with this.
(2) Top each with a little of the crabmeat then with about 1 teasp. of the mayonnaise.
(3) Stud with the grapes. Garnish with a tiny sprig of mint or parsley.

Roast Leg of Mutton with Oysters
(Kate Dickens's Recipe)

Parboil some well-fed oysters, take off the beards and horny parts, put to them some parsley, minced onions and sweet herbs boiled and chopped fine, and the yolks of 2 or 3 hard boiled eggs, mix all together, and make 5 or 6 holes in the fleshy part of a leg of mutton, and put in the mixture and dress it in either of the following ways; tie it up in a cloth and let it boil gently 2½ or 3 hours according to the size, or braise it, and serve it with a pungent brown sauce.

Duck en Casserole with Curaçao Sauce

Serves 4–5

About 4 lb. disjointed duck
1 level tablesp. flour and 2 level
   tablesp. packet celery soup
2 chopped onions
4 oz. mushrooms
$\frac{1}{4}$ pt. ($\frac{1}{2}$ cup) water
Juice of 1 orange
3 tablesp. curaçao
1 teasp. salt and a little pepper
1 teasp. dried basil
3 oranges
Maraschino cherries

(1) Preheat oven to 350° or No. 4.
(2) Heat fat in pan.
(3) Coat the joints in the dry mixture.
(4) Fry joints in fat until lightly browned and place in casserole dish.
(5) Fry onions and wash sliced mushrooms for 2 minutes, then add water, orange juice, curaçao, seasoning and basil. Stir well and when boiling pour over the duck joints.
(6) Cover and bake for $1\frac{1}{2}$–2 hours, or until duck is tender. Time will depend on age of duck. An older one will need as much as 3 or $3\frac{1}{2}$ hours. Reduce heat to 300° or No. $2\frac{1}{2}$ after 20 minutes.
(7) Peel and slice oranges and place on enamel plate. Heat through just before serving. Top each with a cherry.

Apple Pudding (Victorian Recipe)

Serves 6

This is really a mouth-watering
   Meringue Pie!
6 large cooking apples
8 oz. (1 cup) brown sugar
2 oz. butter
2 eggs, separated
1 lemon
1 lb. short pastry

(1) Wet the edge of a pie dish and line with strips of pastry 3 inches wide. Arrange a $\frac{3}{4}$-inch strip on rim and decorate with pinches and fork marks. Preheat oven to 425° or No. 5.
(2) Peel and slice apples, removing all core. Place in saucepan with the sugar and grated rind and juice of the lemon. Boil until soft.
(3) Remove from heat and add butter. Whisk in the yolks. Pour into the pie-dish. Bake for 20 minutes.
(4) Beat whites to a very stiff froth then fold in 4 rounded tablesp. sugar. Pile on top of apple. Return to oven and cook for about 20 minutes at a low heat, until meringue is crisp.

Pears in Sherry with Coated Bananas

Serves 6

$1\frac{1}{2}$ lb. pears or 1 large can
2 teasp. small sago
4 oz. ($\frac{1}{2}$ cup) sugar
5 tablesp. sherry
6 or more bananas
Milk, sugar, coconut

(1) If pears are fresh, cook with $\frac{1}{2}$ pint (1 cup) water and the sugar and sago. When tender lift on to a serving dish. Add sherry to syrup and pour into sauce-dish.
(2) If canned pears are used, cook the sago in the syrup until transparent.
(3) Peel bananas. Dip first in milk, sweetened with a little sugar, then in desiccated coconut. Arrange around the pears.

Pencil sketch of Dickens by George Cruikshank, 1838

After a Ride with Friends

Early November 1837

BY WAY of recreation after the long hours of writing, sometimes six to eight at a stretch, Dickens loved to mount a horse and take to the country roads out of London. Epping Forest, Richmond and Twickenham, Barnes Common, Hampstead Heath, Greenwich and Chiswick were some of the spots within one-horse power perimeter.

Usually one or more of his friends would accompany him and if they started out before lunch, would stop and eat at a roadside inn. Sometimes it was a "red hot chop" at Jack Straw's Castle on Hampstead Heath, "Mr. Codlin's" Stew at the Spaniard Inn, or eel-pie at Twickenham. Sometimes they would do a round trip. For instance, out through the Vale of Middlesex by Twyford Abbey and home by Harrow—or out through Acton's narrow high street, by orchard-bordered lanes to Chiswick and home to dinner by Shepherd's Bush and the Scrubs.

During those carefree years the men seldom bothered to change into riding gear, nor did they hire particularly noble beasts. This evidently amused the neighbours who, seeing them so indifferently mounted, laughingly called them "those Cockney riders". Not that they would have cared. They were young, gay, witty and intelligent and sufficient unto them was the glorious day ahead.

Sometimes Kate would drive out to join them. At first she had a small chaise with a pair of small ponies, but because of their disconcerting habit of "suddenly rushing up side streets or standing immovable at night beside ditches" the outfit had to be changed to something more suitable to a lady.

On that November day the three friends who rode with Dickens were Forster, Harrison Ainsworth and Thomas Noon Talfourd, later to become a judge and knighted. Like the other three he was a writer (though mainly of plays), but he is remembered particularly for his strenuous efforts to protect authors from plagiarism of their work. His Copyright Bill was eventually presented to Parliament, but was unsuccessful and was thrown out in October 1837. It was finally passed in 1842. Dickens had a great admiration and fondness for him and dedicated to him his *Pickwick Papers*.

The riders returned together to Doughty Street, no doubt all in good appetite and ready for one of Kate's hearty dinners.

A KATE DICKENS MENU	**MODERN MENU (DINNER)**
(6–7 persons)	(4 or more people)
Vegetable Soup	*Pâté Maison (or a bought French Pâté)*
Roast Fillet of Veal	*Stuffed Roast Fillet of Veal*
Boiled Knuckle of Ham	*Pears and Prunes*
Greens. Browned Potatoes	*Green Vegetable. Roasted Potatoes*
Apple Tart (p. 164) Custards (p. 202)	*Apple Snow. Caramel Custards (p. 202)*

Vegetable Soup   *Serves 4–6*

1 oz. (1 rounded tablesp.) butter or margarine
2 peeled, chopped onions (8 oz.)
2 level tablesp. packet celery soup
2 chicken or veal cubes
1 pint water
3 cups finely chopped mixed vegetables
Salt and pepper

(1) Melt fat in large pan. Add chopped onions and fry for 2 minutes.
(2) Add soup powder and water, then cubes, vegetables and seasoning.
(3) Bring to the boil, then simmer for about 1 hour, or until vegetables are soft.

Pâté Maison   *Serves 8*

1½ lb. calves or lambs liver, skinned
¾ lb. bacon rashers
½ lb. pork sausages
1 large Spanish onion
1 egg, beaten
¼ pint cream, white sauce or evaporated milk
1 teasp. salt, pepper, crushed clove of garlic (optional)
3 tablesp. brandy (optional)

(1) Cut liver into pieces and place in pan.
(2) Remove rinds from bacon and put 6 oz. of it with the liver.
(3) Add chopped onions and ¼ pint water. Simmer for 20 minutes.
(4) Drain liquid into a bowl. Mince all the cooked ingredients together. Tip into a large bowl. Add 4 tablesp. of the liquid and the salt and pepper. Mash in sausages.
(5) Mix in the cream, sauce or milk and beaten egg. Add garlic if desired. Stir well.
(6) Line a 2-lb. loaf pan with the rest of the bacon. Tip in the mixture and press down well. Cover with foil.
(7) Cook for 1¼ hours. Pour off liquid. If desired pour over 3 tablesp. brandy. Cool a little then turn out.

Stuffed Roasted Fillet of Veal with Pears

2½–3 lb. fillet of veal (thick end of leg) with a pocket for stuffing
3 tablesp. fat

Stuffing
3 oz. (1½ cups) soft breadcrumbs
1 good tablesp. prepared sage and onion stuffing (dry)
6 oz. prunes, cooked and stoned
2 oz. chopped walnuts
½ teasp. salt
3 teasp. butter

(1) Preheat oven to 350° or No. 4.
(2) Mix all ingredients for stuffing and mash in the butter. This is all the binding needed.
(3) Push stuffing into cavity and secure with thread or tiny skewers.
(4) Heat fat in meat dish in oven.
(5) Pour a little fat over the meat, then wrap it in foil. Put into baking tin and roast for 2 hours. Remove foil after 1¾ hours and test meat. Continue cooking uncovered until tender.

Roasted Potatoes. Peel and parboil potatoes for 3 minutes in salted water. Drain and arrange around the meat, turning once so that they are covered with the fat. Sprinkle them with salt and pepper. Roast with the meat.

Pears with Redcurrant Jelly. Heat halved cooked or canned pears. Place around the meat and fill centres with redcurrant jelly.

Apple Snow   *Serves 6–7*

1 large can of apple-sauce or stewed apple, concentrated (1¼ pints)
The rind and juice of 2 lemons
¾ lb. sugar (if canned apple is unsweetened) or to taste
2 level tablesp. small sago and ½ teasp. salt
1 packet powdered gelatine (½ oz.)
The whites of 3 eggs
Cream or brandy cream (p. 40)

(1) Tip apple and sugar into saucepan. Add lemon rind and juice, sago and salt.
(2) Simmer for 20 minutes until sago has disappeared.
(3) Mix gelatine with 2 tablesp. cold water, allow to dissolve in the apple mixture. Cool to lukewarm.
(4) Whisk egg whites until so stiff they will not fall from the bowl if it is turned upside down. Fold into the apple. Tip into serving dish. Serve with cream.

Dining House Food

Bleak House

MR. GUPPY of the legal firm of Kenge and Carboy, Lincoln's Inn, is about to go out for midday dinner with his Junior Mr. Smallweed, and his friend Mr. Jobling, a market gardener from Deptford. They are both his guests.

Accordingly they betake themselves to a neighbouring dining-house known by its frequenters by the denomination of Slap Bang. Unaffected by the seductive show in the window of artificially whitened cauliflowers and poultry, verdant baskets of peas, coolly blooming cucumbers and joints ready for the spit, Smallweed leads the way to his favourite box. He is well known. It is no use trying him with anything less than a full sized 'bread' and in the matter of gravy he is adamant. He orders veal and ham and fresh beans for three, adding, "and don't forget the stuffing Polly". Three pint pots of half and half are superadded.

Amidst a general flush of steam of hot joints the legal triumvirate appease their appetites. Jobling makes such a speedy end of his plate of veal and ham bringing it to a close before the others are mid-way in theirs that Mr. Guppy proposes another. "Thank you Guppy," says Mr. Jobling, "I really don't know, but what I will take another." "Will you take any other vegetable? Grass? Peas? Summer cabbage?" "Thank you Guppy. I will take Summer cabbage." Order given; with the sarcastic addition from Mr. Smallweed of, "without slugs". Cabbage produced. Jobling getting over the ground in excellent style.

"Now Smallweed," says Mr. Guppy. "What would you recommend about pastry?" "Marrow puddings," says Mr. Smallweed instantly. Three marrow puddings are produced and to these succeed, "Three Cheshires", and to those, "Three small rums." This apex of the entertainment happily reached, Mr. Jobling puts his legs up on the carpeted seat (having his own side of the box to himself) and leans back. "What am I to do? How am I to live? Ill fo manger you know," says Mr. Jobling pronouncing that word as if he meant a necessary fixture in an English stable. "I'll pay," says Mr. Guppy. "What will it be?" Smallweed instantly replies; "Four veal and hams is three, and four potatoes is three and four, and one summer cabbage is three and six, and three marrows is four and six, and six breads is five, three Cheshires is five and three, and four small rums is eight and three, and three Pollys is eight and six. Eight and six is half a sovereign and eighteenpence out."

The First Christening Party

December 9th, 1837

CHARLES Dickens Junior had been given three names, Charles Culliford Boz. Culliford was a Dickens family name and Boz the amusing *nom de plume* Dickens gave himself when he first submitted his *Sketches* to a London editor. It was a cold-in-the-dose rendering of Mose, short for Moses, the pet name of his young brother Augustus, and taken from one of his favourite works, *The Vicar of Wakefield*. One wonders what Kate thought of it and whether she would have preferred for the third name something representing her own side of the family—George, for instance, after her father, or her own maiden name of Hogarth. But, in those days, still forty-five years before the Married Women's Property Act (1882), the husband was not only completely in possession of all his wife's property and money but also of all decisions regarding the children —names included.

The baby's godmother was a young lady of great wealth, Angela Burdett-Coutts, whose father was the radical reformer, Sir Francis Burdett, and mother the daughter of Sir Thomas Coutts, founder of the Bank that still has its branches in London. Dickens met her at the home of Edward Majoribanks and from the beginning a lifelong friendship was born. The 280 letters from Dickens to Miss Burdett-Coutts, collected and edited by Edgar Johnson, reveal the friendship as totally platonic, based on their mutual concern for the less fortunate in the community, notably girls who because of poverty and homelessness had to live by prostitution. Miss Burdett-Coutts had the money and the will to use it compassionately—Dickens had the drive and imagination to channel it into causes of the greatest need. Their fine work was done without publicity and it was many years before it became known. In 1871 Miss Coutts was elevated to the peerage and became the Baroness Burdett-Coutts. She outlived Dickens by thirty-six years.

The christening took place at the New St. Pancras Church and afterwards there was a party at Doughty Street. Besides the two families and godmother, the guests included the William Halls, Edward Chapman and Mr. and Mrs. S. C. Hall, an early editor of the *New Monthly*. At an evening party the other friends bidden were John Forster, John Ross (an uncle by marriage), Tom Mitton and Mr. and Mrs. Tom Beard.

(8–10 persons)

Scotch Mutton Broth

Roast Goose
Mutton Curry Rice
Cold Pigeon Pie (p. 164)
Salad
Broccoli.   Mashed Potatoes

Eve's Pudding

Toasted Cheese.   Watercress

A MODERN MENU

French Onion Soup

Roast Goose with Raisin and Orange Stuffing
Green Vegetable.   Roasted Potatoes
Side Salads (p. 201)

Mother Eve's Pudding, Modern Recipe

Biscuits and Cheeses

French Onion Soup

Serves 10

2 oz. (2 tablesp.) butter
1 lb. onions, peeled and chopped
1 oz. (2 level tablesp.) flour
3 pints stock, or water plus
  3 chicken or veal cubes
2 level teasp. of salt and a little
  pepper
Grated cheese
Paprika pepper

(1) Melt butter in large pan.
(2) Add onions and fry for 3 minutes browning lightly. Add flour and fry for another 2 minutes.
(3) Pour in stock or water with cubes.
(4) Bring slowly to the boil stirring well. Add seasoning. Add more salt if necessary.
(5) Cook until onions are soft.
(6) Pour into heated bowls and sprinkle with grated cheese and paprika pepper. Traditionally the soup is poured on to toasted bread, but for a dinner party this would be too filling.

Roast Goose with Raisin and Orange Stuffing

1 goose, usually 8–10 lb.

Stuffing
5 oz. (2½ cups) soft breadcrumbs
1 level teasp. salt and a little pepper
1 small can mandarin orange
  segments, drained
3 oz. stoned raisins
1 small chopped onion
1 teasp. dried sage
3 teasp. butter

(1) Preheat oven to 325° or No. 3.
(2) Make stuffing: combine breadcrumbs, salt and pepper, orange segments, raisins, onion and sage. Mash in the butter.
(3) Fill goose cavity, sew up and secure with tiny skewers. Sprinkle with salt and pepper.
(4) Cover bird with foil, but leave part of underneath so that fat can run out. Goose is a very fat bird!
(5) Roast for 3½–4 hours, slowly. Now and again pour off fat. Reduce heat to 300° or No. 2½ after 1 hour.
(6) Remove foil after 2½ hours and allow bird to brown.

Serve with Orange Sauce (p. 116)

Eve's Pudding (Kate Dickens's Recipe)

Mix together $\frac{1}{2}$ lb. breadcrumbs, $\frac{1}{2}$ lb. chopped apples, $\frac{1}{2}$ lb. currants, $\frac{1}{2}$ lb. suet, 6 oz. sugar, 4 beaten eggs, nutmeg and 2 oz. citron and lemon peel. Butter a mould. Boil for 3 hours.

Note. In those days, this would have been covered with a cloth and tied with string. Now we can cover securely with foil. The water should reach only half-way up the pudding basin during boiling. Add more water if necessary. It should be boiling.

Mother Eve's Pudding

Serves 10

This is an old English recipe, too, but a little different from Kate's.

4 eggs
1$\frac{1}{2}$ lb. apples
10 oz. (1$\frac{1}{4}$ cups) sugar
4 oz. (2 cups) soft breadcrumbs
Grated rind and juice of 2 lemons
2 oz. butter
A little nutmeg

Brandy Cream
To $\frac{1}{4}$ pint whipped cream add 1 level teasp. sugar and 1–2 tablesp. brandy

(1) Preheat oven to 350° or No. 4.
(2) Have an 8$\frac{1}{2}$-inch deep ovenware dish. Melt the butter in this in oven. Do not allow to brown.
(3) Break eggs into a bowl and add sugar. Beat until thick and foamy.
(4) Peel apples and chop finely. Add to egg mixture. Add lemon and breadcrumbs. Remove dish from oven, pour melted butter into mixture.
(5) Tip into dish and dust with nutmeg. Bake for about 45 minutes.

Serve with Brandy Cream. If the pudding is served cold the Cream could be piled on top.

Toasted Cheese (Victorian Recipe)

6 oz. Gloucester cheese
1 beaten egg
2 oz. (1 cup) soft breadcrumbs
1 teasp. made mustard
1 level teasp. salt
A little pepper and a few grains of cayenne
3 tablesp. beer
Slices of bread

(1) Heat griller.
(2) Combine all ingredients.
(3) Toast bread on both sides and remove crusts. Spread with butter, then with some of the mixture.
(4) Put under grill and toast until sizzling.

Garnish with parsley.
A simple Toasted Cheese may be made by merely putting the grated cheese on to the buttered toast, sprinkling with salt and pepper and grilling until melted.

Housekeeper's Food

Hard Times

MRS. SPARSIT, housekeeper to Mr. Bounderby the Banker, considered herself as some sort of Bank Fairy. But the townspeople, who saw her every day at the window of her afternoon apartment, preferred to think of her as the Bank Dragon!

Mrs. Sparsit's tea was just set for her on a pert little table with its tripod legs in an attitude and the light porter placed the tea tray on it, knuckling his forehead as a form of homage. "And what," said Mrs. Sparsit, pouring out her tea, "is the news of the restless wretches of the town today?" "Still uniting and leaguring and engaging to stand by one another," returned Bitzer, a clear headed, cautious, coldly calculating young man. Having satisfied himself on his Father's death that his Mother had a right of settlement in Coketown, this excellent young economist had asserted that right for her with such steadfast adherence that she had been shut up in the Workhouse ever since, and he held the respectable office of general spy and informer.

"We are constantly hearing from the restless wretches ma'am concerning their wives and families, till it becomes quite nauseous. I don't want a wife and family ma'am, why should they?" "Because they are improvident," returned Mrs. Sparsit, her nose becoming more Roman and her eyebrows more Coriolanian in severity. "If they were more provident, and less perverse, they would say while my hat covers my family I have only one to feed, and that's the person I most like to feed." "To be sure," assented Mrs. Sparsit, eating a muffin. "Is there anything else that I could fetch you ma'am?" "Nothing just now," Mrs. Sparsit answered, brushing away crumbs. "Thank you ma'am, I shouldn't wish to disturb you at your meals ma'am, particularly tea knowing your partiality for it, but there's a gentleman has come across the road as if he were going to knock." Mrs. Sparsit, wiping her mouth and adjusting her mittens said, "If it is part of my duty to Mr. Bounderby, I will see him."

Mrs. Sparsit took the precaution of concealing her little table with all its appliances upon it in a cupboard and decamped upstairs that she might reappear in the Board room in the manner of a Roman matron going outside the city wall to treat with an invading general.

Gruesome Visits, then Home to Dinner

Doughty Street, April 30th, 1837

THESE visits were made, with friends, to the Coldbath Fields House of Correction and Newgate Prison. We know that Dickens's concern for the poor and downtrodden extended also to the plight of prisoners incarcerated in conditions so deplorable that they seemed deprived of all humanity. In this he was supported by his friend-in-philanthropy, Angela Burdett-Coutts. Coldbath Fields especially interested her. Her father, from whom she had inherited her radical beliefs had, a generation before, brought furious wrath down upon himself for daring to expose the treatment of inmates there. So the visit could have been part of their joint campaign.

On the way home the men visited Newgate Prison, an even more gruesome place. Opposite was a pillory, a whipping post and gallows, where hangings were still held in public. This was a practice Dickens abhorred. He was certain that people who watched the horrible spectacle were debased by it and that crime was thus increased. In spite of his persistent efforts it was many years before hangings were removed behind the prison walls, but undoubtedly London was a more wholesome city as a result. Newgate ceased to function in 1880 and was later demolished. In its place stands the Central Criminal Court, Old Bailey, E.C.4.

The four who accompanied Dickens were William Macready, the top actor of the day and another of Mr. and Mrs. Dickens's lifelong friends, John Forster, George Cattermole, painter and illustrator who did drawings for *The Old Curiosity Shop* and *Barnaby Rudge* (and also Scott's *Waverley Novels*), and Halbot Browne, better known as "Phiz", the artist who was as successful as Cruikshank in plucking from Dickens's novels the exact images as seen in their creator's mind.

After the visits they returned to Doughty Street for dinner. Four other guests had been invited—J. P. Harley, Kate's parents and Mr. G. L. Banks, brother-in-law of the artist Daniel Maclise.

At this time Dickens was writing both *The Pickwick Papers* and *Oliver Twist*, submitting them alternately once a fortnight. In September *Pickwick* was finished and on the 18th Dickens gave the first of the famous book dinners. It was held at the Prince of Wales Hotel in Leicester Street with Thomas Talfourd as the guest of honour. A set of ladles, each one depicting a character in *Pickwick*, was designed by Cruikshank and presented to Dickens at the dinner by Chapman & Hall. They may be seen at the Dickens Museum at 48 Doughty Street, London.

A KATE DICKENS MENU	*A MODERN MENU*
(8–10 persons)	(4 or more people)
Giblet Soup	*Giblet Soup*
Baked and Stuffed Haddocks (*p.* 199)	*Sole Véronique*
Roast Haunch of Mutton *Stewed Onions. Brown Potatoes* *Roast Pheasant* (*p.* 200)	*Pheasant en Casserole* *Sauté Potatoes. Cauliflower with* *Asparagus Sauce*
Pound Pudding (*p.* 200)	*Quick Pear Meringue*

Giblet Soup   *Serves 8–10*

Giblets from the two pheasants
1 tablesp. butter or oil
2 level tablesp. flour
2 large onions, peeled and chopped
6 sticks of celery
2 rashers of bacon
2½ pints water with 2 chicken cubes
Bouquet garni
Salt and pepper to taste

(1) Melt fat in large saucepan.
(2) Cut up the giblets and add. Add chopped onion, then flour. Fry all together for about 4 minutes.
(3) Add celery, chopped bacon, water, cubes, bouquet garni and plenty of salt and pepper.
(4) Stir well and bring to simmering point.
(5) Simmer, covered, for about 1–1½ hours.
(6) Strain and mash through as much of the vegetable as possible. Reheat and serve.

Sole Véronique   *Serves 8*

2½ lb. skinned and filleted sole
¾ lb. white grapes, pitted
1½ level tablesp. butter
1½ level tablesp. flour
¼ pint milk and ¼ pint white wine
1 bay leaf
Salt and pepper

(1) Poach fish in covered pan, adding ¼ cup water or wine, 1 bay leaf and salt and pepper. Poach for about 15 minutes.
(2) Pit the grapes.
(3) Melt the butter, then stir in flour and cook together without browning for 2 minutes.
(4) First whisk in the milk and when thick add the wine. Season well with salt and pepper.
(5) Lift fish into ovenproof dish. Tip fish liquid into sauce. Cover fish with the sauce, then sprinkle with the grapes. Garnish with chopped parsley. Cover and keep warm in oven.

Pheasant en Casserole

Serves 8

2 fat pheasants
1 cup cooked rice
2 teasp. butter
6 oz. washed sliced mushrooms
1 small finely chopped onion
½ teasp. basil
Salt and freshly ground pepper
4 tablesp. oil or butter
1 large chopped onion
6 sticks celery, chopped
1½ level tablesp. flour
¼ pint (½ cup) water and ½ pint (1 cup) red wine
1 level teasp. salt and a little freshly ground pepper

(1) Preheat oven to 300° or No. 3.
(2) Have the birds well cleaned.
(3) Fry mushrooms and small onion in the butter for 5 minutes then combine with the rice, basil and seasoning.
(4) Fill cavities with this stuffing. Truss both birds.
(5) Put chopped onion and celery in a large casserole. Sprinkle with salt and pepper.
(6) Heat the 4 tablesp. oil or butter then brown the two birds all over. Lift them on to the vegetables.
(7) Tip away all but 1 tablesp. of the hot fat. Add the flour and fry until browned. Stir in the water, wine and more seasoning. Cook and stir until thickened a little. Pour around the birds.
(8) Cover with lid and cook in oven for 1½ hours or longer. Make sure that birds are really tender.

Cauliflower with Asparagus Sauce

1 large cauliflower
Salted water
1 can asparagus soup
Chopped parsley

(1) Cook cauliflower in salted water until tender, but not squashy.
(2) Drain and lift into vegetable dish.
(3) Heat soup and pour over. Sprinkle with chopped parsley.

Quick Pear Meringue

Serves 10–12

2 cans (each 29 oz.) pears
2 cans (each 1 lb.) creamed rice
⅓ pint pale sherry
4 eggs, separated
4 good tablesp. chocolate chips or bits
7 good tablesp. castor sugar for meringue

(1) Open cans of pears and drain syrup away well. Put pears into 1 large or 2 smaller deep ovenproof dishes.
(2) Open cans of rice, tip into bowl and add sherry. Drop in unbeaten egg yolks and whisk until well blended.
(3) Spread on top of pears. Sprinkle with the chocolate.
(4) Whisk whites of eggs until dry stiff. Gently fold in the sugar, a little at a time, so that the egg white remains stiff. Pile on top of rice and rough into peaks. Bake in slow oven, 225° or No. 1½ for about 25 minutes, or until meringue is crisp on the outside.

Prison Food

Little Dorrit

IN A villainous prison in Marseilles languished two men. One was a Frenchman, Monsieur Rigaud, the other an Italian, John Baptist Cavalletto.

A prison taint was on everything. The imprisoned air; the imprisoned light, the imprisoned damp, the imprisoned men were all deteriorated by confinement. Like a well, like a vault, like a tomb, the prison had no knowledge of the brightness outside; and would have kept its polluted atmosphere intact, on one of the spice islands of the Indian Ocean.

The prison keeper appeared saying to his little daughter, "She shall feed the Birds." "This loaf is for Signor John Baptist. We must break it to get it through into the cage. This sausage in a vine leaf is for Monsieur Rigaud. Again this veal in savoury jelly is for M. Rigaud. Again these three little white loaves, again this strachino cheese, again this wine, again this tobacco, all for M. Rigaud, Lucky bird!"

Perhaps Cavalletto glanced at the Lyons sausage, perhaps he glanced at the veal in savoury jelly, but they were not long there to make his mouth water. M. Rigaud soon dispatched them and proceeded to suck his fingers clean as he could and to wipe them on his vine leaves; "How do you find the bread?" "A little dry, but I have my old sauce here," returned John Baptist, holding up his knife. "How sauce?" "I can cut my bread, so, like a melon. Or so, like an omelette. Or so, like a fried fish. Or so, like a Lyons sausage," said John Baptist demonstrating cuts.

"Here!" cried M. Rigaud. "You may drink. You may finish this." It was no great gift, for there was mighty little wine left; but Signor Cavalletto received the bottle gratefully, turned it upside down in his mouth and smacked his lips. Rigaud was now rolling his tobacco into cigarettes by the aid of little squares of paper which had been brought with it. "Here! You may have one." "A thousand thanks," said John Baptist, and sat down on the pavement holding one of his ankles in each hand and smoking peacefully.

The jailer turned his basket upside down to beat out the crumbs and said; "I have expended all the money I received; here's a note of it. Adieu my birds." "Adieu my poor birds," added the pretty child.

Chapman & Hall are Entertained

Doughty Street, January 28th, 1838

IN A letter to Forster inviting him to this dinner Dickens writes: "Little Hall and his wife and big partner are going to dine here on Saturday next at half past five . . . the illustrious George (Cruikshank) and his stout lady are coming too. . . ." The "Little Hall and big partner" were of course Chapman & Hall, the firm that for many years were to be Dickens's publishers and friends.

They had a shop in the Strand, No. 186, and it was from there that Dickens, back in 1833, had bought the *Monthly Magazine* in which he hoped to see his first anonymous *Sketch* in print. To his delight there it was! *A Dinner in Poplar*, published! Describing his ecstasy he confesses that he found difficulty in mastering his emotion and keeping back the tears of joy as he walked into Westminster Hall on his way to the Gallery. Such success tempted him to try again and soon he had submitted six more articles to the same magazine. All were printed. Two years later he was destined again to encounter Chapman & Hall, but this time not as a youth trembling with anxiety, but a man confident in his ability and vocation. William Hall called at Furnival's Inn with an offer. It was to write a series of linked sketches of a sporting nature, each to appear as a monthly number at 1*s*. each with a fee for him of £14 per month. Dickens gladly accepted and thus was born *The Pickwick Papers*. At the time of this 1838 dinner the Papers had been published in book form and was still selling in enormous numbers.

In another part of the above letter, Dickens had said: "I start on my pilgrimage to the cheap schools of Yorkshire (a mighty secret) next Monday morning. . . ." Reports had reached him that there were still schools where cruelty, neglect and starvation were perpetuated and he decided to make a first-hand investigation. Taking his friend Halbot Browne (the illustrator "Phiz") he set off for Yorkshire on January 30th. Even before they reached the school their suspicions were confirmed. Mr. Barnes, the Attorney of Barnard Castle to whom they had had a letter of introduction revealed the truth. "It would be better," he said, "to let them run errands, hold horses or fling themselves in any way upon the mercy of the world than consign them to such dens." They saw the schools and as a result Dickens returned at once to London and began his first number of *Nicholas Nickleby*. On February 9th it was finished and was published in April. Thereafter the numbers continued until October 1839.

A KATE DICKENS MENU

(8–10 persons)

Barley Broth
(see Scotch Broth, p. 19)

Fried Whiting with Shrimp Sauce
(p. 31)

Lobster Patties

Stewed Kidneys

Roast Saddle of Mutton
(see Roast Lamb, p. 19)
Boiled Turkey
Knuckle of Ham
Mashed and Brown Potatoes

Swiss Pudding

A MODERN MENU

Lobster Stuffed Tomatoes

Braised Kidneys

Roast Saddle of Lamb (see Roast Lamb, p. 19)
Roasted Potatoes.   Peas.   Candied Carrots (p. 8)

Chocolate Mousse
or
Stuffed Peaches (p. 128)

Lobster-stuffed Tomatoes

Serves 8

4 large tomatoes or 8 smaller ones
8 oz. flaked lobster
4 tablesp. mayonnaise
4 good tablesp. chopped gherkins
2 teasp. sugar and salt and freshly
   ground pepper to taste
Lettuce

(1) Cut tomatoes in half crosswise. Scoop out flesh and seeds. To get a serrated edge to the tomatoes, cut with a sharp pointed knife a zig-zag around the circumference, then pull apart.
(2) Combine lobster, mayonnaise, gherkins and a little of the tomato flesh. Season with the sugar, salt and pepper.
(3) Fill tomato halves and garnish each with a tiny sprig of parsley.
(4) Place each in a cupped lettuce leaf.

Lobster Patties

Makes 24

24 puff pastry patties
   (from the pastrycook)
1 lb. flaked lobster
½ pint parsley sauce (pkt. or
   home-made)
1 tablesp. anchovy
4 oz. cooked shrimps for garnish.
   Also sprigs of parsley

(1) Combine the lobster, sauce and anchovy Taste and add seasoning.
(2) Fill cases. Garnish each with a shrimp and heat well.
(3) Top each with a sprig of parsley.

Braised Kidneys
Serves 8

½ lb. streaky bacon
16 lamb's kidneys
2 medium-sized onions (8 oz.)
Flour
½ pint water with 1 chicken cube
1 level teasp. mixed mustard,
    1 teasp. sugar and salt and pepper
    to taste
4 tablesp. sherry (or extra water)
Parsley

(1) Remove rinds from bacon. Cut in halves and roll up. Fry until cooked and fat has run out. Remove to an ovenproof plate and keep warm.
(2) To the bacon fat, add the chopped onions and fry for 3 minutes.
(3) Remove skin and fatty tissue from kidneys and roll in flour. Fry with the onions until lightly browned.
(4) Add water, cube, and seasonings. Bring to simmering point. Cover and simmer for about 30 minutes or until kidneys are tender. Pressure-cooking time: 10 minutes at 15 lb. pressure.
(5) Add sherry. Serve garnished with bacon rolls and sprigs of parsley.

Chocolate Mousse
Serves 10

8 oz. dark cooking chocolate
8 oz. (1 cup) sugar
2 pints (4 cups) milk
1 level teasp. salt
3 level tablesp. cornflour
4 eggs, separated
2 packets powdered gelatine
    (2 level tablesp.)
2 teasp. vanilla essence
2 oz. finely chopped walnuts
Whipped cream sweetened with a
    little sugar and laced with brandy

(1) Put 1 pint of the milk into a pan. Add sugar and chocolate, broken roughly into pieces. Heat.
(2) Mix cornflour with 2 tablesp. cold water and stir in. Stir and cook until thickened. Add salt.
(3) Separate egg yolks and whites. Whisk yolks into sauce. Cook for just 1 minute. Remove from heat. Add vanilla.
(4) Mix gelatine with 2 tablesp. cold water. Add to sauce and allow to dissolve. Pour into bowl and put away until almost set.
(5) Whisk whites until dry stiff and fold into the half set mixture. Pour into serving dish or dishes, and when set sprinkle with chopped walnuts. Serve with the cream

Swiss Pudding (Kate Dickens's Recipe)

Butter your dish, lay in it a layer of breadcrumbs grated very fine, then boil 4 or 5 apples very tender, add a little butter, nutmeg and fine sifted sugar. Mix up all together and lay on the breadcrumbs, then add pieces of fresh butter on the top, and bake in a slow oven for ¼ hour until it becomes a delicate brown. It may be eaten hot or cold.

Charles, Kate and Georgina by Maclise

Summer Guests Destined for Fame

4 Ailsa Park Villas, Twickenham, June 1838

ALTHOUGH Dickens was destined to meet an enormous number of people during his brilliant career, friends made in the early days remained close through all the triumphs and vicissitudes of the ascending years. He was interested in people from all walks of life, but found it impossible to accommodate all the admirers who sought his friendship. Man-like he gave Kate the unenviable task of keeping them at bay and this she did with commendable tact. Writing to Forster he confessed, "I thank God most heartily for having given me a quiet spirit, and a heart that won't hold many people."

On March 6th of this year a daughter was born to Charles and Kate. She was christened Mary Angela in memory of Kate's young sister who died so tragically in May of the previous year, but was always called Mamie. Again Charles decided that good country air would benefit them, so for June and July he took a cottage at Twickenham and for August one at Broadstairs.

At both places Kate and Charles entertained generously and at this dinner all four guests were destined for fame. They were John Forster, Daniel Maclise, William Makepeace Thackeray and Douglas Jerrold. Thackeray, one year older than Dickens, had been a contender, after the death by suicide of the artist Robert Seymour, for the job of illustrator of *The Pickwick Papers*, but lost to Halbot Browne, the very successful "Phiz". As a novelist, particularly as the author of *Vanity Fair*, *Pendennis*, and *The Newcombes*, he was to find fame almost as great as Dickens himself. He died in 1853 at the age of 52.

Douglas Jerrold was another writer whose name is listed amongst the famous Victorians. He was the author of over seventy plays and many novels, some of which appeared serially in *Punch*. Two of his plays were *Rent Day* and *Black-Eyed Susan*, and his best known novel was *Mrs. Caudle's Curtain Lectures*. He was nine years older than Dickens and died in 1857, aged 54.

Maclise, too, was moving towards fame. He had recently been elected A.R.A. and was soon to be chosen as one of the artists invited to decorate the new House of Lords. Forster described him as a man full of Irish charm, wit and humour and wrote: "A greater enjoyment than the fellowship of Maclise at this period it would indeed be difficult to imagine."

A KATE DICKENS MENU

(8–10 persons)

Vermicelli Soup
Oxtail Soup

Turbot and Smelts (p. 196). Soles
Cod's Head.   Stewed Eels

Fricassee of Chicken
Oyster Patties (p. 195)
Stewed Kidneys (p. 48)
Sweetbreads
Two Boiled Fowls.   Ham
Saddle of Mutton
Three Woodcocks.   Hare
Two Wild Ducks
Mashed Potatoes.   Broccoli

Apple Tart (p. 164) Orange Fritters
Charlotte Russe
Italian Cream (p. 120)
Macaroni (p. 104)
Toasted Cheese (p. 40)

A MODERN MENU

(For a large dinner party)

Oxtail Soup with Vermicelli
Asparagus Hollandaise

Crumbed Sweetbreads with Bacon

Coq au Vin
Creamed Potatoes.   Broccoli.   Beans

Charlotte Russe
Apple and Orange Tart (p. 164)

Toasted Cheese (p. 40)
or
Biscuits and Cheeses

Quick Oxtail Soup with Vermicelli   *Serves 10*

2 packets oxtail soup
3½ pints water
1 cup uncooked vermicelli
2 teasp. sugar
3–4 tablesp. brandy (optional)

(1) Put soup powder, sugar and water into large pan. Add vermicelli.
(2) Bring to the boil, then simmer for about 15 minutes or until vermicelli has softened.

Just before serving, add the brandy.

Asparagus Hollandaise   *Serves 10*

2 lb. asparagus, either from a can
or cooked

Hollandaise Sauce
4 oz. butter
3 eggs
1 tablesp. lemon juice
1 teasp. sugar
3 tablesp. water
¼ teasp. salt

(1) Cook asparagus, if fresh, and not canned, first removing tough ends.
(2) *Make Sauce:* have a double-boiler and in the bottom part put water and allow to come to the boil.
(3) In the top part, put butter, chopped into pieces, beaten eggs, lemon juice, water and seasoning.
(4) While water boils underneath, cook and whisk sauce until thick. Remove from heat and continue beating for another minute.
(5) Put warm spears on individual plates and spoon a little sauce on the side of each.

Coq au Vin
Serves 8–10

5 lb. disjointed chicken
Flour
½ lb. streaky bacon rashers
1 large Spanish onion, finely chopped
  (about 10 oz.)
½ lb. mushrooms
1 clove garlic (optional)
¼ pint water
½ pint red wine or cooking sherry
Bouquet garni
Salt and freshly ground pepper

(1) Preheat oven to 300° or No. 2½–3.
(2) Remove rinds from bacon. Cut into 2-inch pieces and begin to fry in frypan.
(3) Skin chicken joints and coat well with flour. Peel and chop onions and wash and slice mushrooms.
(4) When bacon has cooked and a lot of fat has run out, lift out with a slotted spoon on to a plate.
(5) Have bacon fat very hot, then fry the chicken joints until lightly browned all over. Place them in casserole dish. Add bacon.
(6) Add onions and mushrooms to fat left in pan and fry for 2 minutes. Add 1 teasp. flour and cook for another minute.
(7) Add crushed garlic if desired, then stir in the water, wine, bouquet garni and seasoning.
(8) Bring to the boil and pour over the chicken. Cover with lid and bake slowly for about 1½ hours or until chicken is very tender. Remove bouquet garni.

Crumbed Sweetbreads with Bacon
Serves 8

½ lb. bacon rashers
1 lb. blanched and ready prepared
  sweetbreads
1 beaten egg with 3 tablesp. water
Crisp breadcrumbs
Salt and pepper

(1) Fry rashers.
(2) Cut sweetbreads into ¾-inch slices.
(3) Add 1 level teasp. salt and a little pepper and water to beaten egg.
(4) Dip sweetbreads into this, then into breadcrumbs.
(5) When bacon is cooked and fat has run out, lift it on to a plate and keep warm.
(6) Fry sweetbreads in the bacon fat until lightly browned on both sides. Serve with the bacon.

Charlotte Russe
Serves 6

Sponge fingers
Sherry
1 cup mashed fruit
  (fresh or canned)
Sugar to taste (make it sweet)
½ pint (1 cup) evaporated milk or
  cream
1 level tablesp. powdered gelatine
2 egg whites

(1) Line a spring-form mould (or bottomless cake tin placed on a flat dish) with lady fingers standing up all around. Sprinkle with sherry.
(2) Heat fruit and stir in gelatine.
(3) Add to cream or evaporated milk and whisk well. Set to the wobbly stage.
(4) Whisk egg whites until very stiff and fold in. Pour into mould. When set lift off mould. Decorate.

Schoolboy's Food

The Life and Adventures of Nicholas Nickleby

NICHOLAS had accepted the post of junior master at Mr. Squeer's school, Dotheboy's Hall and on his way he met, at the Saracen's Head, Snow Hill, Mr. Squeers and some of his unfortunate pupils. They had arranged to travel together the rest of the way to Yorkshire. But first they had to have breakfast.

Nicholas found Mr. Squeers sitting at breakfast with five little boys. Mr. Squeers had before him a small measure of coffee, a plate of hot toast and a cold round of beef, but was intent on preparing breakfast for the little boys.

"This is twopenn'orth of milk is it waiter?" said Mr. Squeers looking down into a large blue mug and slanting it gently so as to get an accurate view of the quantity of liquid contained in it. "That's two penn'orth Sir." "Fill that mug up with luke warm water." "To the wery top Sir? Why the milk will be drowned."

"Never mind that. Conquer your passions boys and don't be eager after vittles." Mr. Squeers took a large bite out of the cold beef. "Sit down Mr. Nickleby," he said. "Here we are a breakfasting you see." Nicholas bowed and looked as cheerful as he could. "Oh that's the milk and water waiter? Don't forget the thick bread and butter for three." At this the five little boys looked very eager and followed the waiter with their eyes.

"When I say Number one," said Squeers with his mouth full of beef and toast, putting the blue mug before the children, "the boy on the left nearest the window may take a drink and when I say Two the boy next him, and so on. Subdue your appetites my dears. Number one may take a drink." Number one seized the mug ravenously and had just drunk enough to make him wish for more when Mr. Squeers gave the signal for number two until the milk and water terminated with number five.

Dividing the bread and butter for three into as many portions as there were children, Squeers said; "You had better look sharp with your breakfast for the horn will blow in a minute or two and every boy leaves off." The boys began to eat voraciously and in desperate haste. In a short time the coach horn was heard. Jumping up, Squeers produced a small basket. "Put what you have not had time to eat in here boys. You'll want it on the road," he said.

Nicholas was considerably startled by these economical arrangements.

A Christmas Dinner

Doughty Street, December 1838

THIS was the second and last Christmas spent at Doughty Street. The next was celebrated at their new home in Devonshire Terrace near Regent's Park and Marylebone Road.

It is a dinner worth recording as it shows that Dickens was as aware as the rest of us of the danger that might lurk around the corner if some superstitions were flouted. Charley, then just under 2 years old, writes in later life: "I am not at all sure that the first recollection of my father is not more derived from tradition than actual memory. Indeed, as I had at the time attained the ripe age of two or thereabouts, I suppose it must have been so. But I seem to remember very well one Christmas Day dinner at Doughty Street when, owing to the non-appearance of one of the guests the party consisted of thirteen and I was brought down from the nursery to fill the gap and afterwards set on a footstool on the table close to my father at dessert time. It was one of his few superstitions, by the by, this thirteen at the table."

All through their married life Kate and Charles looked on Christmas as a very important family occasion. Kate always had the table looking bright and pretty and the food presented in the best Christmas tradition. The pudding had its own special dish of coloured "repoussé" china ornamented with holly and it came in with the brandy alight and flaming. Charles always did his best to make Christmas a season of generosity and gaiety and later, as we know, he exhorted all Scrooges to open their hearts and their purses.

It is difficult for us today to realize that Christmas cards were not exchanged until after 1846 and then only amongst a few and that Christmas Day was a lone holiday with everyone back at work on the 26th. Boxing Day was the time for opening the "alms-boxes" either in churches or other places and distributing the contents to the poor and needy. There would be no Christmas tree, either, twinkling in the front window or standing gaily bedecked in a corner. Such an idea was at that time quite unknown and it was not until after 1840 when the German Prince Albert married the young Victoria that it was introduced by him into England. This is borne out by Dickens's descriptions of Christmas in his works. His decorations are always confined to holly and ivy and he had to make the most of the brightness of the berries to create the right festive atmosphere.

A Victorian Christmas Dinner

As Kate Dickens has not given us a menu for her Christmas dinners, we have to assume that she thought it too traditional and cut-and-dried to record.

Giblet Soup (p. 43)

Turbot with Lobster Sauce

Roasted Turkey with Boiled Ham, Bread Sauce and Cranberry Sauce

Christmas Pudding with Brandy Sauce

Assorted Nuts, Olives, Crystallized Fruits, Mints

Turbot with Lobster Sauce
Serves 6

2 lb. turbot
1 small grated onion
1 bay leaf
3 tablesp. white wine or pale sherry
1 level teasp. salt and a little pepper

Sauce
6 oz. flaked lobster
$\frac{1}{4}$ pint cream of tomato soup
$\frac{1}{4}$ pint fresh cream
2 level teasp. sugar
1 tablesp. anchovy sauce
1 level teasp. salt and a little pepper

(1) Preheat oven to 350° or No. 4.
(2) Cut turbot into portions and place in ovenproof dish.
(3) Sprinkle with the onion, pour the wine over and add bayleaf. Sprinkle with salt and pepper.
(4) Cover with lid and bake for about 20–25 minutes.
(5) For the sauce, combine all ingredients and heat through. Do not allow to boil.
(6) Tip fish liquor into sauce. Serve a little with each fish portion. Garnish with parsley.

Stuffing for Turkey

Sausage and Chestnut Stuffing. Combine $\frac{1}{2}$ lb. chestnuts (weighed after cooking and shelling) with 1 lb. sausage meat. Add 1 finely chopped onion, 1 tablesp. chopped parsley, 1 teasp. thyme, 2 level teasp. sugar, 1 level teasp. salt and a dash of pepper.

Prune and Walnut Stuffing. Combine $\frac{1}{2}$ lb. cooked, stoned, chopped prunes with 4 oz. chopped walnuts and 2 cups (4 oz.) soft bread-crumbs. Add 1 teasp. basil, 1 teasp. salt and 2 teasp. sugar.

Bread Sauce

Put $1\frac{1}{2}$ cups cubes of bread into a small pan. Add $\frac{1}{2}$ grated onion, 2 whole cloves, 1 cup milk, $\frac{1}{2}$ teasp. salt and a little pepper. Cook gently for 5 minutes. Remove cloves.

Stuffed Roasted Turkey

1 turkey, size to your own choice
Two types of stuffing for cavities
  (*see previous page*)
6 rashers of streaky bacon
Fat
Foil

(1) Preheat oven to 350° or No. 4.
(2) Make stuffings and fill both cavities. Secure with thread. Truss.
(3) Arrange rashers over breast, and wrap completely in foil.
(4) Put into baking dish with 2 tablesp. fat and $\frac{1}{4}$ cup water.
(5) Allow the following times: 10–12-lb. turkey, 30 minutes to the lb. 13–16 lb. 25 minutes to the lb. and a larger turkey 18 minutes to the lb. This is for slow cooking, reducing heat to 300° or No. $2\frac{1}{2}$ after 1 hour.
(6) Half an hour before cooking time is up, remove foil and bacon and allow bird to brown.

Christmas Pudding
Serves 10–12

2 lb. mixed dried fruit
$\frac{1}{4}$ lb. blanched sliced almonds
12 oz. ($2\frac{1}{3}$ cups) S.R. flour
4 oz. (2 cups) soft dry breadcrumbs
$\frac{1}{2}$ lb. prepared suet
6 oz. ($\frac{3}{4}$ cup) brown sugar
5 eggs
Juice of 1 large orange
1 tablesp. golden syrup
1 teasp. mixed spice and $\frac{1}{2}$ teasp. ground nutmeg
1 teasp. each vanilla and almond essences
3 tablesp. brandy

(1) Combine fruits and almonds.
(2) Sieve flour into bowl and add breadcrumbs, suet, salt, brown sugar and spices.
(3) Grease one large or two smaller pudding bowls.
(4) Beat eggs and add to them the orange juice and syrup.
(5) Stir this mixture into dry ingredients, then add fruits, essences and brandy.
(6) Let everyone have a stir for luck then put into bowl or bowls.
(7) Have a large saucepan (or saucepans) one-third filled with boiling water.
(8) Cover pudding with greaseproof paper then tightly with foil. Put into water and boil, covered with lid, for about 6 hours. Add a little more boiling water when necessary. Quantity will make one 4 lb. or two 2 lb. puddings.

Brandy Sauce. Make your usual white sauce and to each $\frac{1}{2}$ pint add 1 beaten egg, 1 level tablesp. sugar and an extra 2 teasp. butter. Stir in 2 tablesp. brandy.

Family Food

A Christmas Carol

THE Ghost of Christmas Present wafts Ebenezer Scrooge to the home of his clerk Bob Cratchett who pockets but fifteen copies of his name per week.

Tiny Tim on his active little crutch was escorted by the two young Cratchetts to his stool beside the fire while Bob, turning up his cuffs, as if poor fellow they were capable of being made more shabby, compounded some hot mixture in a jug with gin and lemons. Master Peter and the ubiquitous young Cratchetts went to fetch the goose from the bakers. You might have thought a goose a feathered phenomenon to which a black swan was a matter of course, and in truth it was something very like it in that household. Mrs. Cratchett made the gravy (ready beforehand in a little saucepan) hissing hot. Master Peter mashed the potatoes with incredible vigour. Miss Belinda sweetened the apple sauce. Martha dusted the hot plates; Bob took Tiny Tim beside him at a tiny corner of the table; the two young Cratchetts crammed spoons into their mouths lest they should shriek for goose before their turn came. There never was such a goose, its tenderness, size and cheapness were the theme of universal admiration. Indeed as Mrs. Cratchett said with great delight (surveying one small atom of bone upon the dish) they hadn't ate it all! Yet everyone had had enough and the youngest Cratchetts were steeped in sage and onions to the eyebrows.

Mrs. Cratchett left the room alone, too nervous to bear witnesses to take the pudding up and bring it in. Halo! A great deal of steam! The pudding was out of the copper. A smell like washing day! That was the cloth. A smell like an eating house and a pastrycooks next door to each other with a laundress next door to that; That was the pudding. In half a minute Mrs. Cratchett entered, flushed but smiling proudly with the pudding like a speckled cannon ball, so hard and firm blazing in half of half a quarten of ignited brandy and bedight with Christmas holly stuck on top. Everybody had something to say about it, but nobody said it was at all a small pudding for a large family. Any Cratchett would have blushed to do such a thing. Bob served out the hot stuff in the jug and proposed a toast. "A Merry Christmas to us all my dears. God bless us", which all the family echoed.

"God bless us every one," said Tiny Tim, the last of all.

An Impromptu Birthday Party

Doughty Street, February 7th, 1839

EVIDENTLY there had been no celebration plans for Dickens's twenty-seventh birthday. In a letter to the actor-manager J. P. Harley he wrote: "This is my birthday. Many happy returns to you and me. I took it into my head yesterday to set up an impromptu dinner on this auspicious occasion—only my own folks, Leigh Hunt, Ainsworth and Forster. I know you can't dine here in consequence of the tempestuous weather on the Covent Garden shores, but if you will come in after . . . you will delight me greatly. . . . Lord bless my soul. Twenty seven years old! Who'd have thought it. I never did. But I grow sentimental."

At 27 Dickens was already famous—known not only for his exceptional gifts as a novelist but also as a reformer with a great pity and understanding of the downtrodden and oppressed. To those who objected to the novel *Oliver Twist* as being "coarse and shocking" he replied: "I have yet to learn that a lesson of the purest good may not be drawn from the vilest evil. Nor did I doubt that there lay festering in St. Giles's as good material towards truth as any to be found in St. James's."

Two of the guests, Harrison Ainsworth and John Forster, have already been mentioned. Leigh Hunt was a much older man and at that time, 55. In his young days, when Dickens was a babe of 1 year, he was imprisoned for two years and fined £500 for what was considered to be a libel against the Prince Regent. He is remembered for much fine literary work and as the Editor of the radical magazine of his day, *The Examiner*. He spent a great deal of his time in Italy with Shelley and Byron and it was while he was staying with Shelley that he wrote the book, *Lord Byron and Some of His Contemporaries*. His long poem *The Story of Rimini* was also written in Italy. Dickens found him always a charming and endearing companion. He died in 1859.

At this time Dickens had just emerged from a battle with publishers. In the early days when they were eager to sign him up he found that he had contracted to supply far more work than could be executed by any human being, no matter how industrious. Furthermore, as his popularity soared, he found that others were pocketing the spoils while he made "little more than a genteel subsistence". Both Macrone and Bentley had insisted on getting their pound of flesh from the contracts and in so doing lost a gold-mine. Forster came to the rescue and extricated him and in a series of financial manœuvres, set him on a course with Chapman & Hall.

A KATE DICKENS MENU

(8–10 persons)

Vegetable Soup (p. 35)

Fried Sole with Shrimp Sauce
(p. 7)

Roast Fillet of Beef. Stuffed Kalecannon
Minced Mutton with Bacon
Savoury Omelette

Raspberry Jam Sandwiches

(These would be similar to the old traditional Poor Knights of Windsor, see recipe below)

A MODERN MENU

(6 or more people)

Shrimp and Celery Cocktail

Filet de Bœuf Entouré

Scalloped Tomato and Onion (p. 20)
Green Vegetable.   Scalloped Potatoes (p. 16)
Side Salads (p. 201)

Poor Knights of Windsor

Biscuits and Cheeses

Shrimp and Celery Cocktail
Serves 10

12 oz. cooked shrimps
6 sticks tender part of celery,
    chopped into tiny bits

Pink Cocktail Sauce
1 cup cream of tomato soup
2 teasp. sugar
2 teasp. Worcester Sauce
$\frac{1}{4}$ teasp. salt and a little pepper
2 teasp. vinegar

(1) Put shrimps into cocktail glasses.
(2) Combine all ingredients for sauce.
(3) Stir celery into sauce.
(4) Pour over shrimps and garnish with tiny lemon wedges and parsley.

Chill.

Filet de Bœuf Entouré
Serves 6–8

1 fillet of beef (about 3 lb.) trimmed
    and tied by the butcher
4 oz. streaky rashers of bacon
1 Spanish onion
8 oz. mushrooms
3 tablesp. soft breadcrumbs
$\frac{1}{2}$ teasp. salt and a little pepper
1 crushed clove of garlic (optional)
1 lb. puff pastry

(1) Preheat oven to 425° or No. 7.
(2) Make stuffing: remove rinds from rashers and cut into 1-inch pieces. Begin to fry.
(3) Add finely chopped onion and sliced mushrooms. Fry together gently for 10 minutes. Garlic may be added.
(4) Brush fillet with butter and bake in the hot oven for 20 minutes.
(5) Remove string and skewers and spread with stuffing. Roll up again.
(6) Roll out pastry. Put fillet in centre and wrap around securely with pastry. Pinch all edges together.
(7) Brush with beaten egg and bake for about 30 minutes, or until crust is crisp and brown.

Kalecannon (Kate Dickens's Recipe)

Boil 3 or 4 carrots tender, some young greens and a few turnips, a few potatoes. Cut off outside of carrots, chop very fine. Chop greens, mash turnips and potatoes. Place it all in a melon-shape to form stripes of colours, filling up interior of mould with all the vegetables chopped up together with pepper and salt. Cover mould and boil ½ hour.

Poor Knights of Windsor
Serves 8–10

10 or more thin slices of bread, from large square loaf
3 eggs
8 tablesp. milk
2 level tablesp. sugar
3 rounded tablesp. butter or margarine
½ teasp. vanilla essence
Jam

(1) Remove crusts from bread.
(2) Beat eggs and add milk, sugar and vanilla essence.
(3) Melt some of the fat in a large frying-pan.
(4) Put some of the egg mixture on to a large plate. Dip bread into this, lightly coating both sides.
(5) When fat is very hot, fry bread on both sides. Fry all bread this way, adding more egg mixture to the plate and more fat to the pan.
(6) Spread each slice with jam and roll up.

Your guests will never guess! They will think they are eating delicious pancakes.

Savoury Omelette
Serves 8–10

To be able to serve omelettes as a late course of a dinner, one would certainly need a "treasure" in the kitchen, and no Victorian middle-class home was without one. If two large omelettes were made, they could be divided into small portions.

8 eggs
4 tablesp. water
1 level teasp. salt and a little freshly ground pepper
6 oz. grated cheese
8 oz. chopped ham
Butter

(1) Whisk 4 eggs for the first omelette. Add 2 tablesp. of the water and half salt and pepper.
(2) Heat large pan, then melt in it 1 tablesp. butter.
(3) When very hot, but not brown, pour in the egg mixture. Cook for 1 minute, then move mixture about so that top uncooked egg may run on to the bottom of the pan.
(4) When all has set, sprinkle with half the ham and cheese. With a palette knife fold the omelette over and slide out on to a plate.
(5) Repeat with the rest of the eggs, etc.

Nice Food

Sketches of Young Couples

Mr. and Mrs. Chirrup are a nice Young Couple. He has the smartness and something of the brisk manner of a small bird, she is the prettiest of all little women and has the prettiest little figure conceivable.

To dine with Mr. and Mrs. Chirrup is one of the pleasantest things in the world. She is one of the most engaging little women in the world, and if there is one branch of housekeeping in which she excels to an utterly unparalleled extent it is the important one of carving. A roast goose is universally allowed to be the great stumbling block in the way of young aspirants to perfection; many promising carvers beginning with legs of mutton, and preserving a good reputation through fillets of veal, sirloins of beef, quarters of lamb, fowls and even ducks, have sunk before a roast goose and lost caste and character for ever.

To Mrs. Chirrup the resolving a goose into its smallest component parts is a pleasant pastime. No handing the dish over to an unfortunate man upon her left or right, no wild sharpening of the knife, no hacking and sawing at an unruly joint, no noise, no splash, no heat, no leaving off in despair; all is confidence and cheerfulness. The dish is set upon the table, the cover is removed; for an instant, and only an instant you observe that Mrs. Chirrup's attention is distracted from your story; meanwhile the glittering knife is slowly upraised, both Mrs. Chirrup's wrists are slightly but not ungracefully agitated, she compresses her lips for an instant, then breaks into a smile, and all is over. The legs of the bird slide gently down into a pool of gravy, the wings seem to melt from the body, the breast separates into a row of juicy slices, the smaller and more complicated parts of his anatomy are perfectly developed, a cavern of stuffing is revealed, and the goose is gone.

Mr. Chirrup talks and laughs and drinks his wine and laughs again until it is time to repair to the drawing room, where coffee served and over, Mrs. Chirrup prepares for a round game calling to Mr. Chirrup to assist her which Mr. Chirrup does. In course of time a nice little tray appears, on which is a nice little supper and, when that is finished and you have said, "Goodnight," you find yourself repeating as you ride home that there was never such a nice little couple as Mr. and Mrs. Chirrup.

Gathering of Relatives

Doughty Street, May 1839

THERE can be little doubt that the character of Micawber in the novel *David Copperfield* evolved from Charles's own father, John Dickens. The similarity would not appear to be absolutely exact because the people and events that poured into Dickens's mind always came out expanded and remoulded, but in essence faithful to the original. This was the phenomenon of a unique brain. The feat has never been repeated with the same magic and perhaps never will be—not until another mind with the same permutation of cells is born.

Like Micawber, John Dickens expressed himself both verbally and in letters in a long-winded and involved fashion. This is especially evident in a letter to Coutts Bank, asking for a loan while his son Charles was abroad. It is a letter of some 350 words. The Bank declined in 60. Like Micawber, John Dickens found it impossible to keep within the confines of his income and, like Micawber, had advised Charles (or David) that "if a man had twenty pounds a year and spent nineteen pounds nineteen shillings and sixpence he would be happy, but that a shilling spent the other way would make him wretched". Still, Charles had not forgotten the lovable side of his father and had in consequence made Micawber a kind, generous fellow who when in funds would willingly share his bounty with friends.

Obviously John Dickens had instilled into his son a sense of duty towards relatives. In March Charles had gone to Exeter and had taken and fitted up a cottage for his parents and now, in faithfully keeping up an annual event, he is having to refuse an invitation he might have enjoyed more. Writing to his friend William Longman, a publisher and bookseller, he says: "On Friday I have a family dinner at home, uncles, aunts, brothers, sisters and cousins—an annual gathering. But what fatality is it that you always ask me to dine on the wrong day!"

The generosity of Dickens was not confined to his close relatives. His hand was continually in his pocket, either pressing silver into palms or sending off cheques and bank-notes. In those days the widows of men who died while the family was still dependent had to be helped and many times Dickens and his friends hastily got up theatrical performances and gave the proceeds to the widows. For instance, when his friend and first publisher, John Macrone, died, he with others compiled a book of sketches and other writings written by themselves and edited by Dickens, and gave the proceeds of the sales to Mrs. Macrone. They called it *The Pic-nic Papers*, hoping that the fame of *The Pickwick Papers* would give it a boost.

A KATE DICKENS MENU	A MODERN MENU
(8–10 persons)	*(6 or more people)*
Oxtail Soup (p. 51)	*Oysters on the Shell*
Cod with Oyster Sauce	*Almond Soup*
Roast Saddle of Mutton	*Crown Roast of Lamb*
Pork Cutlets	*Roasted Potatoes. Peas and Carrots*
Kalecannon (p. 60)	*Mint Sauce*
Mashed and Brown Potatoes	*Side Salads (p. 201)*
Roast Pheasants (p. 200). Salad	*Frozen Layer Pudding*
Soufflé Pudding (p. 8)	*Biscuits and Cheeses*
Mince Pies (p. 111)	
Anchovy Toast (p. 68)	

Almond Soup
Serves 8–10

2 level tablesp. butter
2 level tablesp. flour
$1\frac{1}{2}$ pints (3 cups) milk
3 chicken cubes
1 pint water
2 level teasp. salt and a little pepper
1 level tablesp. sugar
4 level tablesp. ground almonds
1 teasp. almond essence
$\frac{1}{4}$ pint whipped cream and
  1 tablesp. brandy (optional)

(1) Melt butter in large saucepan. When sizzling, add flour. Cook for 2 minutes without browning.
(2) Add milk. Whisk and cook until thickened.
(3) Add cubes, water and seasoning.
(4) Just before serving add the essence and the almonds.
(5) The soup may be topped with whipped cream laced with brandy

Cod with Oyster Sauce
Serves 8–10

$2\frac{1}{2}$ lb. cod fillets, skinned
1 tablesp. butter
1 bay leaf
4 tablesp. white wine or water
1 level teasp. salt and a little pepper

Oyster Sauce
1 pint white sauce
1 beaten egg
2 tablesp. anchovy sauce
18 oysters, bearded

(1) Preheat oven to 350° or No. 4.
(2) Wash fillets and place in ovenproof dish.
(3) Top with butter and bay leaf. Pour in wine or water and sprinkle with salt and pepper. Cover and cook in oven for about 25 minutes.
(4) To the white sauce add the beaten egg and anchovy. When fish has cooked tip in the liquor. Bring barely to the boil and remove from heat. Add the oysters. Do not boil again. Serve with the fish.

Crown Roast of Lamb

1 or 2 crown roasts, allow 2 chops per person
Fat

Celery, Mushroom and Onion Stuffing
2 cups soft breadcrumbs
2 cups finely chopped celery
1 cup finely chopped onions
$\frac{1}{4}$ lb. washed sliced mushrooms
1 teasp. thyme, 1 level teasp. salt and a little pepper
1 tablesp. softened butter

(1) Preheat oven to 400° or No. 6.
(2) Have the butcher prepare 2 smaller or 1 very large crown roast.
(3) Wrap each chop-tip in foil to prevent charring in oven.
(4) For stuffing, combine all ingredients and bind with the softened butter. Fill centre or centres of roast.
(5) Put meat into baking dish with 2 tablesp. fat. Bake at the high heat for 10 minutes.
(6) Add potatoes which have been par-boiled in salted water for 3 minutes first, and turn over in fat. Reduce heat to 300° or No. 2$\frac{1}{2}$ and bake slowly for about 2 hours.

Mint Sauce

Serves 8–10

4 tablesp. chopped fresh mint
8 tablesp. boiling water
4 tablesp. vinegar
3 level tablesp. sugar
1 level teasp. salt and a little pepper

(1) Pour boiling water on to vinegar.
(2) Add all the other ingredients.

Frozen Layer Pudding

Sponge cake
Sherry or fruit juice
Ice-cream
Strawberries or any fresh or cooked fruit
Whipped cream

(1) Put a $\frac{1}{2}$-inch layer of sponge cake on the bottom of refrigerator ice-cream tray or trays.
(2) Pour over enough sherry or fruit juice (or both) to dampen the cake.
(3) Cover with a 1-inch layer of ice-cream, any flavour you fancy. Chocolate ice-cream would blend with chocolate or coffee sponge.
(4) Cover this with fruit, then with another layer of sponge. Sprinkle with more sherry or juice. Leave in freezing compartment for 1 hour or longer.
(5) To serve, either turn out and top with whipped cream, or serve from the trays.

Snake bracelet, a personal possession of Kate Dickens

Bouquet holder

Remote and Distant Parts

Petersham, Early July 1839, then Broadstairs

KATE and Charles repeated their 1836 choice for the first part of their summer holiday and settled into Elm Cottage for about a month. Writing from there to Lamon Blanchard (another literary friend and one of the first editors to recognize Dickens's talent) he depicts the Petersham of those days as a quiet retreat. "Living in these remote and distant parts," he wrote, "with the chain of mountains formed by Richmond Hill presenting an almost insurmountable barrier between me and the busy world. . . ." (Days that have gone, gone, gone for ever.)

Dickens was always generous in his invitations to his friends and relatives and we know that this year among those invited were the Macreadys, Cattermoles, J. P. Harley, Maclise, Tom Mitton and his legal partner Charles Smithson with their wives, Harrison Ainsworth and Dickens's two sisters, Mrs. Burnett and Mrs. Austin and their husbands.

The grounds of the Petersham cottage were perfect for games. Forster says:

> extensive garden-grounds admitted of much athletic competition, from the more difficult forms of which I, in general modesty, retired, but where Dickens for the most part held his own against even such accomplished athletes as Maclise and Mr. Beard. Bar-leaping, bowling and quoits were among the games carried on with the greatest ardour; and in sustained energy, or what is called keeping it up. Dickens certainly outdistanced every competitor. Even the lighter recreations of battledore and bagatelle were pursued with relentless activity; and at such amusements as the Petersham races, in those days rather celebrated, and which he visited daily while they lasted, he worked much harder himself than the running horses did.

It was while at Petersham that Dickens wrote to Forster suggesting a notion for a new type of periodical. "I should be willing to commence on the thirty-first of March, 1840 a new publication consisting entirely of original matter, of which one number, price threepence, should be published at regular intervals," he said. Thus was launched *Master Humphrey's Clock*, the periodical that was to carry *The Old Curiosity Shop* and *Barnaby Rudge*.

In September they went to Broadstairs again, then returned to London in time for Kate's third confinement.

A KATE DICKENS MENU	A MODERN MENU
(6–7 persons)	(6 or more people)
Turbot with Lobster Sauce (p. 55)	*Peach Salads*
Fried Sole with Shrimp Sauce (p. 7)	
Roast Pig with Oyster Patties (p. 195)	*Asparagus au Beurre*
Fricandeau of Veal	*Stuffed Roasted Pork with Apple*
Mutton Cutlets. Curry Rabbit	*Sauce or Apple Rings*
Roast Beef (p. 103)	*Roasted Potatoes. Broccoli*
Apple Fritters (p. 200)	*Strawberries Romanoff*
Macaroni (p. 104)	
Sweet Omelettes (p. 8)	*Biscuits and Cheeses*
Croquettes of Rice (p. 116)	*or*
	Anchovy Toasts

Peach Salads   Serves 6

8 oz. cream cheese
2 tablesp. mayonnaise
1 teasp. sugar
1 level teasp. salt and a little pepper
1 tablesp. chopped parsley
Lettuce
3 peaches

(1) Combine cheese with mayonnaise, sugar, salt, pepper.
(2) Place small lettuce-heart leaves on individual plates.
(3) Put a heaped tablesp. of the cheese mixture in the centre of each.
(4) Cut peaches in quarters and arrange 2 on each pile, one on either side.
(5) Put a small sprig of parsley or mint on top of each. Chill.

Stuffed Roasted Pork   Serves 7

5–6 lb. leg of pork
Olive oil
Salt
Fat
Celery, mushroom and onion
  stuffing (p. 64)

Apple Sauce or Apple Rings. To make these, core and peel apples, cut into slices and put into ovenproof dish. Bake until tender with the meat. Sprinkle with sugar. Put a cherry in the centre of each and arrange around meat.

(1) Preheat oven to 450° or No. 8.
(2) See that crackling has been cut finely by the butcher and that he has cut a good pocket for the stuffing.
(3) Fill cavity with stuffing and secure with thread, or small skewer.
(4) Rub crackling with oil, then sprinkle with salt. Put 2 tablesp. fat in meat dish.
(5) Place meat in dish and put into the very hot oven. Let the crackling bubble for about 12–15 minutes. Reduce heat to 300° or No. 2½ or 3 and roast until tender. Allow about 4 hours slow cooking.

Roasted Potatoes. Boil potatoes in salted water for a few minutes, then drain and put around the meat. Baste once with fat.

Strawberries Romanoff

Serves 7

1 lb. strawberries
1 pint vanilla ice cream
2 level tablesp. castor sugar
½ pint whipping cream
3 tablesp. Cointreau

(1) Hull and halve strawberries. Large ones should be quartered. Sprinkle with sugar.
(2) Have ice-cream keeping firm in refrigerator.
(3) Whip cream with the Cointreau.
(4) To serve, place a portion of ice cream on individual dishes. Spoon strawberries over, then top with cream.

Asparagus au Beurre

Serves 6–7

1 lb. cooked asparagus spears, tough ends removed
Juice of 1 lemon
4 oz. butter, melted

(1) Arrange 6 or more spears on each individual plate. They should be just warm.
(2) Sprinkle with lemon juice—just a few drops for each.
(3) Serve melted butter separately.

Fricandeau of Veal

Serves 6–7

3 lb. fillet of veal
4 rashers of bacon
2 onions (about ¾ lb.)
6 sticks of celery
½ teasp. thyme, bay leaf and salt and pepper
2 tablesp. butter or margarine
2 level tablesp. flour
¾ cup water or wine

(1) Preheat oven to 300° or No. 2½.
(2) Remove rinds from bacon and fry rashers until fat runs out. Remove to a plate.
(3) Add the butter or margarine to the bacon fat and heat.
(4) Fry the veal in this until browned all over.
(5) Meanwhile chop onions and celery and tip into a deep ovenproof dish. Add the thyme and bay leaf and sprinkle with salt and pepper.
(6) Place browned veal on top of these vegetables. Arrange bacon on top.
(7) To the fat remaining in the frying pan add the flour. Cook until browned then add water or wine and a little salt and pepper. Cook until thickened.
(8) Pour around the veal. Cover with lid and cook slowly in oven for 3 hours.

Anchovy Toasts

Serves 6–7

6 anchovies
1 tablesp. butter
1 beaten egg
Chopped parsley
Buttered toast

(1) Bone and chop anchovies into small pieces.
(2) Melt butter, then add anchovies and fry for 2 minutes.
(3) Stir in beaten egg and cook gently until thickened.
(4) Spread on to buttered toast.

Rural Food

The Cricket on the Hearth

THE cricket that lived by the hearth of the carrier, John Perrybingle and his little wife, Dot, chirruped gaily when there was happiness in their home and was silent when he sensed sorrow. In this extract the couple are about to make their fortnightly visit to Caleb the toymaker and his blind daughter Bertha.

Lifted to her place in the Carriers' cart by her husband, Dot, looking fresh and rosy called; "John? You've got the basket with the veal and ham Pie and 'things' and the bottles of Beer? I really could not think of going to Bertha's without." The basket was there; and the Baby; and its attendant Tilly Slowboy. As they jogged on, everybody on the road had something to say and Boxer gave occasion for more good natured recognition of, and by, the Carrier than half a dozen Christians would have done. Everybody knew Boxer, especially the fowls and pigs who, when they saw him approaching, with his body on one side and his ears pricked and that knob of a tail making the most of itself, immediately withdrew into remote back settlement. He had business everywhere, fluttering all the pigeons, magnifying the tails of all the cats and trotting into Public houses like a regular customer.

You could watch for Fairy rings in the fields and patches of hoar frost lingering in the shade. January made the fireside warmer in possession and the summer greener in expectancy.

Long before they reached the door, Caleb and his blind daughter were waiting on the pavement. Dot's friend May was there, and Tackleton her future bridegroom had brought a cold leg of mutton and a tart besides. In addition there were the Pie and 'things'; chiefly nuts and oranges and cakes and such small beer. The repast was set forth, flanked by Caleb's contribution which was a great wooden bowl of smoking potatoes for he was prohibited by solemn compact from producing other viands. In order that the bottled beer might not be slighted, John Perrybingle proposed, "Tomorrow; the wedding day;" and called upon them to drink a bumper before he proceeded on his journey. When he returned in the evening he called for Dot and took another rest. This was the order of the day on all Pic-nic occasions and had been ever since their institution.

Showing Off a New Home

Devonshire Terrace, Early January 1840

THE arrival of a third baby in October 1839 after only three and a half years of marriage posed a problem. In Dickens's mind circumstances and calculations were not difficult to equate and the answer that came up was plain. More babies inevitable—larger house essential.

In house-hunting as in everything else Dickens was single-minded and thorough. Refusing an invitation to dally with Forster he wrote: "Barnaby has suffered so much from the house-hunting that I mustn't chop today." Several leaseholds were offered, but as soon as Dickens saw No. 1 Devonshire Terrace he brought Kate to see it and they made their decision. Writing excitedly, again to Forster, he said: "A house of great promise and great Premium, undeniable situation and excessive splendour is in view. Mitton is in treaty and I am in ecstatic restlessness." Later, in more sober mood, when he realized just what he had taken on, he said: "It appeared to me then to be a frightfully first class mansion involving awful responsibilities." But he went ahead nevertheless.

The furniture from Doughty Street was sufficient for only one floor of the larger house but the demand for the novels and the satisfactory income that they brought allowed them to order from Heals in Tottenham Court Road suites of furniture, new carpets, elegant drapes, white window blinds and all the extra bits and pieces necessary to the Victorian home. They moved in December and soon were ready to receive their friends and relatives.

All the old friends already mentioned came and with them many others who were to share Dickens's friendship in the long years ahead. Amongst these were Clarkson Stanfield, George Henry Lewes, the Landseers, Charles and Edwin, and T. J. Thompson. Stanfield, nineteen years older than Dickens, was by then a famous artist and had been made an R.A. in 1835. Dickens affectionately called him "Good Old Stanny" and roped him in to paint the scenery in many of their amateur productions. G. H. Lewes was the essayist and critic who in 1854 flouted the conventions and lived with the novelist George Eliot until his death in 1878. Of the Landseers, Edwin was the one who became famous for his paintings of dogs and deer and for Londoners as the sculptor who gave them the great lions of Trafalgar Square. T. J. Thompson was another of Dickens's intimate friends. He married the girl Dickens suggested for him and later became the father of a famous artist, Lady Butler.

A KATE DICKENS MENU	A MODERN MENU

A KATE DICKENS MENU

(12–14 persons)

Mock Turtle Soup (p. 202). Hare Soup
Oxtail Soup (p. 51)

Cod's Head with Oyster Sauce (p. 63)
Soles with Shrimp Sauce (p. 7)
Stewed Eels with Oyster Sauce (p. 63)

Roast Turkey (p. 56). Sausages. Ham
Sweetbreads (p. 52). Curry Lobster
Haunch of Mutton. Broccoli
Browned Potatoes
Pigeon Pie (p. 164)
Oyster Patties (p. 195)
Maintenon Cutlets. Potatoes
Boiled Turkeys with Oyster Sauce (p. 63)
Two Woodcocks. Hare. Four Snipes

Cabinet Pudding
Apple Tart (p. 164)
Charlotte Russe (p. 52)
Jelly

A MODERN MENU

(For a large dinner party)

Artichokes Vinaigrette
or
Hors d'œuvres (pp. 127 and 175)

Vichyssoise Soup (chilled)

Soles with Shrimp Sauce (p. 7)

Roast Turkey (p. 56)
Roasted Potatoes. Vegetables

Cabinet Pudding
English Apple Pie (p. 196)

Anchovy Toasts (p. 68)

Biscuits and Cheeses

Artichokes Vinaigrette

1 globe artichoke per person

Vinaigrette dressing
  (recipe is enough for 8)
8 tablesp. best oil
4 tablesp. wine vinegar
1 teasp. sugar
½ teasp. salt and a little freshly
  ground pepper
1 tablesp. chopped parsley

(1) Remove outer tough leaves of artichokes and cut stem off close to the leaves. Cut off tops of inner leaves with scissors.
(2) Put into salted water with the juice of half a lemon and cook until thick ends of leaves are tender, about 40 minutes. Drain upside-down, then put on individual plates and serve with little dishes of the dressing.
(3) To make dressing, whisk in electric mixer the oil, vinegar, sugar and seasoning. Lastly add the parsley.

Vichyssoise Soup
Serves 12

3 level tablesp. butter or margarine
1 lb. leeks
1 level tablesp. flour
1½ pints (3 cups) water
3 teasp. celery salt
2 chicken cubes and a little pepper
2 lb. potatoes
1 tablesp. chopped parsley
¼ pint cream

(1) Melt butter in large saucepan.
(2) Wash and cut up leeks and add. Fry for 2 minutes, then add flour and fry for 2 more minutes without browning.
(3) Add water. Stir and cook until thickened.
(4) Add potatoes and cook until tender then add milk, cubes, salt and pepper.
(5) Strain and put away until chilled. Serve topped with whipped cream.

Maintenon Cutlets

Serves 12

12 thick chump chops
1 tablesp. butter
½ lb. mushrooms
1 onion (about 6 oz.)
2 oz. (1 cup) breadcrumbs
Salt and pepper
Fat

Espagnole Sauce: below

(1) Have the butcher cut a pocket in each chop for stuffing.
(2) Preheat oven to 350° or No. 4.
(3) Melt fat in frying-pan. Chop onion and add. Then add washed, sliced mushrooms. Fry together for 5 minutes.
(4) Add to breadcrumbs. Season with salt and pepper.
(5) Push a little of this mixture into each cavity. Secure with tiny skewers.
(6) Put 3 tablesp. fat in baking dish and allow to get hot in oven. Coat chops with flour then put into the hot fat, turning over to coat both sides.
(7) Bake for 1–1¼ hours, reducing heat a little after 30 minutes.
(8) Serve with Espagnole Sauce.

Espagnole Sauce

1 rasher of streaky bacon
1 onion (about 6 oz.)
1 level tablesp. butter
2 level tablesp. flour
1 beef cube
Bouquet garni
½ pt. tomato juice or peeled sliced tomatoes
2 teasp. Worcester Sauce
2 teasp. sugar
Salt and pepper

(1) Remove rind from bacon and cut into 1-inch pieces. Fry until fat runs out. Add butter and allow to get hot.
(2) Add chopped onions and fry for 10 minutes gently, without browning.
(3) Add flour and cook for 1 minute. Add tomato and also ¼ cup water, beef cube and bouquet garni.
(4) Cook and stir until thickened, then add sauce and seasonings. Simmer for about 15 minutes.
(5) Strain before using.

Cabinet Pudding

Serves 12

1 tablesp. apple jelly
1 bottle of maraschino cherries and a few strips of angelica
¾ pint milk
2 level tablesp. sugar
3 beaten eggs
1 teasp. vanilla
24 sponge fingers
1 level tablesp. powdered gelatine
2 tablesp. hot water
Cream and blanched almonds (sliced)

(1) Heat jelly and coat a 3-pint mould with it. Arrange on the bottom halved maraschino cherries and up the sides a few strips of soaked angelica.
(2) Make custard with the milk, sugar and beaten eggs. Cook until the mixture coats the spoon. Do not allow to boil.
(3) Mix gelatine with hot water and stir into custard. Add vanilla. Allow to dissolve thoroughly. Cool.
(4) Line sides and bottom of mould with sponge fingers. Break the rest up and put into mould with more halved cherries.
(5) Pour custard over and put away until set. Unmould and decorate with whipped cream and blanched sliced almonds.

Stately Food

Household Words

In 1848 Dickens wrote some personal letters in the character of an American visitor to England and pretended that he was authorized to inquire into the state of the agriculture there. He signed himself "Major General the Hon. C. Dickens (Richmond, Va.)".

Picture to yourself a large old castle approached by an ancient keep, portcullis etc., filled with company, waited on by six and twenty servants. On arrival your name is announced and your portmanteau immediately taken into your chamber. If you leave your chamber twenty times a day after using your basin, you would find it clean and the pitcher replenished on your return. You cannot take your clothes off, but they are taken away, brushed, folded, pressed and placed in the bureau. At the dressing hour before dinner you find your candles lighted, your clothes laid out, your shoes cleaned, the dress clothes laid out and folded in the nicest manner and cold water, hot water and clean napkins in the greatest abundance. Everything undertaken eventuates the most magnificent hospitality.

All the wines, fruit glasses, candlesticks, lamps and plate are taken care of by the Butlers who have underbutlers for their adjuncts. Ladies never wear white satin shoes or white gloves more than once. Dinner napkins are never left upon the table but are thrown into your chair or under the table.

In this mansion I always came down to breakfast at 9 precisely and found the Duchess at her breakfast. About half past nine the Duke would come in, and the ladies one by one soon after. At breakfast the side table would have on it cold ham, cold chicken, cold pheasant or partridge, which you ask for, or which, as is most common, you get up and help yourselves. On the breakfast table were several kinds of the best breads possible, butter always fresh made that morning, as I have found at all these houses and if you ask for coffee or chocolate, it would be brought to you in a silver coffee pot and you help yourself; if for tea you would have a silver urn to each guest, heated by alcohol, placed by you, a small teapot and small caddie of black and green tea to make for yourself or the servant for you. At breakfast the arrangements were made for the day, and if you were to ride, choose your mode and at the minute, the horses and servants would be at the door.

The labouring people are especially well cared for and looked after. At a future time it will be my duty to report on the turnips, mangel-wurzels, ploughs and live stock.

Come!

Broadstairs, June 1840

DICKENS's letter of June 2nd to his dear Maclise was an enticement to visit. Giving Broadstairs a boost he wrote: ". . . this place is, as the Guide Book most justly observes, 'unsurpassed for the salubrity of the refreshing breezes, which are wafted on the ocean's pinions from far distant shores'." But the accommodation had no such eulogy. "Come to the bower which is shaded for you in the one-pair front," he adds, "where no chair or table has four legs of the same length and where no drawers will open till you have pulled the pegs off and then they keep open and won't shut again." Nevertheless he put, all on its own, the welcoming word,

COME!

With the other friends who had also chosen Broadstairs for their summer exit, they bathed, played games and danced, with Dickens always the gayest and most energetic of them all. Not that he neglected his work. He was as strict with his writing hours there as in London and worked each day from 10 a.m. until 2. He had begun *The Old Curiosity Shop* now being serialized in his periodical, *Master Humphrey's Clock.*

The idea for the book was born earlier in the year when on a visit to Bath. A chance story heard there led to the theme and the character of Little Nell and at first he thought of making it into a short story to be included in the material for one number of *Master Humphrey's Clock.* But he found that this did not please his readers. They had become accustomed to a long serialized story by Boz and when it was not forthcoming, many ceased to buy the paper. So Dickens decided to bow to popular demand and make it into a long novel.

Its success was tremendous. So deeply had his characters penetrated into the minds of his readers that the death of Little Nell was a personal tragedy for each. In America they awaited anxiously for the news that would arrive by ship and as it docked they were on the pier as would parents in need of instant truth. "Was Little Nell saved—or was she . . . ?" When they knew, the grief was unbearable. It was a miracle of writing. Of the other families who were at Broadstairs that summer, the Salas are worth a mention. George Sala was the father of Augustus Henry Sala (then 14) who from 1851 to 1856 wrote regularly for Dickens's *Household Words* and later became war correspondent for the *Daily Telegraph.* He is remembered for many fine novels and travel books and for his part in the founding of Temple Bar in London.

A KATE DICKENS MENU	A MODERN MENU
(4–5 persons)	(A cold holiday luncheon)
Asparagus Soup (*p.* 27)	*Crabmeat Cocktail*
Salmon Smelts	*Platter of Cold Chicken,*
Forequarter of Lamb	*Sliced Tongue and Ham*
(*see Roast Lamb, p.* 19)	*Tossed Salad*
Fricassee of Chicken	*Rice and Raw Mushroom Salad*
New Potatoes. Peas	*or*
Lobster Patties (*p.* 47)	*Potato Salad*
Noyau Jelly. Ice Pudding	*Noyau Jelly Cream*

Crabmeat Cocktail
Serves 5–6

8 oz. crabmeat
Shredded lettuce
Cocktail Sauce (p. 59)
Sliced olives for garnish

(1) Put a little shredded lettuce on the bottom of each cocktail glass.
(2) Arrange crabmeat on top and sprinkle with a little salt and pepper.
(3) Pour a few teaspoons of the sauce over each and garnish with slices of olive.

Tossed Salad
Serves 5–6

1 large or 2 smaller well hearted lettuces
2 grated carrots
2 oz. grated cheese
1 cup cooked green peas
/ ½ cup finely sliced radishes

Spinach Salad
Replace lettuce with 2 cups washed spinach

(1) If desired rub salad bowl with a cut clove of garlic.
(2) Tear lettuce hearts into penny-sized pieces and drop into bowl.
(3) Add carrots, cheese, peas and radishes. Sprinkle with a little salt and pepper. Toss about.
(4) Serve with French dressing or mayonnaise, or dress the salad by first adding about 2 tablesp. oil, then half the quantity of vinegar. Move about to coat vegetables well. Do not add this dressing until just before serving.

Rice and Raw Mushroom Salad
Serves 5–6

4 half-pint cups of cooked rice
6 oz. washed sliced mushrooms
1 tablesp. vinegar
1 level tablesp. sugar
4 peeled, sliced tomatoes
Salt and pepper

(1) Cover sliced mushrooms with vinegar and sugar and allow to marinate for half an hour or longer.
(2) Put cooked rice into salad bowl and sprinkle with salt and pepper.
(3) Add sliced tomatoes, then the mushrooms with the liquid.
(4) Mix lightly.

Potato Salad
Serves 5–6

1½ lb. new potatoes cooked and drained
3 tablesp. chopped spring onions
Chopped parsley, chervil and tarragon may be added
5 tablesp. mayonnaise

(1) Cut cooked potatoes into cubes or slices and put into salad bowl.
(2) Add all other ingredients and move around without breaking up the potato.

Fricassee of Chicken
Serves 5–6

2½–3 lb. disjointed chicken or fowl
1 pint water
1 good teasp. salt and a little pepper
1 bay leaf
1 onion, quartered
2½ level tablesp. flour
½ pint milk
1 hard boiled egg
Chopped parsley

(1) Skin chicken or fowl and place in large saucepan. Add 1 pint water and seasoning.
(2) Add quartered onion and bay leaf. Cover and simmer until tender. 1–1½ hours for chicken, 2½–3 hours for fowl.
(3) Melt butter in another saucepan. Add flour and cook for 2 minutes without browning.
(4) Add milk and whisk and cook until thick. Add ½ pint (1 cup) of the chicken liquid. When blended taste and add necessary seasoning.
(5) Add the chopped hard-boiled egg.
(6) Lift chicken on to serving dish and pour sauce over. Sprinkle with the parsley.

Noyau Jelly Cream
Serves 5–6

1¼ pints (2½ cups) milk
¼ pint (½ cup) heavy cream
3 level dessertsp. powdered gelatine
2 level tablesp. cornflour
4 level tablesp. sugar
1 tablesp. lemon juice
3 tablesp. noyau liqueur
¼ teasp. salt
2 egg whites
2 oz. blanched sliced almonds
Cream

(1) Dissolve gelatine in 3 tablesp. cold water.
(2) Heat milk with sugar. Mix cornflour with 2 tablesp. cold water and stir in. Cook and stir until thick. Add cream.
(3) Stir in the gelatine and allow to dissolve. Add lemon juice, noyau and salt. Put away and allow to set to the wobbly stage.
(4) Beat whites until very stiff. Fold into the half set cream. Tip into serving dish and put away until set.
(5) Decorate with blanched sliced almonds and serve with cream.

Bird Food

Barnaby Rudge (1841)

FROM the Maypole Inn at Chigwell, Barnaby, with Grip the Raven in his basket, goes home to his Mother's cottage.

They made a strange pair, Barnaby with long red hair hanging in disorder about his face and clothes of tattered green cloth trimmed with odds and ends of tawdry lace and ruffles. His hat was decorated with three broken peacock feathers, he wore at his side the hilt of an old sword and used a long staff with which he could leap over hedges and ditches, the big black bird always close to his Master, waking or sleeping.

"We have been afield Mother," said Barnaby after he had kissed her a hundred times. "The wind has been blowing. The rushes and young plants, the cowards bending to it. Grip, brave Grip when the wind rolls him over turns to bite it!" The Raven, hearing his name began crowing like a cock, barking and gravely croaking "I'm a devil, keep up your spirits. Never say die. Bow wow wow."

"Jump then," said Barnaby and the Raven hopped on his Master's shoulder, from that to his extended hand and so to the ground. With his head very much on one side and his bright eye shining like a diamond he replied, in a voice so hoarse and distant that it seemed to come through his thick feathers rather than out of his mouth, "Halloa, halloa, what's the matter now? Polly put the kettle on, kettle put the polly on," and then began to whistle and flapped his wings against his body as if he were bursting with laughter. He came to Barnaby not in a hop or a walk, but a pace like that of a very particular old gentleman with exceedingly tight boots on, trying to walk over loose pebbles.

"Let's to supper lad," cried Barnaby, "I'm hungry and Grip has not eaten since broad noon." The Raven held his beak open ready for snapping up lumps of meat. Of these he received about a score without the smallest discomposure. "More," croaked Grip, "More," but no more was to be had, and while his Master made a hearty meal, Grip disgorged the morsels from his mouth and hid them in various secret corners to be dragged out later and eaten with the utmost relish.

"*Invitation to Dine*"

Devonshire Terrace, January 21st, 1841

Tʜɪs dinner is mentioned by Macready in his Diaries. "Invitation to dine Sunday sennight," he wrote, using the old-fashioned word for a week—the space of seven days.

Mrs. Macready was also called Kate and it is obvious from reading the daily entries that he was a most devoted husband and father as well as an affectionate friend to Dickens. He is remembered even today as one of the greatest Victorian actors. His style was "declamatory" or "ham", and he brought to it the utmost in tragedy, joy, villainy or sorrow. Of Dickens he spoke always with admiration. The novels were a source of constant wonder and the fate of the characters almost as important to him as that of his own family. Preparing himself to read the numbers of *The Old Curiosity Shop* containing the death of Little Nell he wrote, "I dread to read it, but I must get it over. I have never read numbers that gave me such pain. I could not weep for some time. Sensation, sufferings have returned to me that are terrible to awaken. It is real to me. I cannot criticise it."

Although Macready does not tell us whether or not there were other guests present, Forster gives a list of friends who enjoyed with him at this time the "social entertainment". They were (besides Macready), Thomas Talfourd, Clarkson Stanfield, Dr. John Elliotson, the Landseers, Sydney Smith, Edward Bulwer Lytton, Proctor, poet and father of the poetess Adelaide Proctor who wrote for a time under the name of Miss Berwick; Fonblanque editor of the radical paper, *The Examiner*; Emerson Tennant, author and M.P.; Count d'Orsay, elegant friend of Lady Blessington; Dr. Quin, exponent of homoeopathic medicine; the Rev. Harness, writer and cleric; Sir David Wilkie, a famous Scottish artist and Sam Rogers, wealthy bachelor, banker and poet. What a noble and learned lot! Not a business tycoon in sight.

At this time Grip the raven (immortalized in the novel *Barnaby Rudge*) was a lively member of the household. Kate found his wicked ways rather trying, but Dickens and the red-headed groom Topping adored him. When Grip died, Dickens, in a long letter to Maclise, gave a full account of his death and Maclise rose to the occasion by doing the amusing drawing showing Grip flying up to Heaven. Soon afterwards Dickens obtained an older, larger Grip. "A man cannot go ravenless," he said.

A KATE DICKENS MENU

(8–10 persons)

Scotch Mutton Broth (p. 19)

*Fried Oysters.   Shoulder of Mutton
Boiled Fowl with Bacon
Mashed and Brown Potatoes
Stewed Onions.   Salad*

*Bath Pudding
Macaroni with Bacon (p. 104)*

A MODERN SUMMERTIME BUFFET SUPPER

(12 or more people)

*Olives, Nuts, Gherkins and
Cocktail Snacks with the Drinks*

*Mousse de Jambon with
Cold Chicken and Asparagus
Tossed Green Salad (p. 75)
Hot Scalloped Potatoes (p. 16)
or
Potato Salad (p. 76)
Tomato and Cucumber Salad*

N.Z. Pavlovas

Fried Oysters

4 oz. lard or cooking oil
6 or more oysters per person
Flour
Beaten egg, seasoned
Fine dry breadcrumbs
Bacon Rolls

Note. Oysters may be dipped in batter instead of egg and breadcrumbs. Fry in the same way.

(1) Begin to heat lard or oil in small rather deep frying-pan.
(2) Beard oysters. Coat lightly with flour.
(3) Beat the egg, add $\frac{1}{2}$ teasp. salt, a little pepper and 2 tablesp. water.
(4) Dip oysters into this, then into the breadcrumbs.
(5) When fat is quite still with a faint white mist rising (about 375°) fry oysters until lightly browned all over.
(6) For Bacon Rolls, remove rinds from bacon rashers, cut into 5- or 6-inch lengths and roll up. Fry or grill.

Mousse de Jambon

Serves 10–12

$\frac{3}{4}$ lb. cooked ham
1 packet celery soup powder
   (needing $1\frac{1}{2}$ pints liquid)
$\frac{1}{2}$ pint water, 1 pint milk and
   $\frac{1}{4}$ pint fresh cream
2 packets powdered gelatine
   (2 level tablesp.)
3 eggs separated

Note. A salad dressing may be made with the yolks. Beat then cook with 1 tablesp. vinegar, 4 of water and a little sugar, salt, pepper and mustard. Do not allow to boil.

(1) Have one 4-pint mould, or two 2-pint ones.
(2) Mince ham finely, twice.
(3) Add cold water and milk to soup powder and simmer until cooked.
(4) Mix gelatine with 2 tablesp. cold water and stir in. Allow to dissolve.
(5) Add cream and ham. Check for seasoning.
(6) Put away in a bowl until almost set.
(7) Whisk egg whites until as stiff as possible and fold into mixture. Tip into mould or moulds and put away until set.
(8) Unmould on to serving dish or dishes and decorate top with halved sliced tomatoes and parsley.

Tomato and Cucumber Salad
Serves 12

3 lb. tomatoes
2 cucumbers
3 level tablesp. sugar
2 level teasp. salt and a little pepper
6 tablesp. vinegar

(1) Remove skins from tomatoes by either dipping first into boiling water, or holding them on a fork over a gas flame. Cut into slices.
(2) Arrange a double layer of the slices in one large or two smaller dishes, or salad bowls. Sprinkle with a little of the sugar and salt and pepper.
(3) Arrange peeled sliced cucumber over in two layers and sprinkle with salt and pepper.
(4) Repeat the layers, then pour vinegar over. Allow to stand for an hour or longer.

N.Z. Pavlova with Pineapple or Strawberries
Serves 12

Two Pavlovas with the following quantities each will be needed:
4 egg whites
10 oz. (1¼ cups) sugar
1 teasp. vinegar
1 teasp. cornflour
½ pint whipped cream
Pineapple slices or pieces
Maraschino cherries
Strawberries laced with a little
   Kirsh and sugar may be used.

(1) Preheat oven to 200° or No. 1. Put a piece of greased greaseproof paper on an oven tray.
(2) For one Pavlova use the 4 eggs, etc. Beat eggs until stiff on electric mixer.
(3) Sprinkle in the sugar, 1 tablesp. at a time keeping the mixer at full speed.
(4) Add vinegar and cornflour. When mixture is stiff enough to stand alone in peaks it is ready.
(5) Tip on to greased paper, making a pile about 8 inches in diameter. Bake for 1 hour, or until outside is crisp. The inside should be like a marshmallow.
(6) Slide off on to a flat serving dish. Cover with about 1 inch of whipped cream and decorate with pieces of pineapple and maraschino cherries.

Bath Pudding-Pie
Serves 4–6

½ lb. short pastry
1½ oz. (1½ level tablesp.) ground rice
½ pint milk or cream or half and half
2 oz. (2 tablesp.) butter
3 oz. (4 level tablesp.) sugar
½ teasp. vanilla essence
½ teasp. salt
2 eggs, beaten

(1) Preheat oven to 350° or No. 4.
(2) Roll pastry out very thinly and line an 8- or 8½-inch pie dish about 1½–2 inches deep, wetting edge of dish first. Put a strip of pastry around edge and pinch and cut to decorate.
(3) Heat milk or cream. Mix rice with a little water and stir in. Add sugar and salt. Cook and stir until thickened, add butter, beaten eggs and vanilla. Pour into pie shell.
(4) Bake for about ¾ hour. Reduce heat a little after 20 minutes.

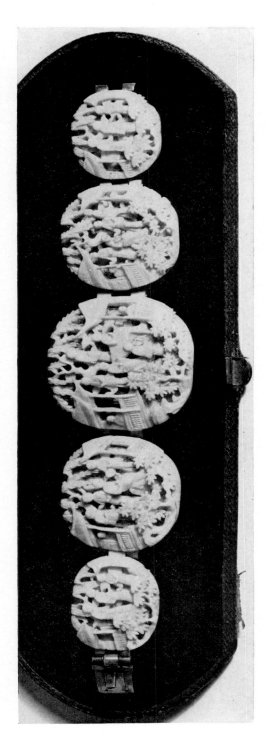

Nutmeg grater

Bracelet belonging to Kate Dickens   A favourite vase of Charles Dickens

Famous Scottish Guests

Devonshire Terrace, Early April 1841

BY THIS time Dickens knew without doubt that the power of his pen went far beyond story-telling. When he met Carlyle in 1840 and discussed with him the great issues of the day, notably the reform legislation that was meeting such strong opposition in Parliament, he knew that he must continue to use this power to arouse the public conscience. As a young man he had prowled the poorer parts of London and found horrors that appalled him. He knew that children were exposed to the vice and evil of the opium houses and other dens of iniquity that thrived in the rat-infested and bug-ridden quarters of the poor and that this laid the foundation for their own future crimes. Even then, in his early twenties, long before he had met Carlyle, his great intelligence told him that it was *education* and not preaching, proselytizing and praying that was the only hope of alleviation. In no other way could the chain of reaction of festering evil to which the children of the poor were subjected be combated.

Other dedicated people were trying to find solutions, but their call was too diffused for strength. Dickens worked in a far more effective way. In the case of *Oliver Twist* he took just one small boy, gave him a guileless and lovable character, planted him firmly in the heart of every reader, then made him the innocent victim of authority's heartless injustice. The anguish of a nation over one small boy "asking for more" and being denied moved the mountains of entrenched complacency and led to an outcry for reform and justice. That was power indeed.

At this dinner the two Scottish guests were Thomas Carlyle and his wife and Lord Jeffrey, down from Edinburgh. Some may know Carlyle best for his famous *Sartor Resartus*, but the books Dickens carried around with him and devoured were *The Chartists* and *The French Revolution*. Jane his wife sounds rather a caustic lady. She thought that Mrs. Dickens's dinner table was rather overdone with its great dishes of dessert and the vases of artificial flowers. She prefers Lady Ashburton's idea of "just four cowslips in china pots"!

Lord Jeffrey had come to London to persuade Dickens to visit his city and enjoy the generous and warm hospitality of Scotland. He accepted and in June began the tour that has been fully described in all the biographies.

<table>
<tr><td>

A KATE DICKENS MENU

(4–5 persons)

Baked and Stuffed Haddock (p. 199)

Broiled Fowl with Mushrooms
(see Fried Chicken, p. 84)
Minced Collops
Mashed and Brown Potatoes

Raspberry Jam Sandwiches
(see Poor Knights of Windsor, p. 60)

</td><td>

A MODERN MENU

(Medium size)

Bouillabaisse

Fried Chicken Maryland
Crumbed Bananas.   Sweetcorn Fritters
Mushroom Gravy
Duchess Potatoes.   Green Vegetable

Ambrosia Apples

Biscuits and Cheeses

</td></tr>
</table>

Bouillabaisse Serves 8–10

¼ pint olive oil
1½ lb. assorted fish such as cod,
  haddock, John Dory or other types
2 large leeks
1 large Spanish onion
1 lb. potatoes
1 crushed clove of garlic
¼ teasp. powdered saffron
½ lb. peeled tomatoes
Bouquet garni
Salt and pepper
2 teasp. sugar
1½ pints (3 cups) water
¼ lb. cooked shrimps
¼ lb. flaked lobster or crabmeat

(1) Heat oil and add chopped leeks and onions. Fry for 5 minutes without browning. Add tomatoes and bouquet garni.
(2) Add peeled, sliced potatoes, garlic, water and fish. Leave shrimps and lobster until the last. Bring to the boil and simmer for about 30 minutes.
(3) Add saffron, sugar and plenty of salt and pepper.
(4) Lastly add the shrimps and lobster or crabmeat.
(5) Serve very hot in heated bowls.

Minced Collops (Kate Dickens's Recipe)

Take 2 lb. of the fillet of beef, chopped very fine. Put it in a stewpan, and add to it pepper and salt and a little flour. Add a little good gravy with a little ketchup and Harvey's sauce and let it stew for 20 minutes over a slow fire. Serve up very hot garnished with fried snippets of bread. This quantity of beef makes a good-sized dish.

Beef Collops (another Victorian Recipe)

Follow Kate Dickens's recipe and while it is cooking line a pie dish with mashed potatoes. Tip in the cooked collops and serve hot.

Fried Chicken Maryland

Serves 5–6

3 lb. disjointed chicken
1 cup cooking oil
3 tablesp. flour
1 teasp. salt and a little pepper
1 beaten egg
Fine dry breadcrumbs
6 bananas
Batter and sweetcorn
Mushroom gravy

(1) Begin to heat the oil in a deep wide pan.
(2) Put flour, salt and pepper into paper bag. Put chicken pieces, one at a time into bag and shake so that they are coated.
(3) Add 2 tablesp. water to the beaten egg. Put breadcrumbs on to a large plate.
(4) Dip floured chicken pieces first into egg, then into breadcrumbs.
(5) When oil is still with a faint white mist rising (about 375°F) fry chicken until browned all over.

Crumbed Bananas. Cut bananas in halves lengthwise. Dip into milk then into fine dry breadcrumbs and fry in butter until golden.

Sweetcorn Fritters. Make $\frac{1}{2}$ pint batter with your usual recipe or with a batter-mix. Season well with salt and pepper and add 2 teasp. sugar. Add 1 small can of sweetcorn kernels to the batter. Have 1 cup oil or 6 oz. lard very hot (see step 5 above) and make fritters with dessertspoons of the mixture.

Mushroom Gravy. Wash and slice 6 oz. mushrooms. Fry in any oil left from chicken or fritters. Add 1 level tablesp. flour and continue frying for 2 minutes. Add $\frac{1}{2}$ pint milk and $\frac{1}{4}$ pint water and stir well until cooked and thickened. Season with pepper and salt.

Duchess Potatoes. $1\frac{1}{2}$ lb. floury potatoes, cooked and mashed with butter, milk and salt and pepper. Add 1 beaten egg and mix well. With potato nozzle and forcing bag, make little pyramids on to greased oven tray. Bake for about 15–20 minutes or until tipped with gold.

Ambrosia Apples

Serves 5–6

1 or 2 large eating apples per person
Christmas mincemeat
$\frac{1}{2}$ pint sherry or white wine
2 level tablesp. sugar
$\frac{3}{4}$ pint ($1\frac{1}{2}$ cups) water
Cream

(1) Core apples then make a slit in the skin around the circumference of each.
(2) Peel about $\frac{3}{4}$ inch of skin from tops. Fill holes with mincemeat.
(3) Pour water into oven baking dish and add sugar.
(4) Lift in the apples. Pour a little of the sherry over them, letting as much as possible seep down into the mincemeat.
(5) Bake for about 20–30 minutes (depending on size and ripeness). Add more water as syrup evaporates.
(6) When apples are just soft, but not broken, add the rest of the sherry or wine to the syrup. Place apples on serving dish and surround with the delicious syrup. Serve with cream.

Workhouse Food

Oliver Twist

THIS is the famous scene in which the poor little half-starved workhouse orphan, Oliver, dares to "ask for more".

The room in which the boys were fed was a large stone hall with a copper at one end out of which a thin gruel was ladled at meal times. Of this festive composition each boy had one porringer, and no more except on occasions of great public rejoicing when he had two ounces and a quarter of bread besides. The bowls never needed washing. The boys polished them with their spoons; then they would sit staring at the copper with such eager eyes as if they would have devoured the very bricks of which it was composed. Boys have excellent appetites. Oliver and his companions had suffered the tortures of slow starvation and, at last, they got so voracious and wild with hunger, that one boy, who was tall for his age, hinted darkly to his companions that, unless he had another basin of gruel per diem, he was afraid he might some night happen to eat the boy who slept next him, a weakly child of tender age. He had a wild and hungry look and they implicitly believed him. A council was held; lots were cast who should walk up to the Master after supper and ask for more; and it fell to Oliver Twist.

The evening arrived; the boys took their places; a long grace was said over the short commons. The gruel disappeared; the boys winked at Oliver; his next door neighbour nudged him. Child as he was, he was desperate with hunger and reckless with misery. He rose from the table; and advancing to the Master, basin and spoon in hand, said somewhat alarmed at his own temerity, "Please Sir, I want some more."

The Master was a fat and healthy man, but he turned very pale. He gazed in stupefied astonishment at the small rebel and clung to the copper for support. The pauper assistants were paralysed with wonder; the boys with fear. "What?" said the Master at length in a faint voice. "Please Sir, I want some more," replied Oliver. The Master aimed a blow at Oliver's head with the ladle and shrieked aloud for Mr. Bumble the Beadle.

Walter Landor Attends
the Christening of Walter Landor

Devonshire Terrace, December 1841

A SECOND son had been born in April of this year and again Charles chose for him the name of a dear friend. This time it was Walter Savage Landor, well-known poet, writer and critic. The christening ceremony took place at the end of the year and the two Walter Savage Landors (one with Dickens added) met for the first time. No doubt their first greetings, had they been recorded for posterity, would have been something in the nature of "Goo-goo" and "Boo-boo", but that is merely guesswork. A man of such literary stature as Landor might possibly have found something more eloquent to say. After all, he was sixty-six years older than his young namesake and his works are still considered to be classics.

At that time he was living in Bath and Dickens and his friends made several pilgrimages there to bask in his eloquence, charm and learning. He had led a remarkably varied life. Most of it had been spent on the Continent and while there he had raised an army and accompanied it to fight the Peninsular War. When he returned to England he bought Llanthony Abbey in Wales and wrote his *Imaginary Conversations*, published in 1829. *The Pentameron* appeared in 1837. He died in Florence in 1864.

For some time Dickens had been toying with an idea. He knew that if he were to extend his creative faculty to its utmost his mind needed constantly to absorb new scenes and new experiences. In the maze of streets and lanes of London he had found a wealth of material and had used it, as we know in miraculous ways. But now he felt the urge to move further afield—very much further.

Across the Atlantic was a vast new country, unfettered as yet by tradition, and he longed to know what type of nation was emerging from the conglomeration of peoples who were shaping it. America was *there* and so must be seen, savoured and assessed. Kate hated the idea and every time it was mentioned she dissolved into tears. To pacify her Charles tried to find a way of taking all the four children with them, but friends who had made the Atlantic crossing advised strongly against it. In the end the Macreadys offered to take the children into their home while they were away and Kate became more or less reconciled to the idea of the great and terrifying adventure.

A VICTORIAN CHRISTENING TEA

Christening Cake
(see Christmas Cake, p. 111)
Assorted sandwiches
Buttered Pikelets
Queen Cakes
Scotch Shortbread
Petit Fours (bought)

A MODERN CHRISTENING TEA

Christening Cake
Cheese and Bacon Savouries
Assorted Sandwiches
Chocolate Cream Queen Cakes
Scotch Shortbread
Coffee Sponge Cake

Pikelets   *Makes 18*

1 egg
1 level tablesp. sugar
5 oz. (1 cup) S.R. flour
$\frac{1}{2}$ level teasp. salt
$\frac{1}{4}$ pint ($\frac{1}{2}$ cup) milk

(1) Heat plate of electric cooker, or a frying- or griddle-pan.
(2) Beat egg and sugar.
(3) Add flour and salt, then half the milk.
(4) Mix, then add the rest of the milk. Stir briskly until smooth.
(5) Brush hot pan or plate with butter. Drop mixture from end of tablespoon to make $2\frac{1}{2}$–3-inch pancakes. When bubbles appear, flip pancakes over and cook until golden. They take only a few minutes.

Cheese and Bacon Savouries

4 oz. streaky bacon
4 oz. grated cheese
Pepper
Accent

(1) Remove rinds from bacon and cut into $\frac{1}{2}$-inch pieces. Combine with the cheese and add a little pepper and $\frac{1}{8}$ teasp. Accent.
(2) Spread thickly on to square slices of bread. Place on oven trays and bake until cheese and bacon have melted and blended together.
(3) Afterwards, remove crusts and cut into fingers. Serve hot.

Sandwich Fillings

Cucumber. Peel and slice the cucumber very finely. Place in a bowl and add salt, pepper and a little lemon juice or vinegar. Allow to stand for about 1 hour, then drain well. Have the bread cut very thinly and buttered well.

Egg and Cheese. Beat 2 eggs. Add 6 tablesp. milk and 4 oz. grated tasty cheese. Season with 1 teasp. sugar, $\frac{1}{2}$ teasp. salt and a little pepper and Accent. Melt 2 teasp. butter in small saucepan, and scramble the egg and cheese. Cool before using.

Scotch Shortbread

8 oz. butter
4 oz. castor sugar
8 oz. flour
4 oz. rice flour

(1) Preheat oven to 325° or No. 3½.
(2) Cream together the butter and sugar.
(3) Work in the flour and rice flour gradually. When all is blended, do not knead any more. The less it is kneaded the better.
(4) Press into an 8-inch square or round shallow pan, and pinch the edges to decorate. Prick all over with a fork.
(5) Bake until crisp, about 1–1¼ hours. Reduce heat if the shortbread is browning too quickly. It must be only a pale gold. Cut into pieces while hot, but leave in pan until cold.

Queen Cakes
Makes 20–22

4 oz. (½ cup) butter
6 oz. (¾ cup) sugar
2 large eggs
6 oz. (1 cup plus 1 tablesp.) S.R. flour
¼ teasp. salt
1 teasp. vanilla essence
3 tablesp. water

(1) Preheat oven to 350° or No. 4.
(2) Cream butter and sugar. If the weather is cold, add 1 tablesp. hot water and reduce final water to 2 tablesp.
(3) Add 2 teasp. flour, then drop in one unbeaten egg. Whisk well, then add more flour and the other egg. Beat very well.
(4) Sift in the rest of the flour, the vanilla and remaining water. Blend well but do not beat again.
(5) Put into greased patty pans and bake for 15–20 minutes.
(6) Ice, then cut off tops, scoop out a little of the cake and fill with sweetened whipped cream.

Chocolate Cream Queen Cakes. Follow above recipe, but replace 1 tablesp. of the flour with 1 tablesp. cocoa. Ice with chocolate butter icing and fill with cream in the same way.

Coffee Sponge Cake. Make batter as shown in Queen Cakes, and instead of the water add 3 tablesp. black coffee. Bake in one 8-inch square pan, well greased, and with butter papers on the bottom. Bake for about 40–45 minutes. Ice with coffee butter icing.

Chocolate Butter Icing. To 6 oz. (1 cup) icing sugar add 1 tablesp. butter, one of boiling water and one of cocoa. Flavour with ½ teasp. vanilla.

Coffee Butter Icing. To 6 oz. (1 cup) icing sugar add 1 tablesp. butter and 1 bare tablesp. boiling black coffee. Flavour with ½ teasp. vanilla essence.

Late Night Food

"Parliamentary Notes" in *Sketches by Boz*

DICKENS, with his usual observations of detail, gives a vignette of the Club used by Members of Parliament.

A superlative Club servant is the butler Nicholas, an unrivalled compounder of salad dressing, an admirable preparer of soda water and lemon, a special mixer of cold grog and punch, and above all, an unequalled judge of cheese. If the old man had such a thing as vanity in his composition, this is certainly his pride. When you had taken your seat in the kitchen and duly noticed the large fire and roasting jack at one end of the room, and the little table for washing glasses and draining jugs at the other—the clock over the window opposite St. Margaret's Church —the deal tables and wax candles, the damask table cloths and bare floor—plate and china on the table and the grid iron on the fire, you may observe a Member of Parliament who has feasted within these walls many a time.

If he is eating his supper now at half past midnight, at what hour can he possibly have dined! A second solid mass of rump steak has disappeared, and he ate the first in four minutes and three seconds, by the clock over the window. Mark the air with which he gloats over the Stilton as he removes the napkin which has been placed beneath his chin to catch the superfluous gravy of the steak, and with what gusto he imbibes the porter which has been fetched especially for him in a pewter pot. Listen to the hoarse sounds of that voice, kept down as it were by layers of solids and deep draughts of rich wine and tell us if you ever saw such a perfect picture of a regular gourmand.

Other members arrive in a great bustle to report that, "The Chancellor of the Exchequer's up", and to get glasses of brandy and water to sustain them. Suddenly a bell is heard to ring with tremendous violence and a cry of "Division" is heard in the passage; away rush the Members pell mell. The room is cleared in an instant; you hear the creaking of the last boot upon the stairs, and are left alone with the leviathan of the rump steaks.

A Farewell Luncheon

Devonshire Terrace, January 1st, 1842

THE little 1200-ton ship that was to take the travellers to America, the S.S. *Britannia*, had arrived at Liverpool and with it had come a great packet of letters containing "all sorts of cordialities, anticipations, and stretching out of hands in token of the welcome awaiting them".

They were to sail on January 4th and on the first they gave a farewell luncheon at Devonshire Terrace. Besides the members of their families, the guests were Mr. and Mrs. Macready (who were taking the children into their own home), Daniel Maclise and John Forster. The house had been let to General Sir John Wilson, but apparently he was not to have access to the wine cellar! Dickens, with the help of Forster, sealed it up, but first they opened "some sparkling Moselle in honour of the ceremony, and drank it then and there to his happy return".

Maclise, knowing how distressed Kate had been at the thought of leaving her children, had done a special drawing of them, just the right size for travelling. It proved to be a great comfort and wherever they went in America it was excitedly unpacked and displayed in their bedroom.

The three-week voyage in the small unstable ship was made doubly miserable by violent storms. The passengers may have been terrified of the raging sea, but Dickens, with his analytical mind, saw even more ghastly possibilities. "I never will trust myself upon the wide ocean if it please Heaven, in a steamer again," he wrote to Forster:

> . . . Consider two of their dangers. First, that if the funnel were blown overboard the vessel must instantly be on fire from stem to stern. . . . Secondly, each of these boats consume between London and Halifax 700 tons of coals; and it is pretty clear from this enormous difference in weight in a ship of only 1200 tons burden in all, that she must be too heavy when she comes out of port, or too light when she goes in. Add to this that by day and night she is full of fire and people, that she has no boats, and that the struggling of that enormous machinery in a heavy sea seems as though it would rend her into fragments—and you may have a pretty consider-able damned good sort of a feeble notion that it don't fit nohow . . .

No wonder they decided to return by sail!

A KATE DICKENS MENU	A MODERN MENU
(4–5 persons)	(6 or more people)
Asparagus Soup (p. 27)	*A Combination Soup*
Turbot with Shrimp Sauce (p. 67)	*Casserole of Pigeons*
	or
Roast Saddle of Mutton	*Bœuf à la Bourguignonne*
(see Roast Lamb, p. 19)	*Saffron Rice (p. 28). Green Vegetable*
Stewed Pigeons	
Mashed and Brown Potatoes	*English Trifle or Zabaglione*
Broccoli. Salad	
	Fried Mushrooms on Toast
Pound Pudding (p. 200)	*or*
Macaroni (p. 104)	*Biscuits and Cheeses*

Combination Soups

Using packet or canned soups, make any interesting combination. For instance, Lobster/Celery, Chicken/Asparagus, Oxtail/Mushroom, Onion/Celery/Tomato, Pea/Vegetable, and so on. The combinations are almost endless.

Casserole of Pigeons — *Serves 5*

5 plump young pigeons
5 rashers of bacon
2 peeled, chopped onions
2 level tablesp. flour
$\frac{1}{2}$ pint (1 cup) water with 1 chicken cube
5 tablesp. red wine or cooking sherry
Salt, pepper, and 1 teasp. sugar
$\frac{1}{2}$ teasp. fresh thyme or $\frac{1}{4}$ teasp. dried

(1) Preheat oven to 300° or No. $2\frac{1}{2}$–3.
(2) Buy prepared pigeons and cut each down the centre. Wash and remove sharp little bones.
(3) Remove rinds from rashers and cut into 2-inch pieces. Fry in a pan, adding the onion. Fry for about 3 minutes, then sprinkle in the flour and continue frying for 2 minutes.
(4) Add water and cube, then wine or sherry. Add sugar, plenty of salt and pepper and thyme.
(5) Put pigeons in casserole and pour the sauce over. Cover with lid and cook slowly for 2 or more hours. Older pigeons will need 3 hours at least. Add more water or wine if necessary.

Bœuf à la Bourguignonne
Serves 6

2 lb. rump steak, cut into 1½ inch cubes
½ lb. bacon, in a ½-inch slice
3 tablesp. oil or butter
1 large Spanish onion, peeled and chopped
3 level tablesp. flour
2 sliced carrots
1 bay leaf, 1 teasp. thyme
1 pint canned consommé, or water with 2 beef cubes
1 dozen tiny onions
4 oz. button mushrooms
½ pint red Burgundy
2 teasp. sugar, 2 teasp. salt and a little freshly ground pepper
2 tablesp. brandy

(1) Preheat oven to 250° or No. 2.
(2) Melt oil or butter and fry the meat for a few minutes.
(3) Add onion and flour and continue frying for 5 minutes.
(4) Add consommé and cook and stir until thickened. Add carrots, bay leaf, thyme, seasoning and wine.
(5) Cut bacon into ½-inch cubes and add.
(6) Put into large casserole dish. Cover and cook slowly in oven for 3 hours.
(7) After 2 hours, add the small onions, button mushrooms and the brandy. Taste and add more salt if necessary.

Note. 1 or 2 crushed cloves of garlic may be added.

English Trifle
Serves 6

1 unfilled sponge sandwich
Raspberry jam
1 egg
½ pint (1 cup) milk
1 level tablesp. sugar
½ teasp. vanilla essence
6 tablesp. port wine
Ratafias
Whipped cream, almonds and cherries

(1) Break sponge cake into pieces and spread with jam. Put into a glass serving dish.
(2) Make custard by heating milk with sugar, then adding beaten egg. Cook gently but do not allow to boil. The custard is ready when it will coat the spoon.
(3) Pour wine over cake. Allow custard to cool to lukewarm and pour over.
(4) Cover with a layer of ratafias.
(5) Whip cream and spread on top. Decorate with blanched sliced almonds and glacé cherries.

Zabaglione
Serves 6

4 eggs, separated
2 level tablesp. sugar
1 level teasp. powdered gelatine in 3 teasp. water
6 tablesp. marsala
¼ teasp. salt
¼ pint whipping cream

(1) Separate eggs and drop yolks into top of double boiler.
(2) Add water, gelatine mixed with the cold water, and the marsala.
(3) Have water boiling underneath and stir and cook until mixture has thickened. Remove from heat and whisk until cool.
(4) Beat egg whites with salt until very stiff and stir in.
(5) Add half the cream. Pour into stemmed glasses. Top with a blob of cream and serve with a wafer.

Guilty Food

Great Expectations

UNDER the grudging care of his sister who was married to kindly Joe Gargary, the boy, Pip, endures a festive meal with a conscience that is far from clear!

We were to have a superb dinner consisting of a leg of pickled pork and a pair of stuffed fowls. A handsome mince pie and the pudding was already on the boil.

I opened the door to the company and last of all Uncle Pumblechook; a large hard breathing middle aged slow man, with a mouth like a fish, dull staring eyes, and sandy hair standing upright on his head, so that he looked as if he had just been choked and had, at that moment, come to. "I have brought you, Mum, a bottle of port wine," said Uncle Pumblechook, carrying the two bottles like dumb bells.

I was squeezed, with a corner of the table in my chest, and the Pumble-chookian elbow in my eye. I was regaled with scaly tips of drumsticks and with those obscure corners of pork of which the pig, when living, had had the least reason to be vain. I might have been an unfortunate little bull in a Spanish arena, I got so smartingly touched up with moral goads, until Uncle Pumblechook led the company back to the theme of food; "Pork regarded as biled, is rich, ain't it?" he said. "Have a little brandy Uncle," said my sister.

I held tight to the leg of the table under the table cloth with both hands and awaited my fate, while my sister went for the stone bottle and poured his brandy out. Instantly, after he drank the company were seized with consternation owing to his springing to his feet, turning round several times in an appalling spasmodic whooping-cough dance and rushing out of the door.

I had filled up the stone bottle with tar-water with which I was some-times horribly dosed.

Uncle Pumblechook asked for hot gin and water, and I still held the leg of the table and pressed it to my bosom as if it had been the companion of my soul. Now my sister went out to fetch the pie which I alone knew was not on the larder shelf. I have never been absolutely certain whether I uttered a shrill yell of terror merely in spirit or in the bodily hearing of the company.

I released the leg of the table, and ran for my life.

Triumph in America

A Transatlantic Menu

THE moment their fiery little cockleshell of a ship arrived at Halifax, then later at Boston for the final embarkation the enthusiastic welcome began. Dickens, with his love of having fun with words called it an *enthoosymoosy* welcome. This was no exaggeration. In one of his first letters to Forster he says: "How can I give you the faintest notion of my reception here; of the crowds that pour in and out the whole day; of the people that line the streets when I go out; of the cheering when I went to the theatre; of the copies of verse; letters of congratulation; welcomes of all kinds, balls, dinners, assemblies without end . . .".

All this Kate shared as well. But for her the triumphs were in the early stages dampened by toothache and a swollen face. With her charming new dresses, her peaches and cream complexion and large blue eyes, she should have been a sensation, so how cruel of Fate to mar her great debut in this way. Fortunately she did recover eventually and was able to enjoy the great dance and dinner given to them in New York. But as the tour proceeded her enjoyment was often marred by her propensity for getting into the wars. To Forster Dickens wrote: "I say nothing about Kate's troubles—but you recollect her propensity? She falls, into, or out of, every coach or boat we enter; scrapes the skin off her legs; brings great sores and swellings on her feet; chips large fragments out of her ankle-bones; and makes herself blue with bruises. She really has, however, since we got over the first trial . . . *made a most admirable traveller* in every respect. . . ." (She must have needed that boost!)

Dickens's appearance surprised the Americans. They could hardly believe that this young man, still in his twenties, with the fresh, almost girlish face, keen laughing eyes and (to them) foppish dress could be the author whose pen could wield such power for good and reveal such a depth of human understanding. Perhaps they expected that such a man should be powerful in his build and countenance and to stalk their land like a giant. But Dickens too had some surprises. He expected mainly to be welcomed as a successful novelist, but instead he found that it was his interest in reform and education that excited the greatest adulation. "Dickens," cried Daniel Webster, "had done more already to ameliorate the condition of the English poor than all the statesmen Great Britain had sent to Parliament."

AN AMERICAN BANQUET

Avocado and Orange Cocktail

———

Oyster and Shrimp Chowder

———

Capon in Champagne with
Corn and Raisin Stuffing
Peas in Baskets. Scalloped Potatoes (p. 16)
Asparagus
Individual Salads (any Green Salad)

———

Banana Cream Pie
Apricot Chiffon Pie (p. 132)

———

Olives, Nuts, Celery

———

Crackers and Cheeses

Avocado and Orange Cocktail   *Serves 6–8*

2 Avocado pears
1 can orange segments
1 level tablesp. sugar
A little Kirsch

(1) Peel pears, remove stones and cut into cubes.
(2) Drain orange segments well. Add to cubes with sugar. Allow to stand until sugar has dissolved.
(3) Spoon into cocktail glasses and pour a little Kirsch over each. Top with a cherry.

Oyster and Shrimp Chowder   *Serves 8–10*

1 quart oysters
½ lb. prepared shrimps
1 packet cream of mushroom soup
1 large can of lobster cream soup
Water (1 cup)
Milk (1 cup)
1 tablesp. chopped parsley

(1) Shell and beard oysters.
(2) Add ½ pint water and ½ pint milk to mushroom soup. Cook the required time given on the packet.
(3) Add cream of lobster soup and heat.
(4) Add shrimps then oysters and parsley. Just bring to the boil, but do not continue cooking. Taste and add salt and pepper if necessary.

Capon in Champagne

1 capon

Stuffing
1 can sweetcorn kernels
2 oz. (1 cup) soft breadcrumbs
1 cup seedless raisins
1 teasp. salt, a little pepper
1 teasp. dried basil
2 teasp. butter

1 split champagne
½ lb. mushrooms
2 tablesp. butter
1 tablesp. flour

(1) Preheat oven to 350° or No. 4.
(2) Combine ingredients for stuffing and add butter, softened. Fill cavity and truss.
(3) Place capon in baking dish and pour champagne over. Cook for 30 minutes, basting twice.
(4) Tip champagne into a jug or bowl. Add 2 tablesp. fat to pan and when hot, baste capon.
(5) Roast for about 1½ hours, or until tender.
(6) Fry mushrooms in butter. Add flour, then pour in champagne. Cook and stir until thick. Season with salt. Serve this sauce with capon.

Peas in Baskets

Makes 12

12 thin slices of bread 4 inches square
Butter
1 large packet frozen peas, or fresh cooked ones.

(1) Spread the bread with butter. Fit into patty pans with the four corners standing up.
(2) Bake in a moderate oven with capon or other poultry or meat. Remove when crisp and golden.
(3) Fill with cooked green peas. Place on serving dish around capon.

Banana Cream Pie

Serves 8

8 oz. crushed cookie or wafer crumbs
1 level tablesp. sugar
4 oz. melted butter
½ teasp. vanilla essence
1 pint (2 cups) milk
2 level tablesp. cornflour
2 eggs
2½ oz. (4 level tablesp.) sugar
2 tablesp. lemon juice and grated rind
3 or 4 peeled sliced bananas
About ½ pint whipped cream

(1) Combine crumbs (any sweet biscuits, cookies or wafers), sugar, melted butter and vanilla. Press into and line a 9- or 9½-inch pie dish about 2 inches deep. Put away in 'frig.' until firm.
(2) Heat milk and add sugar. Mix cornflour with 2 tablesp. water and stir in. Cook until thick.
(3) Beat eggs and stir in. Cook until the mixture just comes to the boil. Remove from heat and add lemon juice and rind.
(4) Cool, then add sliced bananas. Tip into shell.
(5) Top with a thick layer of whipped cream.

The serialized copies of *Bleak House*, showing some of the advertisements used

Festivities and Theatricals

From America to Canada, May 1842

THE one note of discord in the whole triumphant tour of America is so well known that it is now part of history. Dickens, always incensed at any sort of injustice, spoke at a dinner in Boston of the need for legal enforcement of International Copyright. He was appealing, he said, not only on his own behalf, but on that of all authors whose works were printed and sold in other countries without one penny coming to the author in royalties or any other type of payment.

The next day he received bad press reports and indignant snubs, but he had struck the first blow against an injustice which today would be considered intolerable. Many great American writers were in agreement on this question, notably Washington Irving who at a dinner in New York's City Hotel gave the toast, "Charles Dickens, the Nation's guest, coupled with International copyright," then jokingly continued, "it is but fair that those who have laurels for their brows should be permitted to browse on their laurels!" (Smiles all around, but no doubt a little forced on some lips.)

By the end of April, after three and a half months of incessant and often exhausting travel and festivities in all parts of the U.S.A., they reached Canada and the Niagara Falls. As he neared the great spectacle Dickens's excitement was enormous. In one of his fascinating American letters to Forster he wrote: "taking Kate with me I hurried to the Horseshoe Fall. I went down alone, into the very basin. It would be hard for a man to stand nearer God than he does there. There was a bright rainbow at my feet; and from that I looked up—great Heavens! to *what* a fall of bright green water! The broad, deep mighty stream seems to die in the act of falling; and from its unfathomable grave, arises that tremendous ghost of a spray and mist which is never laid. . . ."

In Montreal Dickens was able to indulge in his favourite pastime, theatricals. He was in his element as he threw himself, with a crowd of other enthusiasts, into the production of some private productions at the Queen's Theatre, Montreal. The list of the cast for one of the plays included Mrs. Charles Dickens and on the copy of the programme sent to Forster Dickens had put eight exclamation marks after her name. "Think of Kate playing!" he said, "and playing devilish well!"

A CANADIAN DINNER PARTY MENU

Canadian Fish Chowder
Cheese Soufflé (p. 155)
Breaded Veal Cutlets in Claret Sauce
Riced Potatoes. Green Vegetables
Glazed Sweet Potatoes
Biscuit Tortoni
Peeping Tom Apples

Canadian Fish Chowder — *Serves 8*

2 lb. fish (cod, haddock or any
  suitable type)
4 rashers of streaky bacon
2 large onions, peeled and chopped
1 lb. old potatoes, peeled and
  quartered
1½ pints (3 cups) water
1 pint (2 cups) milk
1 bay leaf
Salt and pepper

(1) Ask the butcher for the heads, backbone, etc., of the fish. Put these into a pan and cook with 1 cup water for half an hour. Strain.

(2) Remove rinds from bacon, cut into 1-inch pieces and fry in large saucepan. Add chopped onions and fry for another 2 minutes.

(3) Add fish liquid, water, then potatoes and bay leaf.

(4) Remove skin from fish and see that there are no bones left. Cut into 2-inch pieces and add to the mixture. Cover and simmer for 30 minutes or until potatoes are mushy. Season well with salt and pepper.

(5) Add milk. Bring to the boil. Serve without straining. Chopped parsley may be added.

Breaded Veal Cutlets in Claret Sauce — *Serves 8*

8 or more veal cutlets
Juice of 2 lemons
1 level teasp. onion salt and 1 bay
  leaf
3 tablesp. fat
Flour
1 beaten egg with 2 tablesp. water
Dry white breadcrumbs
2 level tablesp. flour
¾ pint (1½ cups) water and ¼ pint
  claret or dark sherry
Salt and pepper

(1) Marinate chops in lemon juice with bay leaf and onion-salt for an hour or longer. Turn now and again.

(2) Preheat oven to 350° or No. 4.

(3) Drain cutlets then dip first in flour, then in egg, then in breadcrumbs.

(4) Have fat in baking dish in oven and allow to get hot. Put in cutlets and turn over to coat them on both sides with the fat.

(5) Bake for 1–1½ hours or until tender. Reduce heat if cutlets are cooking too quickly.

(6) When nicely browned lift on to serving dish and keep warm.

(7) Have 1 tablesp. of the fat left in pan. Sprinkle in flour and cook on top of cooker until browned. Add water and claret or sherry. Cook and stir until thick. Season well with salt and pepper. Serve this gravy separately.

Riced Potatoes. Cook floury potatoes and mash. Do not add milk or butter. Press through coarse strainer.

Glazed Sweet Potatoes. Melt together 2 or more tablesp. butter and brown sugar. Drain the boiled sweet potatoes and add. Cook and turn until glazed and lightly browned.

Strawberry Biscuit Tortoni   *Serves 8*

1 cup crushed macaroons
1½ pints strawberry ice-cream
¼ pint whipped cream
Strawberries

(1) Mix macaroons with whipped cream.
(2) Spread ice-cream in trays of refrigerator.
(3) Cover with the macaroons and cream. Put into refrigerator and when firm decorate with strawberries sprinkled with a little sugar. Two tablesp. brandy could be added to the cream and macaroons.

Peeping Tom Apples   *Serves 8*

8 or more smallish eating apples
Maraschino cherries and chopped walnuts
8 oz. (1 cup) sugar
1 pint (2 cups) water
1½ level tablesp. powdered gelatine
Whipped cream
Brandy (optional)

(1) Preheat oven to 350° or No. 4.
(2) Core apples, then peel. Fill hollows with the mixed nuts and cherries, finishing with a whole cherry. Place in baking dish.
(3) Pour the water and sugar around and add the syrup from the jar of cherries.
(4) Baste the apples with the liquid, and cook until just tender, but not broken. Baste several times.
(5) Place apples in cups, one in each with the cherry downwards.
(6) To the hot syrup add the gelatine. When dissolved pour over apples in cups. When set, dip each in hot water and unmould. Any jelly left over could be chopped and used to decorate the dish.
(7) Serve with whipped cream. Brandy may be added.

Boston Food

American Notes (1842)

ON JANUARY 28th, 1842 Kate and Charles, with Kate's maid Anne, arrived in Boston. Dickens wrote:

The tone of society in Boston is one of perfect politeness and good breeding; the ladies are unquestionably very beautiful. Their education is much as with us; neither better nor worse. I had heard some marvellous stories in this respect; but not believing them was not disappointed.

The usual dinner hour is two o'clock. A dinner party takes place at five; and at an evening party they seldom sup later than eleven. I could never find out any difference between a party at Boston and a party in London, saving that at the former place all assemblies are held at a more rational hour; that the conversation may possibly be a little louder and more cheerful; that a guest is usually expected to ascend to the very top of the house to take his cloak off; that he is certain to see at every dinner an unusual amount of poultry on the table; and at every supper at least two mighty bowls of hot stewed oysters, in any one of which a half grown Duke of Clarence might be smothered easily. The Bar is a large room with a stone floor and there people stand and smoke and lounge about all evening. There too, the stranger is initiated into the mysteries of Gin Sling, Cocktail, Sangaree, Mint Julep, Sherry-cobbler, Timber Doodle and other rare drinks.

Tremont-house is full of boarders many of whom sleep upon the premises and contract by week for their board. A public table is laid in a very handsome hall for breakfast, dinner and supper. The advent for each of these epochs in the day is proclaimed by an awful gong which shakes the window frames and horribly disturbs the nervous foreigners.

In our private room the cloth could not, for any earthly consideration, have been laid for dinner without a huge glass dish of cranberries in the middle of the table and breakfast would have been no breakfast unless the principal dish were a deformed beef steak with a great flat bone in the centre, swimming in hot butter and sprinkled with the very blackest of all possible black pepper.

Home!!!!!!!!!

Devonshire Terrace, Early July 1842

THE moment the date was fixed for the return to England and their darlings, the travellers could hardly eat or sleep for excitement. Charles wrote in his last letter to Forster: "we shall soon meet, please God, and be happier and merrier than ever we were . . . Oh, home —home—home—home—home—home—HOME!!!!!!!!!!!!

Dickens's young brother Fred had brought the children from Macready's home to Devonshire Terrace in readiness for the great re-union, but since in those days the exact date of the arrival of a ship could not be known, they were tucked up in bed when their parents burst excitedly into their nursery. Apparently the reunion was so overwhelming that poor little Charley, then 5½, was quite overcome. In later years he wrote:

> I distinguished myself in a most brilliant manner by being frightened into some sort of fit or convulsion on the unexpected appearance of my parents at my bedside. My first really clear recollection is in connection with a certain American rocking chair which he had brought back from the States and in which he often used to sit on an evening singing comic songs to a wondering and delighted audience consisting of myself and two sisters. One of these songs was *The Loving Ballad of Lord Bateman* in the composition of which my father, Thackeray and George Cruikshank were all supposed to have a hand. This was in the days before the great George (Cruikshank) took to teetotalism and to flinging an infinite quantity of cold water over everything. Another favourite song of ours was concerned with Guy Fawkes. Some of Tom Moores' melodies also formed part of the repertoire as well as others I have forgotten, but the impression of the singer as he sat in that rocking chair with us three children about him or on his knee has never in the least faded from my mind.

For some weeks after their return they were kept busy with home-coming festivities both at the homes of their friends and at Devonshire Terrace. Kate's sister Georgina, now 17, was already established in the house when they returned. At first Kate was glad to have her to share the responsibility of a growing family and a famous husband. But as time went on her poor health put her at a disadvantage and when it was too late she found that the reins of the household management had slipped from her. But this did not happen until very much later in her married life. Just now she was very much the charming mistress of Devonshire Terrace.

A KATE DICKENS MENU	A MODERN MENU
(6–7 persons)	*Lobster Newberg*
Fried Flounder with Shrimp Sauce (p. 7)	*Roast Beef with Yorkshire Pudding and Horseradish Sauce Roasted Potatoes. Cauliflower*
Roast Beef Cold Pigeon Pie (p. 164). Peas Potatoes. Salad	*Marrons à la Crème with Ice Cream*
Currant and Raspberry Tart Macaroni	*Biscuits and Cheeses*

Lobster Newberg   *Serves 6–7*

½ lb. lobster meat, flaked
4 oz. washed sliced mushrooms
2 level tablesp. butter
1 small grated onion
2 level tablesp. flour
¼ pint milk
¼ pint cream, single would do
4 tablesp. pale sherry
Salt and pepper

(1) Prepare lobster meat and mushrooms.
(2) Melt butter and grate in the onion. Begin to fry, then add mushrooms. Cook for about 8 minutes.
(3) Add flour and cook for 2 minutes, then add milk. Cook and stir until thick. Add cream and sherry. Season with salt and pepper.
(4) Lastly add lobster. Heat, but do not boil again. Fill scallop shells and sprinkle with breadcrumbs. Dot with butter.
(5) Keep hot in a moderate oven.

Roast Beef

4 or more lb. rolled sirloin, wing rib or other good joint
3 tablesp. fat
Flour and salt and pepper

(1) Preheat oven to 425° or No. 7.
(2) Sprinkle meat with flour and salt and pepper.
(3) Put fat into baking dish and allow to become very hot in oven.
(4) Put meat into dish and baste with hot fat.
(5) Bake at the hot heat for 15 minutes, then reduce heat to 350° or No. 4. Roast for 1½ hours for rare finish, 2–2½ hours for well-done finish.
(6) For Roasted Potatoes, see p. 36.

Horseradish Sauce (Kate Dickens's Recipe)

Stew an onion in a little fish stock until it will pulp, add 1 or 2 spoonfuls of grated horseradish, and one or two spoonfuls of essence of anchovies. Beat all together over a fire, thicken it with a little butter and finish with a spoonful of lemon pickle or lemon juice. Vinegar may be substituted, in which case it must be mixed with the horseradish and boiled with it, while the lemon pickle (being of delicate flavour) should only be warmed.

Yorkshire Pudding
Serves 4–6

1 egg
4 oz. flour
$\frac{1}{2}$ teasp. salt and a little pepper
$\frac{1}{2}$ cup milk and $\frac{1}{2}$ cup water

Note. Some prefer to cook the Yorkshire pudding around and under the meat. To do this, lift meat on a trivet first.

(1) Beat egg in a bowl and add the water.
(2) Sieve in flour and seasoning and beat until smooth. Add milk.
(3) Have 3 tablesp. of the fat from the meat in a square pan. Let it heat on top of the cooker until it is still with a faint white mist rising (about 375°F).
(4) Pour in the batter and bake for about 40–45 minutes in the hottest part of the oven (the top). Cut into slices and arrange around the meat.

Marrons à la Crème
Serves 6–7

1 pint chestnuts
$\frac{1}{2}$ pint (1 cup) milk
4 oz. ($\frac{1}{2}$ cup) sugar
$\frac{1}{2}$ pint whipping cream
3 tablesp. brandy

Note. Canned chestnut purée may be used.

(1) Cook chestnuts in boiling water until shell and skin may be removed.
(2) Peel then cook in the milk until soft. Mash. Add sugar.
(3) Whip cream until stiff (but not into butter!)
(4) Add chestnut purée and brandy.
Serve with ice-cream.

Macaroni Savoury

8 oz. macaroni
4 oz. grated tasty cheese
1 tablesp. anchovy sauce
$\frac{1}{2}$ pint white sauce
Salt and pepper or cayenne pepper
Breadcrumbs and butter
Bacon (optional)

(1) Cook macaroni in salted water until tender. Drain.
(2) Add all the ingredients and tip into one oven dish, or individual ramakins.
(3) Sprinkle with breadcrumbs, dot with butter and bake for about 15 minutes.
(4) May be served with bacon.

American Food

Martin Chuzzlewit

YOUNG Martin Chuzzlewit decided to pawn his possessions and seek a new life in far-off America. He took with him his devoted friend Mark Tapley (always determined on being jolly and coming out strong in the worst possible circumstances) and after the crossing they landed at the port of New York. They were met by the Editor of *The New York Rowdy Journal* and taken to the lodging house of Major and Mrs. Pawkins. Here they experienced their first meal in the United States.

The dining room showed cold white walls and ceiling, a dreary waste of dining table and a collection of cane bottom chairs. In the further region was a stove garnished on either side with a great brass spittoon. The atmosphere of the room was flavoured by a sickly gush of soup from the kitchen and by such remote suggestions of tobacco as lingered within the brass receptacles beforementioned.

At the sound of a bell as loud as a fire alarm, a rush of people came plunging wildly in, their fierce excitement due to dinner being ready. Eighteen or twenty persons, some five or six of these ladies who sat together wedged in a little phalanx, had already begun at a rate which was quite alarming and everybody seemed to eat his utmost in self defence as if a famine were expected before breakfast time. A turkey at the top, a pair of ducks at the bottom and two fowls in the middle disappeared as rapidly as if every bird had the use of his wings and had flown in desperation down a human throat. The oysters stewed and pickled leaped from their capacious reservoirs and slid by scores into the mouths of the assembly. The sharpest pickles vanished with whole cucumbers at once like sugar plums and no man winked an eye. Great heaps of indigestible matter melted away as ice before the sun. It was a solemn and an awful thing to see dyspeptic individuals bolting their food in wedges and spare men with lank and rigid cheeks came out unsatisfied from the destruction of heavy dishes and glared with watchful eyes upon the pastry.

What Mrs. Pawkins felt at dinner time each day is hidden from human knowledge. But she had one comfort. It was soon over.

A Social Whirl for William Longfellow

Devonshire Terrace, Early October 1842

THERE is no doubt that it is the test of time that measures true greatness. In his own day William Longfellow was hailed as a great poet but did his contemporaries realize that right on through his own and our present century his verses would be chanted in schools and colleges in almost every part of the world? "The Village Blacksmith", "The Song of Hiawatha", "The Wreck of the Hesperus" (now more a condition than a story!), "Excelsior", "Paul Revere's Ride" and all those other familiar poems are today as much a part of life as the rising of the Moon or the setting of the Sun. Yet in Dickens's schooldays they were unknown.

While Dickens was in America, Longfellow told him of a trip he had planned to Europe, so it was arranged that as soon as he set foot in England he was to come straight to Devonshire Terrace. He arrived at the beginning of October and soon was in the thick of the social whirl. London teemed with the famous and at the London salons and at dinner at Devonshire Terrace and other homes he met such lions as Lord Tennyson, Bulwer Lytton, Thackeray, Carlyle, Ainsworth, Forster, Sam Rogers, the intellectual and controversial Lady Blessington with Count d'Orsay, Lady Holland and many other bright lights of the literary scene.

Art and the stage were also represented and so were people famous for their contribution to welfare such as Southwood Smith, the great sanitary reformer who brought to the notice of Dickens the sorry plight of young children forced to slave for long hours in mines and factories. Dr. John Elliotson too was around. He was the founder of the Phrenological Society and an exponent of the healing powers of mesmerism. Dickens was impressed by the theory and tried it on his own family, often with success.

Some of London's most brilliant functions were held in Gore House, the home of Lady Blessington. But since her association with Count d'Orsay was not fully explained, many Victorian ladies felt obliged, in case of contamination, to decline her invitations. Gore House was later demolished and in its place rose London's great Albert Hall, completed in 1871. Longfellow wrote home about his stay with the Dickens's family, "I write this from Dickens's study from which so many luminous things have radiated," he said. "The raven croaks from the garden and the ceaseless roar of London fills my ears." He returned to America on the new ship *The Great Western*, thought then to be the ultimate in maritime engineering.

A KATE DICKENS MENU
(14–18 persons)
White Soup (p. 191)
Spring Vegetable Soup

*Boiled Salmon with Lobster Sauce
and Cucumbers (p. 56)*
Mushroom Patties.   Lobster Cutlets

*Lamb's Cutlets with
Cucumber Sauce (p. 119)*
*Rabbit Curry Smothered with
White Sauce*
*Roast Haunch of Mutton
(see Roast Lamb, p. 19)*
Boiled Fowl and Tongues
Spinach Salad (p. 75).   New Potatoes
Duckling.   Guinea Fowl
Asparagus

Clear Jelly
Italian Cream (p. 120)
Marble Cream (p. 201)
Strawberry Cream (p. 201)

Lobster Salad (p. 202)

A MODERN COCKTAIL PARTY MENU
Oyster Patties (p. 195)
Mushroom Patties
*Sweetcorn and Cheese in Choux
Pastry Cases*
Prune Bacon Rolls
Cheese and Bacon Savouries (p. 87)
or
Toasted Cheese (p. 40), Cut Small
Cheese Dip with Yoghurt
Avocado Dip
Savoury Crackers and Large Potato Chips
Cheese Straws
Heated Cocktail Sausages

Choose 4 or more of these savouries depending on the size of the party.

Mushroom Patties (Victorian Recipe)   *Makes 24–30*

½ lb. mushrooms
2 tablesp. butter
½ pint (1 cup) milk
1½ level tablesp. flour
Salt and pepper
24 patty cases, from the pastrycook

(1) Wash and slice mushrooms. Peel if skin is tough.
(2) Melt butter and fry mushrooms for 10 minutes.
(3) Stir in the flour and cook 1 minute, then add milk and seasoning.
(4) Fill pastry cases with this mixture. Reheat before serving.

Sweetcorn and Cheese in Choux Pastry Cases   *Makes 36*

Make or buy 36 choux pastry cases
   about ping-pong ball size
1 can of sweetcorn, cream style
3 oz. grated cheese
Salt and pepper

(1) Combine sweetcorn and cheese and season with salt and pepper.
(2) Fill cases with the mixture and heat in oven for about 20 minutes.

Prune Bacon Rolls
Makes about 36

Prunes
Port wine, ½ cup
1 lb. streaky bacon

(1) Cook prunes in 1 pint water and 2 tablesp. sugar.
(2) When soft, remove stones. Soak prunes in the port wine for an hour or longer.
(3) Remove rinds from bacon and cut into 5-inch lengths. Place 1 or 2 prunes on each piece and roll up. Secure with picks.
(4) Place on oven tray and bake until bacon begins to sizzle. Serve hot, garnished with sprigs of parsley.

Cheese Dip with Yoghurt
Serves 14–16

4 oz. cream cheese
1 jar yoghurt (5 oz.)
2 tablesp. mayonnaise with 2 teasp. sugar
2 teasp. chopped parsley, or chives, or both

(1) Beat together all ingredients and add a little salt and pepper.
(2) Chill. Serve with crisp savoury crackers and potato chips. Small pieces of celery or carrot sticks may also be served with the dip.

Avocado Dip
Serves 12

1 ripe avocado pear
6 oz. cream cheese
2 teasp. sugar
2 tablesp. mayonnaise
2 tablesp. cream or top milk
½ teasp. salt and a little pepper

(1) Cut pear in half, remove stone and scoop flesh into a bowl.
(2) Add cream cheese, mayonnaise, sugar and cream. Season with salt and pepper.
(3) Whisk all together adding more cream if necessary to make a perfect dipping consistency.
(4) See step 2 of above recipe.

Cheese Straws
Makes about 48

1 lb. puff pastry
6 oz. grated tasty cheese
Salt, pepper, cayenne

(1) Either make or buy the pastry.
(2) Roll out to about ¼-inch thickness and spread with the cheese.
(3) Sprinkle with salt, pepper and a little cayenne.
(4) Fold pastry over and roll, then fold and roll again, until the cheese is well incorporated with the pastry.
(5) Finally roll out very thinly—about ⅜ inch. Cut into fingers about ¼ inch wide and 5 inches long. Bake in a hot oven for 10–15 minutes, or until a golden colour.

Banquet Food

The Letters of Charles Dickens (1847)

From the house which he described as "preposterous" (see p. 138) Dickens wrote of a banquet held in his honour.

(see p. 138)

Three gorgeous drawing rooms with ten thousand wax candles in golden sconces, terminated in a dining room of unprecedented magnificence with two enormous transparent plate glass doors in it, looking straight into the kitchen, with cooks in their white paper caps dishing the dinner.

Forth from the plate glass doors issues the Banquet, the most wonderful feast ever tasted by mortal; at the present price of truffles, that article alone costing for eight people at least five pounds.

On the table are ground glass jugs of peculiar construction, laden with the finest growth of champagne and the coolest ice. With the third course is issued Port wine which would fetch two guineas a bottle at any sale.

The dinner done, Oriental flowers in vases of golden cobweb are placed upon the board, and with the ice is issued Brandy, buried for 100 years. To that succeeds Coffee brought from the remotest East for an equal quantity of Californian gold dust.

The Company being returned to the drawing room, tables roll in laden with Cigarettes from the Harem of the Sultan, and with cool drinks in which the flavour of the Lemon, arrived yesterday from Algeria, struggles voluptuously with the delicate orange arrived this morning from Lisbon.

A big table rolls in, heavy with massive furniture of silver and breathing incense in the form of a little present of tea, direct from China.

Even now I have forgotten to set down the half of it, in particular a far larger plum pudding than was ever seen in England at Christmas time, served with a celestial sauce in colour like the orange blossom and in substance like the blossom powdered and bathed in dew.

This item was named "Hommage a l'illustre ecrivain d'Angleterre".

A Christmas Carol

A Five O'clock Gathering at Devonshire Terrace, Christmas 1843

THE salutary story, *A Christmas Carol*, showing how goodwill, kindness and simplicity may be used for the salvation of greed and selfishness, enlarged even further Dickens's reputation as a humanitarian. It was published a few days before Christmas 1843 and was an instant success. Six thousand copies were sold in one day and by early 1844 three editions were already taken by the trade.

Even so, the expense of keeping a large family with various dependents adhering, together with the upkeep and running of a large home, worried him considerably. To Forster he said, "My year's bills are so terrific that all the energy and determination I can possibly exert will be required to clear me. . . ."

The tenderness he showed in the *Carol* permeated his own home life and was recorded many times by his children in their reminiscences of their father. Mamie wrote:

> In our childish days my father used to take us every 24th day of December to a toy shop in Holborn where we were allowed to select our Christmas presents and also any we wished to give to our little companions. Although I believe we were often an hour or more in the shop before our several tastes were satisfied, he never showed the least impatience, was always interested and desirous as we were that we should choose exactly what we liked best. . . .

And later another charming tribute from the same pen:

> My father was the fun and life of Christmas gatherings for he loved to emphasise Christmas in every way and considered that the great festival should be fragrant with the love we should bear one another. Long walks with him were daily treats to be remembered. Games passed our evenings merrily. "Dumb Crambo" was a favourite and one in which my father's great imitative ability showed finely. I remember one evening his dumb showing of the word "frog" was so extremely laughable that even the memory of it convulsed Marcus Stone, the clever artist, when he tried to imitate it.

Another game that had caught on in the Dickens household was the game we now know as "Any Questions", but which was then called "Yes and No". It is described in full in *A Christmas Carol*. The evening was also gay with charades (rehearsed that very morning) and many country dances of home-made invention were strenuously performed. The finale was usually the Sir Roger de Coverley, danced very much in the same manner as at old Fezziwig's Ball in the *Carol*.

CHARLES DICKENS'S PUNCH PARTY

Christmas Cake
Christmas Mince Pies
Assorted Sandwiches
Charles Dickens's Punch
or
Victorian Shrub (a Rum Punch)

CHRISTMAS EGG-NOG PARTY
Christmas Cake
Christmas Mince Pies
Assorted Canapes
Large Egg-nog

Christmas or Christening Cake

4 lb. mixed fruit (including sultanas, raisins, currants, peel and cherries. Add 6 oz. blanched almonds
3 level tablesp. cornflour
1¼ lb. plain flour
½ teasp. baking powder
½ teasp. ground nutmeg
⅛ teasp. ground cloves
½ teasp. cinnamon
1 lb. butter
1 lb. brown sugar
10 eggs
1 teasp. each of lemon, vanilla and almond essences
5 tablesp. brandy
2 tablesp. sherry

Note. If margarine or unsalted butter is used add 1 level teasp. salt

(1) Prepare fruit and almonds and mix with the cornflour.
(2) Sieve together the flour, spices and baking powder.
(3) Preheat oven to 250° or No. 2. Line a 10-inch deep cakepan with 2 thicknesses of greaseproof paper.
(4) Cream together the sugar and butter until light and smooth. Beat the eggs well.
(5) Add 1 tablesp. of the flour, then add the egg a little at a time, beating well between each addition.
(6) When all the egg has been added, stir in fruit, then flour, essences, 2 tablesp. of the brandy and the sherry.
(7) Let everyone have a stir for luck, then turn into lined pan. Smooth the top with a wet knife, then make a depression in the centre so that the cake will rise evenly.
(8) Bake for 5–5½ hours. Heat may be reduced to 225° or No. 1 if cake seems to be cooking too quickly. Everything depends on oven.
(9) When cooked and still hot, pour over the rest of the brandy. Leave cake in pan until cold before turning out.

Christmas Mince Pies   *Makes about 18*

4 oz. butter or margarine
4 oz. (½ cup) sugar
1 egg
8 oz. (1½ cups) S.R. flour, or plain flour with 1½ level teasp. baking powder
½ level teasp. salt
1 jar mincemeat with ½ lb. extra sultanas and a little brandy if desired

(1) Preheat oven to 350° or No. 4.
(2) For the shortcake pastry, cream butter or margarine and sugar.
(3) Add 2 teasp. of the flour, then the egg and beat well.
(4) Add flour and form into a soft dough. Roll out and line deep patty pans.
(5) Fill with the mincemeat, then top with rounds of the pastry. Pinch all around to seal and decorate, or seal with fork marks.
(6) Bake for 20–25 minutes.

Charles Dickens's Punch
3 Pints

Peel into a very strong common basin (which may be broken, in case of accident, without damage to the owners' peace or pocket) the rinds of 3 lemons, cut very thin, and with as little as possible of the white coating between the peel and the fruit, attached. Add a double handful of lump sugar (good measure), a pint of good old rum and a large wine glass full of brandy—if it be not a large claret glass, say two. Set this on fire, by filling a warm silver spoon with the spirit, lighting the contents at a wax taper and pouring them gently in. Let it burn 3 or 4 minutes at least, stirring it from time to time. Then extinguish it by covering the basin with a tray, which will immediately put out the flame. Then squeeze in the juice of the 3 lemons, and add a quart of *boiling* water. Stir the whole well, cover it up for 5 minutes, and stir again.

At this crisis (having skimmed off the lemon pips with a spoon), you may taste. If not sweet enough, add sugar to your liking, but observe that it will be a *little* sweeter presently. Pour the whole into a jug, tie a leather or coarse cloth over the top, so as to exclude the air completely, and stand it in a hot oven for 10 minutes, or on a hot stove one-quarter of an hour. Keep it until it comes to table in a warm place near the fire, but not too hot. If it be intended to stand 3 or 4 hours, take half the lemon peel out, or it will acquire a bitter taste.

The same punch allowed to grow cool by degrees, and then iced, is delicious. It requires less sugar when made for this purpose. If you wish to produce it bright, strain it into bottles through silk.

Egg-Nog, Large
Serves 12

Beat 8 egg yolks with 6 oz. sugar. Add 1½ pints brandy or whisky, ½ pint cream and 1½ pints milk. Lastly whisk the egg whites very stiffly and stir in. Sprinkle with grated nutmeg.

Victorian Shrub (A Rum Punch)

To 2 quarts of rum add ¾ pint (1½ cups) orange juice, ½ pint (1 cup) lemon juice, 2 lb. sugar and the zest of 2 lemons. Put all into a covered jar and allow to stand for 2 days, then add 2½ pints (5 cups) of water and leave to stand for another 12 days before using.

Festive Food

Sketches by Boz

ALL his life Charles Dickens held in his warm heart a special place for Christmas festivities.

Christmas time! That man must be a misanthrope indeed in whose breast something like a jovial feeling is not roused by the recurrence of Christmas. We know nothing more delightful than a Christmas family party, an annual gathering of all the accessible members of the family, young or old, rich or poor. All the children look forward to it for two months beforehand in a fever of anticipation.

Grandmamma in a high cap and slate coloured silk gown, and Grandpapa with a beautifully plaited shirt frill and white neckerchief seat themselves on one side of the drawing room fire upstairs. Children, cousins, the dear little baby and its nurse are seated in front waiting the arrival of expected visitors by hackney coach.

As to the dinner, it is perfectly delightful, nothing goes wrong and everybody is in the best of spirits. Grandpapa relates a circumstantial account of the purchase of the Turkey for which he had toddled all the way to Newgate market and engaged a porter to bring home in triumph behind him. With slight digressions relative to the purchase of previous Turkeys, Uncle George tells stories and carves poultry and takes wine and jokes with the children at the side table. When at last the stout servant staggers in with a gigantic pudding with a sprig of holly in the top, there is such a laughing and shouting and clapping of little chubby hands, and kicking up of fat dumpy legs only equalled by the applause with which the astonishing feat of pouring lighted brandy into the mince pies is received by the young visitors. Then the dessert—and the wine—and the fun!

Good will and cheerfulness doing more to awaken the sympathies of every member of the party and perpetuate good feeling during the ensuing year than half the homilies ever written by half the Divines that have ever lived.

Fill your glass again with a merry face and a contented heart. Our life upon it, but your Christmas shall be Merry and your New Year a Happy one.

Dining with the Leaders of Fashion

Devonshire Terrace, January 6th, 1844

N<small>O WONDER</small> Charles called his two companions Kate and Georgina his "Petticoats". The Victorian husband, seeing his wife undress, must have been astonished at the layers of underwear that were discarded before human flesh was reached. After the dress, off would come several long full petticoats of various weights, then below-the-knee pantaloons, two or more bodices, tightly laced stays and finally the chemise. Not that the husband would see the final revelation—or anywhere near it. He would have to be satisfied to watch each garment emerging from underneath the sturdy and voluminous nightgown that enclosed his wife's modesty like a tent!

Once they were ready for bed—Kate in her long-sleeved neck-to-toe nightgown and Charles in his nightshirt, they would need to combat the cold by wearing headgear. Kate's would be a frilled bonnet tied under her chin and Charles's a woollen cap with a long tassel hanging down on one side.

Influenced by such leaders of fashion as Count d'Orsay and Harrison Ainsworth, Dickens wore stylish and distinctive clothes. Charley, describing the attire of the day says:

> The men arrayed themselves in high shouldered coats with great rolling collars; tight sleeves with the wristbands of the shirt generally turned up over the cuffs. High stiff stocks, tight around the neck tumbled in cateracts of satin over the shirt front and displaying a couple of gold pins attached to each other by a chain. . . . High waistcoats of various brilliant colours just showing themselves. Nether garments cut tightly and strapped over the boot; long gold watch chains encircling the neck and meandering over the waistcoat and long, generally untidy looking hair.

Although Kate was pregnant again and expecting her baby in the middle of this month, they seem to have had a gay Christmas season. Dickens sums it up in a letter to an American friend: "Such dinings," he wrote, "such dancings, such conjurings, such blind-man's buffings, such theatre-goings, such kissings-out of old years and kissings-in of new ones, never took place in these parts before."

Amongst the revellers were, besides the families, Forster, the Macreadys, Count d'Orsay, Ainsworth, Thackeray, Maclise, the Carlyles, Sam Rogers and friends from the early days, William Jerdan, influential editor of the *Literary Gazette*, and his wife.

A KATE DICKENS MENU	A MODERN MENU
(8–10 persons)	(6 or more people)
Carrot Soup	*Carrot Soup*
Turbot with Shrimp Sauce (p. 7)	*Turbot and Celery Salad*
Roast Beef (p. 103)	*Roast Duck, Honey Crisped*
Turkey Poult (p. 56)	*Roasted Potatoes. Riced Potatoes (p. 100)*
Tongue Patties. Pork Cutlets	*Cauliflower with Parmesan Cheese*
Stewed Celery	
Mashed and Brown Potatoes	*Rice Croquettes with Tipsy Pears*
Greens	
Hare. Macaroni (p. 104)	*Biscuits and Cheeses*
Ice Pudding. Clear Jelly	
Cream	
Celery and Beetroot Salad(p. 201)	

Carrot Soup, Quick   *Serves 10*

1 packet onion soup
1 packet chicken soup
3 pints water
¾ lb. grated carrots
2 teasp. sugar
1 tablesp. chopped mint or parsley
Cream if required

(1) Grate the carrots and cook in the water for 10 minutes.
(2) Mix the soups with ¼ pint extra cold water and stir in. Add the sugar and cook for the required time on the packet. Cream may be added.
(3) Lastly add the mint or parsley.

Turbot and Celery Salad   *Serves 8–10*

2 lb. turbot, skinned
8 sticks of celery
French dressing

(1) Cook turbot in 3 tablesp. water or white wine and 4 tablesp. milk. Add 1 teasp. salt and a little pepper. Cook slowly covered, until tender.
(2) Drain and flake into a bowl. Add trimmed and finely chopped celery.
(3) Serve on individual plates in cupped lettuce leaves and pour dressing over.

Tongue Patties   *Makes 24*

½ lb. minced cooked tongue
8 sliced olives
Espagnole sauce
   (p. 72)
24 pastry cases

(1) Make or buy the patty cases.
(2) Combine the tongue, olives and sauce.
(3) Spoon into cases. Reheat before serving. Each may be topped with a slice of stuffed olive.

Roasted Duck, Honey Crisped

3 tablesp. fat
1 duck about 5 lb.
1 good tablesp. thick honey
Stuffing if desired, either your usual
    sage and onion stuffing or the
    prune and walnut stuffing on
    p. 55
Orange slices
Orange sauce or gravy, or both

(1) Preheat oven to 400° or No. 6.
(2) Stuff bird if desired. Truss.
(3) Put fat in pan and place in oven to heat.
(4) Remove pan from oven. Put bird in and baste with the hot fat.
(5) Smear then with the honey. Return to oven. Cook at the high heat for 10 minutes, then reduce heat to 325° or No. 3. Allow about 2 hours. Less if bird is very young, more if old.
(6) For roasted potatoes, boil them first for a few minutes in salted water. Drain and place around the bird. Baste them once.

To serve, arrange heated orange slices around and place a cherry in the centre of each.

Orange Sauce. Melt $1\frac{1}{2}$ level tablesp. butter and add 2 tablesp. flour. Cook for 2 minutes, then add $\frac{1}{2}$ cup orange juice and 1 level tablesp. sugar. Thin with about $\frac{1}{2}$ cup water or cream.

To Boil Cauliflower with Parmesan
(Kate Dickens's Recipe)

Boil a cauliflower, drain it on a sieve and cut it into convenient sized pieces, arrange these pieces in a pudding basin so as to make them resemble a cauliflower on the dish, season it as you proceed, turn it on the dish, then cover it with a sauce made of grated Parmesan cheese, butter and the yolks of a couple of eggs, seasoned with lemon juice, pepper, salt and nutmeg and put Parmesan grated over it. Bake for 20 minutes to brown it.

Rice Croquettes
Serves 6

2 cups cooked rice
2 level tablesp. sugar
2 tablesp. guava, cranberry or other
    pinky-red jelly
2 eggs
Breadcrumbs
2 tablesp. butter or margarine

(1) While rice is still hot, add the sugar and jelly.
(2) Beat eggs. Save 1 tablesp. of this and add the rest to the rice mixture.
(3) Cool on a plate, then form into croquettes.
(4) Add 1 tablesp. water to the egg. Dip croquettes into this, then into breadcrumbs and fry in the butter.

Serve with the pears.

Tipsy Pears. Drain pear halves. Add sherry to the syrup and pour over. Fill centres with cherries.

Palazzo Peschiere, Genoa, 1844

Off to Italy

Farewell Dinner at 9 Osnaburgh Terrace, June 1844

ON JANUARY 15th a fifth child was born to Kate and Charles and called Francis Jeffrey after their Scottish friend Lord Jeffrey. This addition to the family together with the disappointing sales of *Martin Chuzzlewit* set Dickens thinking of ways to economize. One suggestion made by Forster was to let Devonshire Terrace at a good rental then transport himself and his family to Italy. There they could take advantage of the cheaper cost of living and at the same time Dickens could make money by writing about his impressions and experiences.

Dickens liked the idea and set about making plans. He found a tenant, but unfortunately she demanded to move in right away. Evidently in those days tenants were more difficult to find and it was the landlord who had to make the concessions! So rather than lose the tenant, Dickens rented a temporary home, 9 Osnaburgh Terrace, for the intervening period.

They wanted to give a farewell dinner but were so worried about the efficiency "below stairs" that they seriously considered having it either at the Clarendon Hotel in London or the Star and Garter at Richmond. Dickens, in a letter of despair, appealed to Forster for help. "Advise, advise!" he wrote,

> advise with a distracted man. Investigation below stairs renders it, as my father would say, "manifest to any person of ordinary intelligence, if the term may be considered allowable," that the Saturday's dinner cannot come off here with safety. Advise! Advise! List of the invited. There's Lord Normanby; And there's Lord Denman. There's Easthope, wife and sister. There's Sydney Smith. There's you and Mac (Macready). There's Babbage. There's Lady Osborne and her daughter. There's Southwood Smith. And there's Quin. And there are Thomas Chapman and his wife. So many of these people have never dined with us, that the fix is particularly tight. Advise! Advise!

Forster's advice was to drop it altogether, but in the end Kate took the matter into her own hands. The dinner came off at their own, if temporary, home and Charles was no longer a distracted man.

Just before they left for Italy another farewell dinner was given. This time it was at Greenwich and was in honour of Dickens. A notable guest was the famous artist Joseph Turner, then 69. According to Forster, Turner enveloped his throat, that sultry day, in a huge red belcher handkerchief, which nothing would induce him to remove!

A KATE DICKENS MENU

(14–18 or 20 persons)

Asparagus Soup (p. 27)
White Soup (p. 191)

Boiled Salmon with Lobster Sauce (p. 55)
Filleted Soles with Shrimp Sauce (p. 7)

Patties.   Pork Cutlets.   Lobster Cutlets
Grenadines of Veal.   Rabbit Curry
Forequarter of Lamb
(see Roast Lamb, p. 19)
Chickens and Tongue
Spinach.   Potatoes.   Salad
Guinea Fowl.   Pigeons.   Lobster Salad
Asparagus

Cabinet Pudding (p. 72)
Punch Jelly.   Clear Jelly
Charlotte Russe (p. 52)
Italian Cream

A MODERN MENU

(6 or more people)

Melon and Grape Cocktail with Vodka

Grilled Salmon with Cucumber Sauce

Baked Crumbed Pork Chops
with Peaches or Mangoes
Creamed Potatoes.   Vegetable Salad

Lemon Meringue Pie (p. 156)
or
Fresh Fruit and Cheeses

Melon and Grape Cocktail with Vodka   *Serves 6–8*

Melon
Grapes, pitted
Sugar
Vodka

(1) Cut melon into cubes and place in a bowl.
(2) Add pitted grapes, about equal quantities, and 2 tablesp. sugar to 1 medium-sized melon. Allow to stand until a syrup has formed.
(3) Put into cocktail glasses and pour about 1 tablesp. vodka over each. Garnish with cherries. Chill.

Grilled Salmon with Cucumber Sauce   *Serves 6*

About 6 oz. salmon per person for
  this course
Butter and seasoning

Cucumber Sauce
About 6 inches of cucumber
2 tablesp. lemon juice
Salt, pepper and sugar
½ pint white sauce or cream

(1) Make sauce or whip cream. Peel and slice cucumber and cook for a few minutes in 2 tablesp. water and lemon juice. Sprinkle with salt, pepper and a little sugar. Stir into either cream or white sauce.
(2) Spread salmon with butter, add pepper and salt and grill for about 10 minutes on either side. Serve with the sauce. Garnish with sprigs of parsley.

Baked Pork Chops with Peaches or Mangoes

1 or more pork chops per person
Egg, salt and pepper
Fat
Breadcrumbs
Peach halves or mangoes
Cress for garnish

(1) Preheat oven to 350° or No. 4.
(2) Beat egg and add 2 tablesp. water, 1 level teasp. salt and a little pepper.
(3) Trim a little of the fat from the chops. Dip in egg, then in breadcrumbs.
(4) Put 2 good tablesp. fat in pan and allow to get hot in oven. Put chops in and turn over at once so that they are coated on both sides with the fat.
(5) Bake for 1–1½ hours or until tender and browned. Reduce heat a little after 20 minutes.

Serve with drained peach halves or mangoes and garnish with cress.

Grenadines of Veal

Serves 6

1½ lb. fillet of veal cut into ½-inch slices
4 rashers of streaky bacon
2 tablesp. butter or margarine
1 chopped Spanish onion
1½ level tablesp. flour
3 peeled tomatoes
2 teasp. chopped parsley
4 tablesp. claret or cooking sherry
¼ pint water
Salt and pepper
1 teasp. sugar

(1) Remove rinds from bacon and cut into 1-inch pieces. Begin to fry in deep frying-pan.
(2) Add butter or margarine and when hot, fry the slices of veal on both sides. Remove them to a plate.
(3) To the fat remaining in the pan, add the onion and fry for 2 minutes. Add flour and cook for another 2 minutes.
(4) Add tomatoes, claret, parsley and water. Season well with salt and pepper.
(5) Return the meat to the sauce in the pan. Cover and simmer for about 1 hour, or until veal is tender.

Italian Cream (a Kate Dickens's Recipe)

Whip together for nearly an hour a quart of thick scalded cream, a quart of raw cream, grated rind of 4 lemons and the juice, 10 oz. sugar, ½ pint sweet wine. Continue whipping until very thick. Lay a piece of muslin in a sieve and ladle the cream upon it with a spoon. In 20 hours turn it carefully out, but mind it does not break. Garnish with fruit, jelly or with flowers.

Below Stairs Food

The Old Curiosity Shop

IN THIS story Dick Swiveller, lawyer's clerk to Miss Sally Brass and her brother Bevis, conferred in his lighthearted way the title of "The Marchioness" upon the little drudge of a servant.

Sitting on a high stool and whistling cheerfully, Mr. Swiveller was disturbed by a rapping of knuckles on the door. "Come in," said Dick. "Oh please," said a little voice low down in the doorway, "Will you come and show the Lodgings?" Dick lent over the table and descried a small slipshod girl in a dirty coarse apron and bib which left nothing of her visible but her face and feet. She might have been dressed in a violin case. There never was such an old fashioned child in her looks and manner. She must have been at work from her cradle.

"Miss Sally said I wasn't to show the Lodgings, or people wouldn't believe the attendance was good. If they saw how small I was." "This is a queer sort of thing" muttered Dick, "What do you mean to say you are? The cook?"

"Yes, I do plain cooking; I do all the work in the house. Lodgings is 18/- a week and us finding plate and linen. Boots and clothes is extra and fires in winter time is eightpence a day."

The business with the Single Gentleman as Lodger concluded, Dick could not rid his mind of the small servant, and groped his way in darkness down to the door of a back kitchen, a dark miserable place, very low and very damp. The water was trickling out of a leaky butt and a most wretched cat was lapping up the drops with the sickly eagerness of starvation. The grate was wound up and screwed tight so as to hold no more than a little thin sandwich of fire. The coal cellar, the candle box, the salt box, the meat safe were all padlocked. There was nothing that a beetle could have lunched upon. Miss Sally Brass had a leg of cold mutton in her hand and taking a key from her pocket, opened the safe bringing out from it a dreary waste of cold potato, looking as eatable as Stonehenge. After a great show with a large carving knife, Miss Sally held up about two square inches of mutton. "Don't you ever say that you hadn't meat here." With these words Miss Sally locked the mutton away, then stood over the small servant while she finished the potatoes, rapping the child on the head with the blade of the knife, finding it impossible to stand close without administering a few knocks.

A Continental Trek

Italy, 1844–5

Trust Dickens to find a novel, spectacular and sensible way to travel abroad. He decided that he would find a conveyance large enough to hold his entire "menagerie" as he called his entourage, plus their trunks, portmanteaux and cases of necessities, personal and domestic. He found what he wanted at the Pantechnicon, Belgrave Square—a huge lumbering carriage, requiring four sturdy horses to drag it along.

The experiment proved to be a great success. "The children had not cried in their worst troubles, the carriage had gone lightly over abominable roads and the courier had proved himself a perfect gem." Charley, then 7, remembered it and wrote in his reminiscences: "I can remember many walks with my father up apparently interminable hills in the lonely French countryside, many cheery meals and snacks produced, as by the conjuror's art from the innumerable pockets in that wonderful travelling coach. . . . Many wild roadside Inns were in some mysterious way, peculiar to himself, aided and abetted by the excellent courier, Roche. He evolved order out of chaos, comfort out of squalor and cheery kindly attention out of original sulky apathy." Roche also added excitement to the journey by making sure that the news that he was escorting a famous family went on before them and when each night they trundled into the courtyard of an inn, they were received with rapturous delight.

The Villa Bella Vista at Alvaro was far from the house of their dreams. They went in through a rusty creaking gate and overgrown vineyard and garden and drew up before a house that looked to Dickens like a disused pink jail. Inside was as disappointing and Kate's heart sank when she saw the stiff uninviting furniture, the rats and lizards scuttling around the empty rooms and the armies of fleas making a flea-line for Timber Doodle the dog. They decided to move from the Villa of the Beautiful View the moment they could find another abode.

Meanwhile Dickens wrote long letters to his friends, went out to examine the environment and did a crash course in Italian. He had an aptitude for languages and learnt to speak and write fluent French and Italian in a very short time. As Alvaro was a seaside resort, he and the children spent a lot of time in the water. From Mamie's book we learn that the children were as much at home in the water as any known variety of fish and that they "looked in wonder at the so-called bathing of the Italian women. They would come in swarms with the most elaborately arranged hair . . . and the slightest wetting was the equivalent of a bath!"

ITALIAN MENU

Zuppa di Fagioli alla Fiorentina
(Bean Soup)
or
Il Minestrone
(Soup with Vegetables, Tomatoes and Pasta)

———

Polpettone alla Fiorentina
(Meat Balls with Spaghetti)

———

Pizza alla Napoletana
(Cheese Curd Pie)

Zuppa di Fagioli alla Fiorentina   *Serves 6–8*

½ lb. haricot beans
2 pints water
2 peeled and chopped onions
½ lb. tomatoes
1 crushed clove of garlic
Several sprigs of thyme and
    rosemary
2 tablesp. oil

(1) Soak beans overnight in the water.
(2) Add all the other ingredients and boil
    until beans have softened, about 1½–2
    hours. Add more water if necessary.
In pressure pan, allow 40 minutes at 15 lb.
pressure.

Il Minestrone   *Serves 10*

6 oz. kidney beans
3 bacon rashers
1 large Spanish onion
1 crushed clove of garlic
6 celery sticks, cut into small pieces
1 lb. tight white cabbage
½ lb. tomatoes
6 oz. macaroni
1 small packet frozen peas
Salt and pepper and 2 teasp. sugar
1 tablesp. olive oil
Grated cheese

(1) Soak beans overnight in 2 pints water.
(2) Remove rinds from bacon and cut into
    1-inch lengths. Fry in large soup sauce-
    pan. Add beans and water.
(3) Add chopped onion, garlic, celery and
    shredded cabbage.
(4) Simmer, covered, until beans have
    softened, adding another pint of water.
(5) Add macaroni, tomatoes, peas, salt
    (about 3 teasp.), pepper, sugar and oil.
(6) Cook for another 20 minutes.
(7) Serve in heated bowls and sprinkle with
    cheese.

Polpettone alla Fiorentina
(Meat Balls in Sauce with Spaghetti)

Serves 5–6

½ lb. veal or lean lamb
½ lb. lean bacon or ham
2 onions (about ¾ lb.)
1 oz. (½ cup) soft white breadcrumbs
1 teasp. salt, a little pepper and
  1 teasp. thyme (½ teasp. if dried)
1 beaten egg
Fat
1 crushed clove of garlic
1½ level tablesp. flour
¾ pint (1½ cups) water with
  1 beef cube
2 teasp. tomato purée from a tube
1 teasp. sugar
3 or 4 tablesp. wine or sherry

(1) Mince together the veal, bacon and one of the onions. Mix with breadcrumbs, seasoning, thyme and beaten egg.
(2) Form into small balls, roll in flour and fry in hot fat until browned all over. Put on a plate or into a casserole dish.
(3) To remaining fat in pan add the other onion, chopped and the garlic. Fry for a few minutes, then add flour and fry for another 2 minutes.
(4) Add water, tomato, sugar, cube and salt and pepper to taste. Cook until thickened, then add wine or sherry.
(5) Either pour over balls in casserole dish, or put into saucepan and add balls.
(6) Either cook, covered in the oven for 35 minutes, or on the top of the cooker for 30 minutes gently.

Serve with spaghetti.

Spaghetti. Bring 2 pints water to the boil and add 1 teasp. salt. Have ¾ lb. spaghetti and spiral it into the water. Boil for 15–20 minutes. Strain through colander and add 1 tablesp. butter.

Pizza alla Napoletana
(Cheese Pie)

Serves 8

½ lb. short pastry
¾ lb. cream cheese or cottage cheese
2 oz. ground almonds
¼ pint cream
4 oz. (½ cup) sugar
2 tablesp. lemon juice
½ teasp. almond and ½ teasp. vanilla
  essences
2 eggs, beaten
½ teasp. salt

(1) Preheat oven to 325° or No. 3.
(2) Make short pastry (your own recipe) and roll out thinly. Line an 8½-inch pie dish about 2 inches deep, and put a 1-inch strip around the edge. Decorate.
(3) Combine cream cheese, almonds, cream, sugar, lemon juice, essences, beaten eggs and salt.
(4) Tip into lined dish.
(5) Bake for about ¾ hour.

Poor Man's Food

The Chimes

TOBY VECK, the impecunious ticket porter, always trotted on his errands with messages or parcels and returned, still trotting, to his place on the steps of the church. To everybody the little old man was known as "Trotty".

On a bitter winter day the drowsy sound of twelve o'clock just struck was humming like a melodious monster bee all through the steeple. "Dinner time, eh?" Trotty told himself. "There's nothing more regular in its coming round than dinner time, and nothing less regular in its coming round than dinner."

"Why Father, Father," said a pleasant voice in his ear and Trotty looked into the bright dark eyes of his daughter Meg. He kissed the lips belonging to the eyes, and squeezed the blooming cheeks. "Why Pet," he said, "I didn't expect you today." "But here I am," Meg cried. "And not alone!" Trotty looked curiously at a covered basket which she carried. "Smell it Father dear, only smell it. Let me lift up the corner. There. What's that?" Trotty took the shortest possible sniff at the edge of the basket. "Why it's hot!" "It's scalding hot," cried Meg. "Now guess!" Trotty sniffed, the grin upon his withered face expanding as if he were inhaling laughing gas. "It ain't I suppose Polonies?" "No, no nothing like Polonies." "Its mellower than polonies. It improves every moment. Its too decided for trotters. Liver? No, there's a mildness about it it don't answer to liver. It ain't faint enough for pettitoes. It wants the stringiness of cock's head. I know, it ain't sausages. It's chitterlings!" "No it ain't," cried Meg. "What am I thinking of," cried Toby, "Its tripe!" Tripe it was; and Meg in high joy, protested he should in half a minute say it was the best tripe ever stewed, "in a basin tied up in a pocket handkerchief." "Make haste, for there's a hot potato besides an half a pint of fresh drawn beer in a bottle." As he was stooping to sit down on the steps the Chimes rang. "Amen," said Trotty pulling off his hat. "The Bells broke in like a grace Meg my dear."

He made no pause in his attack on the savoury meat before him, but cut and ate and cut and drank and cut and chewed, and dodged about from tripe to hot potato and back again to tripe with unflagging relish.

The Bells Ring Out

The Peschiere, Genoa, November 5th, 1844

IN SEPTEMBER Dickens and his "menagerie" moved from the "lonely, rusty, stagnant Villa" at Alvaro and thankfully established themselves in a beautiful ornate house called the Palazzo Peschiere or the Palace of the Fishponds. It was indeed a palace, with frescoes by Michael Angelo, a huge hall fifty feet high, numerous fountains and ponds, an elegantly laid-out garden and an extensive view over the city of Genoa. All this for about £5 per week.

Nevertheless Dickens was often homesick for his London. "Did I tell you how many fountains we have here," he wrote to Forster, "but if they played nectar, they wouldn't please me half as well as the West Middlesex water-works at Devonshire Terrace." For his study he chose a room with a fine view and settled down, hoping that the beauty and serenity of his surroundings would be an inducement to creative work. But he had failed to take into account the fact that he was in a land of countless churches, convents and monastries and that they all had loud bells to peal. At first the incessant clanging maddened him and interfered with his concentration. But, quite unexpectedly he found that they rang into his mind an idea for a Christmas story. Thus was born the tale of the goblins and bells, *The Chimes*.

He was so delighted at the way the tables had turned that in a letter to Forster he wrote, "Let them clash upon me now from all the Churches and Convents. I see nothing but the old London belfry I have set them in." Then later he added, "I am in regular ferocious excitement with *The Chimes*! Get up at 7; have a cold bath before breakfast and blaze away wrathful and red hot until 3 P.M. or so when I usually knock off for the day." This cold bath habit is mentioned in later years by his daughter, Mamie, "My father was looked upon as an amiable maniac with a penchant for washing," she said.

Dickens was so anxious to read his story to Forster and his other friends that he went all the way back to England to do it. But before he left he and Kate gave a large dinner party. Dickens gives the lists of guests as "our English Consul and his wife; the banker, Sir George Crawford and his wife; the De la Rues, Mr. Curry and some others, fourteen in all . . .".

They were still in Genoa on January 6th to celebrate Charley's birthday party, his eighth. Miss Burdett-Coutts, his godmother, sent as her contribution a huge birthday cake weighing ninety pounds! It had to go to the pastrycook's for repairs after the journey from England and when the word got around all the neighbourhood crowded in to gape at it.

ITALIAN LUNCHEON

Antipasto (Hors d'œuvre)

Il Concion (Mixed Salad)
with Italian Cheeses
or
Maccheroni al Forno
(Macaroni, Baked)

Zabaglione (see p. 92)
or
Pesche Ripiene (Stuffed Peaches)

Antipasto

Anchovies
Sliced tomatoes
Olives
Sliced salami
Chopped hard-boiled eggs with sardines
Marinated mushrooms
Stuffed celery

(1) Arrange in hors d'œuvre platter, the anchovies, tomatoes sprinkled with vinegar, sugar and salt and pepper.
(2) Olives, ripe and green, sardines and egg, sliced salami.
(3) Washed sliced mushrooms first marinated in oil and vinegar, and sprinkled with pepper.
(4) Stuffed celery. Mix cream cheese with a little mayonnaise and season. Fill hollows of tender pieces of celery, about 2 inches long.
Any other hors d'œuvre items may be served.

Il Concion (Mixed Salad)

Tomatoes
Pimientos
Chopped celery
Sliced radishes
Gherkins and olives
Hard-boiled eggs
Basil
Salt and pepper
Shredded chicory may be added

(1) Peel tomatoes by dipping first into boiling then into cold water, or holding them on a fork over a gas flame. Cut into quarters and put into salad bowl (the bowl may first be rubbed with a cut clove of garlic). Sprinkle with a little sugar and salt and pepper. Add sliced pimientos.
(2) Add chopped celery, radishes, gherkins, olives and basil.
(3) Add 3 or more tablesp. oil and mix salad gently, then add a little salt and pepper and half as much vinegar as oil.
(4) Garnish with quartered hard-boiled eggs.

Note. The salad could be served in cupped lettuce leaves.

A Selection of Italian Cheeses

Fresh Cheeses: Mozzarella, Scamorza, Ricotta, Crescenza Stracchino, Cremino and Mascarpone.

Bland Cheeses: Fontina, Bel Paese, Taleggio.

Seasoning Cheeses: Parmesan, Italian Cheddar.

Veined Cheeses: Italian Gorgonzola, Erbo, Moncenisio, Dolcelatte.

Goat's Cheeses: Belarno, Fontini, Caprian.

Maccheroni al Forno
(Macaroni, Baked)

Serves 4

½ lb. macaroni
¾ lb. tomatoes
1 tablesp. butter or oil
4 oz. grated Parmesan
2 teasp. sugar
Salt and pepper
Paprika

(1) Put 1 quart of water and 1 teasp. salt into large pan. Bring to the boil, then add macaroni. Boil until just tender, but not too soft.
(2) Drain well, then tip into oven-proof dish. Add butter or oil and move about until well coated. Sprinkle with more salt.
(3) Peel and slice tomatoes and arrange over macaroni. Sprinkle with sugar, salt, pepper and basil.
(4) Top with the grated cheese and bake until cheese is sizzling and lightly browned. Sprinkle with paprika.

Pesche Ripiene
(Stuffed Peaches)

Serves 6

12 peach halves, stones removed
2 cups cake crumbs
2 oz. ground almonds
1 level teasp. almond essence
4 tablesp. sherry or brandy
A little peach syrup
Cherries for garnish

(1) Combine crumbs with almonds, essence and wine.
(2) The mixture should be moist, but not sloppy. Add a little peach syrup or more wine if necessary.
(3) Pile on to peach halves. Top with cherries.
(4) If the peaches were canned, add a little wine or sherry to the rest of the syrup and either serve separately or pour around peaches in serving dish.

May be served with ice-cream and cream.

Note. Pear or apricot halves may also be used for this dish.

Italian Food

Pictures from Italy (1846)

HAVING established his family in Albaro, Charles Dickens with his brave Courier Roche set off to visit Parma, Modena and Bologna.

I started for Piacenza in the coupé of a machine something like a travelling Caravan in company with my brave Courier and a lady with a very large dog who howled dolefully at intervals all night. It was very wet and very cold. Next morning we changed coaches at Allessandria where we were packed up in another coach in company with a very old priest; a young Jesuit; and a gentleman with a red nose that had an uncommon and singular sheen upon it. We travelled on till four o'clock that afternoon. The coupé had discharged two people and had only one passenger inside, a monstrous ugly Tuscan with a great purple moustache of which no man could see the ends when his hat was on. I took advantage of this better accommodation, and in company with this gentleman (who was very good humoured) travelled on till nearly eleven o'clock at night when we made a halt at Stradella.

I followed a sleepy man with a flaring torch into a great cold room where there were two immensely broad beds on what looked like two immensely broad deal dining tables. This stage in the proceedings is interrupted by the Courier (he had been cooking) saying that supper is ready in the priests' chamber next door, the counterpart of mine. The first dish is a cabbage, boiled with a great quantity of rice in a tureen full of water, and flavoured with cheese. It is so hot and we are so cold that it appears almost jolly. The second dish is some little bits of pork, fried with pigs' kidneys. The third, two red fowls. The fourth two little red turkeys. The fifth a huge stew of garlic and truffles and I don't know what else; and this concludes the entertainment.

Before I can sit down in my own chamber and think it the dampest, the Brave Courier comes in, in the middle of such a quantity of fuel he looks like Birnam Wood taking a winter walk. He kindles this heap in a twinkling and produces a jorum of hot brandy and water; for that bottle of his keeps company with the seasons and now holds nothing but eau de vie.

At four o'clock next morning he is up again fresher than a new blown rose, producing mugs of scalding coffee; and going out into the dark streets roaring for fresh milk on the chance of somebody with a cow getting up to produce it.

Play-Acting

Devonshire Terrace, Late June 1845

DICKENS and his family left Italy for home in June and as soon as they were settled again at Devonshire Terrace he was seized with a desire to indulge in his great love, play-acting. Accordingly he got together with all the friends he thought would be interested and invited them to dinner. After much discussion they agreed to find a theatre and stage Ben Jonson's *Every Man in His Humour* and to take the parts themselves.

The cast-elect were Forster; Jerrold; Cattermole; Maclise; John Leech, an artist and caricaturist who is known for his long association with *Punch* and for his illustrations for Dickens's *Christmas Carol*; T. J. Thompson; Frank Stone, the artist who is purported to have painted the picture showing the Dickens family at their Villa in Rosemont (a clever discovery made by the biographer, Una Pope-Hennessy); and Mark Lemon, founder of *The Field*, first Editor of *Punch* and a successful play-write. All these men remained for always Dickens's close and dear friends.

The play was put on at the Royalty Theatre in Dean Street, London on September 21st and brought rave notices from the critics. Charles played Captain Bobadil and showed himself to be such an outstanding actor that the stage carpenter said regretfully, "Ah, Mr. Dickens, it was a sad loss to the public when you took to writing"! (Some loss!)

While Charles was enjoying all this, Kate was pregnant again and, as always on these occasions, was far from well. Some blame them for not exercising more restraint, but of course they were the victims of an age when mother nature was not thwarted and so was free to continue her ruthless design for keeping the species going.

Charles too was pregnant, but not with human child. His embryo was a newspaper to be called the *Daily News* and intended to be a vehicle for his radical ideas, especially concerning the Ragged Schools for the education of the ignorant poor. As usual in all his philanthropic ventures the great heart of the wealthy Miss Burdett-Coutts was ready for his suggestions. Their concern was not only for the collective poor, but for individuals. Often the needs and the possible rehabilitation of one fallen girl would be studied as carefully as if she were a close relative.

With all this on his plate, Dickens still had time to be an attentive parent. Mamie remembers the little garret room at Devonshire Terrace that she shared with her sister Katie. "My father had taken the greatest pains to make the room as pretty and comfortable as possible," she wrote, "and if we had put up some new print or ornament, he had to be dragged up the steep stairs to see it."

A KATE DICKENS MENU

(8–12 persons)

Cod with Oyster Sauce (p. 63)

*Roast Leg of Mutton with Veal Stuffing
Boiled Fowl. Tongue (p. 192)
Broccoli. Mashed and Brown Potatoes*

*Rice Blancmange
Cream*

Macaroni Savoury (p. 104)

A MODERN MENU

(6 or more people)

*Pineapple and Melon
Minted Cocktail*

*Stuffed Leg of Lamb or Colonial Goose
Mint Sauce (p. 64)
Roasted Potatoes. Peas
Individual Side Salads (any mixed salad)*

Apricot Chiffon Pie

Scotch Woodcock

Pineapple and Melon Minted Cocktail

Serves 6–8

1 can pineapple
1 melon
1 level tablesp. sugar
Peppermint essence
A little green colouring
Cherries

(1) Drain pineapple, chop and put into a bowl.
(2) Add an equal quantity of cubed melon. Cover with sugar and allow to stand until sugar has melted.
(3) Flavour with peppermint to your taste and colour with a little vegetable colouring.
(4) Put into cocktail glasses and garnish each with a cherry. Serve chilled.

Stuffed Leg of Lamb

3–4 lb. leg of lamb (with a large pocket for stuffing)

Forcemeat Stuffing
4 oz. (2 cups) soft breadcrumbs
1 grated onion
1 tablesp. chopped parsley
1 teasp. dried or 2 teasp. fresh thyme
3 teasp. butter
Salt and pepper
Fat

(1) Preheat oven to 400° or No. 6.
(2) Combine all ingredients for stuffing and chop in the butter.
(3) Fill cavity and secure with thread or tiny skewers.
(4) Place in oven with 2 tablesp. fat.
(5) Cook for 10 minutes at the high heat. Then baste with the fat and reduce heat to 250° or No. 2. Allow to cook very slowly for 3 hours, basting again once.

For the Roasted Potatoes, peel and boil in salted water for 3 minutes, drain and place around meat. Baste with the fat. Allow about 2 hours.

Rice Blancmange
(Victorian Recipe and Modern Recipe)

Serves 6

Victorian

1½ oz. (3 level tablesp.) ground rice
2 oz. (4 level tablesp.) castor sugar
1 pint (2 cups) milk
Vanilla pod

(1) Mix rice with 3 tablesp. of the milk.
(2) Bring the rest to the boil and add sugar and pod.
(3) Add ground rice. Cook and stir until thickened.
(4) Simmer for 10 minutes, stirring frequently. Remove pod.
(5) Pour into a wet mould and when cold turn out.

Modern

Follow Victorian recipe to step 4, cool to lukewarm, then add the very stiffly beaten whites of 2 eggs. Pour into serving dish and allow to get cold before serving. May be served with cream and fruit.

Apricot Chiffon Pie

Serves 6

6 oz. any sweet biscuits or wafers, crushed
3 level teasp. sugar
3 oz. melted butter
½ teasp. vanilla essence
1 can of apricots (1 lb.)
1 packet gelatine (1 level tablesp.)
3 level tablesp. sugar
2 eggs, separated
Small can of evaporated milk or a carton of cream, ¼ pint

Note. Brandy or apricot brandy may be added to the cream.

(1) Combine crushed biscuits or wafers, sugar, melted butter and vanilla. Mix well and tip into an 8- or 8½-inch pie dish about 1½–2 inches deep. Press around to line the dish neatly. Put away in refrigerator until firm.
(2) Drain syrup from can and make up to ½ pint with water. Pour into saucepan and bring to the boil, adding sugar.
(3) Mix gelatine with 2 tablesp. water and stir in. Stir until dissolved.
(4) Whisk in the egg yolks then remove from heat.
(5) Add evaporated milk or cream. Whisk well together then put into a bowl and allow to set to the wobbly stage.
(6) Beat whites until very stiff. Chop apricots. Add with whites to the half-set jelly. Pour into crumb shell and allow to set.
(7) Spread with whipped cream.

Scotch Woodcock

Serves 6

2 egg yolks
¼ pint (½ cup) cream
Anchovy paste
Buttered toast
A little cayenne pepper
Parsley sprigs

(1) Beat yolks in a small pan and add cream. Season with salt and pepper and cook until thickened.
(2) Spread buttered toast with anchovy and sprinkle with a few grains of cayenne.
(3) Cut toast into 2½-inch squares and pour egg and cream mixture over. Serve hot garnished with parsley sprigs.

Rosemont, Lausanne

No. 1 Devonshire Terrace

A Christening Party, then Rosemont

Devonshire Terrace, April 1846

AT THE St. Marylebone Church six months after his birth, a fourth baby boy was christened Alfred d'Orsay Tennyson Dickens, a mixture that astonished even those who had come to expect the odd in Dickens's choice of names. One rhymer, Father Prout, wrote:

> What eye but glistens
> And what ear but listens
> When the Clergy christens
> A babe of Boz.

After the ceremony a party was given at Devonshire Terrace for the godparents, namesakes, relatives and friends.

At the beginning of this year Dickens's *Daily News* had appeared with himself as Editor, but a few weeks later, suddenly and uncharacteristically, he threw it up, giving Forster the excuse that he was "tired to death and quite worn out". Did he find that in becoming the Editor of a daily newspaper his great creative ability was being dissipated in petty problems and matters of business?

Again the Continent beckoned him and again Kate was uprooted and transported to strange houses in strange surroundings. They set off on May 31st and after staying at various places on the way, arrived at Lausanne on June 11th. Here, after a few days of concentrated house-hunting, they found the Villa Rosemont and settled in. Dickens, now free to create a new novel, began *Dombey & Son*, with a commission from Chapman & Hall to produce it in the usual monthly numbers.

Charley remembered Lausanne well and in later years talks about his father's recreations after long hours of exhausting writing. He says: "My memories of my father are chiefly concerned with walks along the Lakeside or among the beautiful hills behind the town or to open air fêtes in the heart of the green woods where he was always anxious that I should distinguish myself in the boyish sports going on. There was much cheery intercourse with many charming English families, and he had English house guests too in plenty."

We know that the Haldimands, de Cerjets, Hallams and their American friends the Watsons were there. We also know that Alfred Tennyson, then 37, arrived unexpectedly and at a very opportune moment. Charley tells us that "one autumn evening in the fading twilight, my sister Mamie was sitting at the piano singing Tennyson's 'Queen of the May', when who should stroll in through the window that opened on to the lawn, but the great poet himself!"

A CHRISTENING HIGH TEA

Christening Cake (p. 111)
Date and Walnut Scones
Baking-powder Muffins
Sliced Bread and Butter
Platter of Ham, Tongue and Cold Chicken
Tossed Salad (p. 75).   Oasis Salad
Apple Shortcake
Pineapple Upside-down Cake

Date and Walnut Scones   *Makes about 18*

Use packet scone-mix or the
  following home-made mixture
10 oz. (2 cups) S.R. flour, sieved
1 level teasp. baking powder
1 level teasp. salt
2 tablesp. butter
1 level tablesp. sugar
About ½–¾ cup milk and water
1 cup chopped dates
½ cup chopped walnuts

(1) Preheat oven to 475° or No. 8 or 9.
(2) Rub butter into flour and baking powder
    and add salt and sugar.
(3) Add dates and walnuts.
(4) Mix to a soft dough with the milk and
    water.
(5) Pat out or roll to about ¾ inch thickness.
    Cut into squares or rounds. Brush with
    a little top milk or beaten egg.
(6) Bake for 10 minutes.

Baking Powder Muffins   *Makes about 15*

8 oz. (1½ cups) S.R. flour with ½ teasp.
  salt and ½ teasp. baking powder
1 egg, beaten
1 tablesp. golden syrup
2 tablesp. butter
3 level tablesp. sugar
¾ cup milk

(1) Preheat oven to 425° or No. 5.
(2) Sieve dry ingredients into a bowl. Add
    sugar.
(3) Melt together the syrup and butter.
(4) Add beaten egg, syrup-and-butter and
    milk. Stir until blended, but do not beat.
(5) Put into greased muffin pans (deep patty
    pans) and bake for about 15–20 minutes.

Oasis Salad   *Serves 6*

6 sticks chopped celery
1 cup cubed melon
½ cup chopped dates
½ cup chopped walnuts
4 sliced gherkins
1 cup cooked green peas
Lettuce

(1) The salad bowl may first be rubbed with
    a cut clove of garlic.
(2) Line bowl with lettuce leaves.
(3) In another bowl put the celery, melon,
    dates, walnuts, gherkins and peas.
(4) Mix and tip into salad bowl.
(5) Serve with oil and vinegar or French
    Dressing.

Apple Shortcake
Serves 6–8

4 oz. (4 tablesp.) butter or margarine
4 oz. (½ cup) castor sugar
8 oz. (1½ cups) S.R. flour with ½
   teasp. salt
1 egg
1½–2 cups sweetened stewed apple
   or apple sauce

(1) Preheat oven to 350° or No. 4.
(2) Cream fat and sugar. Add 2 teasp. of the flour, then the egg. Beat well.
(3) Add flour and salt and mix into a dough. Divide into two pieces.
(4) Roll each piece out to fit a 8½- or 9-inch shallow pan. Put one piece in.
(5) Cover with the apple, then with the other piece of rolled-out dough.
(6) Bake for about 40–45 minutes. Leave in pan until cold. Dust with icing sugar.

Pineapple Upside-down Cake
Serves 5

1 egg
4 oz. (½ cup) sugar
2 oz. (2 tablesp.) butter
1 level tablesp. golden syrup
2 tablesp. water
5 oz. (1 cup) S.R. flour
¼ teasp. salt

Topping. 1 tablesp. butter, 1 tablesp. golden syrup, pineapple slices and cherries.

(1) Preheat oven to 350° or No. 4.
(2) Beat together until very light the egg and sugar.
(3) Heat in a small saucepan the butter, syrup and water.
(4) Sieve half the flour into egg and sugar mixture, just folding in. Add half syrup and butter, then the rest of the flour and last of the syrup and butter. Stir, but do not beat.
(5) Melt together the syrup and butter for topping and pour into a 7- or 7½-inch cake pan. Arrange the pineapple slices in the syrup and put a cherry in the hole of each.
(6) Pour the batter over. Bake for about ¾–1 hour. When cooked, loosen sides and turn out.

Hotel Food

The Uncommercial Traveller (1860)

MR. AND MRS. GRAZINGLANDS came by railroad to London and after transacting their business at the Bank of England, went sightseeing. Soon Mrs. Grazinglands felt quite faint with exertion and want of food.

Her tender husband looked in the window of a pastry-cooks where he beheld nothing to eat but butter in various forms, slightly charged with jam, and languidly frizzling over tepid water. Two ancient turtle shells, on which were inscribed the word "Soups", and from a stuffy alcove a ghastly mockery of a dusty marriage breakfast spread out on a rickety table. An oblong box of stale and broken pastry at reduced prices ornamented the doorway. They turned away on the timely remembrance that Jairings Hotel for Families and Gentlemen was but round the corner.

Arriving, they found the second waiter, in flabby undress, cleaning the windows of the empty Coffee room, and the first waiter denuded of his white tie, making up his cruets behind the Post Office Directory. The latter (who took them in hand), was greatly put out by their patronage and instantly smuggled them into a penitential apartment where five invalided old plate warmers leaned up against one another under a melancholy old sideboard. Mr. Grazinglands and his charming partner waited twenty five minutes for the sherry, half an hour for the tablecloth, forty minutes for knives and forks, three quarters of an hour for the chops, and an hour for the potatoes.

On settling the bill, which was not much more than the day's pay of a Lieutenant in the Navy, Mr. Grazinglands took heart to remonstrate against the general quality and cost of his reception. The waiter replied that Jairings made it a merit to have accepted him on any terms, and added, "When indiwiduals is not staying in the 'Ouse, their favours is not looked upon as being worth Mr. Jairing's while; nor is it the style of business Mr. Jairing wishes."

Finally, Mr. and Mrs. Grazinglands passed out of Jairings Hotel for Families and Gentlemen in a state of greatest depression, and did not recover their self respect for several days.

Entertaining in Paris

No. 48, Rue de Courcelles, Fauberg St. Honore,
January 1847

THEY remained at Rosemont until November, then Dickens decided to give his family a taste of Paris. The house they rented was such a mixture of beauty and oddity that Charles called it the "strangest house ever furnished. Quite ridiculous, unparalleled and preposterous. Something between a baby house, a shades, a haunted castle and a mad kind of clock, and not to be imagined by the mind of man!"

To this edifice Forster was invited to stay, but first Dickens had to warn him about the cold. "Cold intense," he wrote, "the water in the bedroom jug freezes into solid masses from top to bottom, bursts the jugs with reports like small cannon, and rolls out on the tables and wash-stands hard as granite!"

Busy still on *Dombey & Son*, he found the place so draughty and strange that concentration was almost impossible. "Couldn't find a corner that would answer my purpose," he continued to Forster, ". . . sat six hours at a stretch and wrote as many lines. . . ."

Just how important calm and order were to Dickens is described by Charley:

> As to his system of work [he wrote] it was the same wherever he was. No city clerk was ever more methodical than he; no humdrum, mono-tonous, conventional task could ever have been discharged with more punctuality or with more business-like regularity than he gave to the work of his imagination and fancy. As to his papers, writing material and quaint little bronze figures which he delighted in having before him, all was as neat and orderly as everything else in and about the house. When he was writing one of his long stories and had become deeply interested in the working out of his plot and the evolution of his characters he lived, I am sure, two lives; one with us and one with his fictitious people.

If difficulties beset Dickens by day, the evenings were gay and many famous Frenchmen came to dine and to meet Forster—Dumas, Eugene Suè, Victor Hugo, Theophile Gautier, Alphonse Karr and Lamartine.

While still here Dickens had to go to England on business, so he decided to take Charley from his school, Kings College, then to a dinner party at Gore House. When the boy sat down to the dinner table he noticed that the chair next to him was vacant. "It's only the Prince," said Lady Blessington "he's always late." And sure enough after the repast had got under way, a "sallow, rather sullen man" came in, and after kissing Lady Blessington's hand, sat down beside Charley. He was Prince Louis Napoleon, afterwards Emperor of the French, who was finally exiled to Chislehurst.

A FRENCH STYLE MENU

Truite au Vin au Beurre de Truffles
(Trout in Wine with Truffles)

Filet Mignon Béarnaise
or
Tournedos Rossini
(Steak with Liver Pâté)
Petits Pois.   Sauté Potatoes

Bavarois aux Fraises
(Bavarian Mousse with Strawberries)
or
Ananas Pierrette
(Strawberries and Pineapple in the Shell)

Truite au Vin au Beurre de Truffles

¼ pint (½ cup) water
¼ pint (½ cup) wine
1 small onion
1 bay leaf
½ teasp. fresh thyme
Sprigs of parsley
Salt and pepper
6 or more river trout
3 oz. (3 tablesp.) butter and
   1 dessertsp. chopped truffles

(1) Combine for the court bouillon the water, wine, onion, herbs, salt and pepper. Boil for 10 minutes.
(2) Have the trout cleaned (but with heads left on). Put them into the bouillon, bring to simmering stage and simmer gently for 10–15 minutes.
(3) Lift out, remove skin and put on to a heated serving dish. Keep warm.
(4) Cream the butter and add truffles. Spread over the trout. Garnish with lemon slices and sprigs of parsley.

Filet Mignon Béarnaise

Fillet steaks about 1½ inches thick.
Butter

Béarnaise Sauce: make Hollandaise Sauce (p. 51) using wine instead of water and lemon, and adding 1 teasp. chopped tarragon and chervil

Thick slices of tomato
Sugar, salt and pepper

(1) Make the sauce.
(2) Preheat griller until very hot.
(3) Spread fillets with butter and grill on both sides at highest heat. For rare finish allow about 4–5 minutes on either side. For well-done finish allow 8 or more minutes on either side.
(4) The tomato slices, sprinkled with a little sugar, salt and pepper could be heating in the grilling pan, or be fried in a little butter.
(5) To serve, put a slice of tomato on to each steak and top with a sprig of parsley. Serve with the sauce.

Tournedos Rossini — *Serves 6*

6 steak fillets about 1 inch thick
Butter, salt and pepper
6 slices of liver pâté
Flour

Madeira Sauce
1 tablesp. butter
2 level teasp. flour
4 tablesp. Madeira or sherry
5 tablesp. water
1 teasp. soy sauce or ½ beef cube
Salt and pepper

(1) Heat butter in heavy frying-pan. Fry fillets for 4 minutes on either side, or until browned and rare inside. For well-done fillets allow about 8 minutes on either side.
(2) Sprinkle with salt and pepper. Put on to a serving dish.
(3) Fry the pâté slices for 1 minute on either side and put one on top of each fillet. Keep warm.
(4) Into drippings in pan, add butter and flour and cook together for 2 minutes. Stir in wine and water and cook until thickened, adding soy sauce or cube. Season well.
(5) Serve in a sauce dish.

Bavarois aux Fraises — *Serves 9*

1 lb. strawberries, hulled
8 oz. (1 cup) sugar
4 tablesp. lemon juice
1 packet (1 level tablesp.) powdered
  gelatine
1 level tablesp. cornflour
¼ pint (½ cup) water
½ cup milk and ½ cup cream
2 egg whites

(1) Mash half the strawberries and cover with sugar and lemon juice.
(2) Mix gelatine with 2 tablesp. cold water.
(3) Heat the water and milk. Mix cornflour with 2 tablesp. water and stir in. Cook until thickened. Add gelatine and stir until dissolved.
(4) Add mashed strawberries and cream. Put away until beginning to thicken.
(5) Whisk egg whites until as stiff as possible. Fold into the half set jelly.
(6) Tip into serving dish. Decorate with the rest of the strawberries and whipped cream. No need to unmould.

Ananas Pierrette — *Serves 4–6*

1 large ripe pineapple
½ lb. strawberries
6 oz. sugar
A little Kirsch
Ice-cream
Cream

(1) Cut pineapple in half crosswise. Remove pulp and cut away the hard core.
(2) Cut pineapple into cubes, and place in a bowl. Add hulled, halved strawberries, sugar and Kirsch. Leave until sugar has melted and formed a syrup.
(3) Fill pineapple shells with the fruit. Place side by side.
(4) Serve with ice-cream and cream.

French Food

Pictures from Italy

DICKENS and his family together with nurse, cook and maid are travelling towards Marseilles in a huge coach drawn by four horses and managed by a postillion wearing immense jack-boots and carrying a very long whip.

In Chalons, arrived at the Hotel de l'Ecu d'Or everyone is open mouthed for the opening of the carriage door. The Courier comes down from the box. The door is opened. Breathless expectation. The lady of the family gets out. Ah sweet lady! The sister of the lady of the family gets out. Great heavens Ma'amselle is charming. First little boy gets out. Ah what a beautiful little boy! First little girl gets out. Oh but this is an enchanting child! Second little girl gets out. The landlady yielding to the finest impulse of our common nature catches her up in her arms! Second little boy gets out. Oh the sweet boy! The baby is handed out. Angelic baby. All the rapture is expended upon the baby. Then the two nurses tumble out; the whole family are swept upstairs as on a cloud. The brave Courier is everywhere, looking after beds, having wine poured down his throat by his dear brother the Landlord and picking up green cucumbers with which he walks about, one in each hand like truncheons. Dinner is announced. There is very thin soup; there are very large loaves, one apiece; a fish; four dishes afterwards; some poultry afterwards; a dessert afterwards and no lack of wine. There is not much in the dishes; but they are very good and always ready instantly.

Under the balcony, when we return from a visit to the Cathedral, the servants of the Inn are supping in the open air; the dish is a stew of meat and vegetables smoking hot and served in the iron cauldron it was boiled in. They have a pitcher of red wine and are very merry.

Next morning everything taken out of the coach is put back again. The brave Courier runs into the house for a parcel containing cold fowl, sliced ham, bread and biscuits for lunch; and runs back again. What has he got in his hand now? More cucumbers? No. A long strip of paper. It's the bill. He has on two belts, one supporting the purse full of five franc pieces, the other a leathern bottle filled to the throat with the best light Bordeaux wine. He never pays the bill till this bottle is full. Then he disputes it!

A Theatre Dinner

No. 3, Chester Place, May 1847

KATE was expecting another baby in April and as she wished to be in England for the confinement, Charles brought his family back earlier than he had intended. Their home at Devonshire Terrace had been let until June to Sir James Duke so he rented for three months No. 3 Chester Place, Regent's Park.

The baby was born a few weeks later on April 18th and named after two more of Dickens's friends—Sydney Smith (Canon of St. Paul's and brilliant wit and essayist) and William Haldimand (once Member for Ipswich and living at Lausanne while the Dickens family were there). The name emerged as Sydney Smith Haldimand Dickens. When Kate was well enough, the entertaining began again. Dickens had a box at the St. James Theatre and one evening, after a dinner at Chester Place, he with Kate, Georgy and their guests went off to see the classical play *Nernani* with Fanny Kemble in the main part. They were Daniel Maclise, Harrison Ainsworth, the Douglas Jerrolds, Clarkson Stanfield, and the French actor François Joseph Régnier and his wife.

With seven children now filling the house, the "patter of little feet" must have seemed more like a perpetual stampede and Dickens, realizing that his wife was yet merely 31, must have wished that the good Lord would be rather less bountiful with His "Little Blessings"! Not that he did not adore his children. His daughter Mamie, writing of his tenderness and concern, says:

> His care and thoughtfulness about home matters, nothing being deemed too small or trivial to claim his attention and consideration, were really marvellous when we remember his active eager restless working brain. No man was so inclined naturally to derive his happiness from home affairs. He was full of the kind of interest in a house which is commonly confined to women and his care of us as wee children did most certainly "pass the love of women". His was a most tender and most affectionate nature.

At the end of this year a sad mishap occurred. Charles had accepted the honour of opening the new Glasgow Athenaeum and on the way, in the train, Kate was taken ill and had a miscarriage. In those days trains were strictly for travel and certainly were not fitted up for miscarriages. Even the ordinary functions were not catered for, and it was not until Queen Victoria began to get about by rail that a special coach was built with an apartment for ladies and a lavatory. Until then the passengers had to wait for one of the frequent stops or carry a potty-in-a-basket!

A KATE DICKENS MENU	A MODERN MENU

A KATE DICKENS MENU

(8–9 persons)

Brill with Shrimp Sauce (p. 7)

Roast Rump Steak Rolled and Stuffed
Boiled Rabbits with Onion Sauce (p. 20)
Potatoes. Brussels Sprouts

Lemon Pudding (p. 152)
Spanish Pudding

Toasted Cheese (p. 40)
Watercress

A MODERN MENU

(4 or more people)

Pea Soup

Stuffed Rump Steak
or
Rabbit Casserole with Onion
Potatoes. Green Vegetable

Lemon Wonder Pudding

Biscuits and Cheeses

Pea Soup   *Serves 4–6*

7 oz. (¾ cup) yellow split peas
2½ pints water
1 ham bone or 4 rashers of bacon
3 chopped onions
1 grated carrot
1 bay leaf
2 good teasp. salt and a little pepper

(1) If the peas have been in the cupboard for a long time they will need to soak all night in 1 pint of the water.
(2) If not, just put them into your large saucepan with all the other ingredients.
(3) Bring to the boil and simmer, covered, for about 2 hours. Taste and add more seasoning if necessary.
(4) Usually served with sippets which are cubes of bread fried until crisp in butter or margarine.

Stuffed Rump Steak   *Serves 4*

2 lb. piece of rump steak about
  2 inches thick
4 rashers of streaky bacon
1 onion, about 6 oz.
4 oz. mushrooms
Salt and pepper
Fat

(1) Ask the butcher to slit a pocket in the steak for the stuffing.
(2) Preheat oven to 375° or No. 5.
(3) Remove rinds from rashers and cut into 1-inch pieces. Begin to fry.
(4) Add chopped onion and fry together for 5 minutes. Add washed sliced mushrooms and fry for another 5 minutes. Season well with salt and pepper.
(5) Fill cavity with this delicious stuffing. Secure with thread or tiny skewers.
(6) Put into baking dish with fat and bake for 2 hours slowly at 300° or No. 2½, basting twice with the fat. Put an enamel plate on top after the first hour.

Rabbit Casserole with Onions

Serves 4–6

1 rabbit
6 rashers of bacon
2 onions (about $\frac{3}{4}$ lb.)
3 level tablesp. flour
1 bay leaf
1 teasp. fresh or $\frac{1}{2}$ teasp. dried thyme
$\frac{3}{4}$ pint ($1\frac{1}{2}$ cups) water
1 chicken cube
2 teasp. salt and a little pepper

(1) Preheat oven to 300° or No. $2\frac{1}{2}$ or 3.
(2) Disjoint rabbit or buy it disjointed.
(3) Remove rind from bacon and begin to fry either in dual-purpose casserole or frying pan.
(4) Add chopped onions and fry until lightly browned. Add flour and fry for another 2 minutes.
(5) Add water, bay leaf, cube, thyme and salt and pepper. One crushed clove of garlic may be added.
(6) Put rabbit pieces into casserole and cover with sauce. Cover and cook for 2 hours or longer. See that rabbit is deliciously tender.

Spanish Pudding
(a Kate Dickens's Recipe)

1 lb. flour. 1 tablesp. yeast. Mix $\frac{1}{2}$ lb. butter in a little milk, add to flour and yeast and mix together. Take 3 eggs, yolks and whites, with a little salt and beat fresh into butter. Mix dough well up till it will leave basin and spoon clear. Rise $\frac{1}{2}$ an hour. Roll up with 6 oz. sugar and 1 teasp. cinnamon, $\frac{1}{2}$ oz. candied orange peel, $\frac{1}{2}$ oz. citron peel. To be served with sauce, with orange flower water poured over, half an hour before being sent to table.

Lemon Wonder Pudding

Serves 6 with Ice-cream

6 oz. ($\frac{3}{4}$ cup) castor sugar
2 oz. (2 tablesp.) butter
  or margarine
1 tablesp. hot water
Grated rind and juice of 2 smallish
  or one very large lemon
2 level tablesp. flour and $\frac{1}{2}$ level
  teasp. salt
2 eggs
$\frac{1}{2}$ pint (1 cup) milk

(1) Preheat oven to 325° or No. 3.
(2) Grease a 8-inch deep ovenproof dish.
(3) Put sugar, butter and hot water into mixing bowl and beat until smooth.
(4) Add flour, salt, lemon juice and grated rind. Mix well.
(5) Separate whites and yolks of eggs, dropping the white into another bowl and the yolks into the mixture. Beat them well in.
(6) Add the milk. Lastly beat whites until very stiff and add to mixture. Do not beat or stir too much.
(7) Tip into dish and bake for about $\frac{3}{4}$ hour. *When cooked there will be a light sponge on top and a delicious lemon sauce underneath!*

Stolen Food

Great Expectations

THE boy, Pip, is terrified by Magwitch the convict and promises to get for him a file for his chains and food for his stomach. The scene was set in a churchyard in the midst of desolate marshes, not far from Dickens's last home, Gad's Hill Place.

I was afraid to sleep even if I had been inclined to, for I knew that at the first faint dawn I must rob the pantry. There was no doing it in the night, for there was no getting of light by easy friction then; to have got one I must have struck it out of flint and steel and made a noise like rattling chains. In the pantry I was very much alarmed by a hare hanging up by the heels, whom I rather thought I caught, when my back was half turned, winking. I had no time for selection and I stole some bread, some rind of cheese, about half a jar of mincemeat (which I tied up in my handkerchief), some brandy from a stone bottle which I decanted into a glass bottle; (diluting the stone bottle from a jug in the kitchen cupboard), a meat bone with very little on it and a beautiful round, compact pork pie. I was nearly going away without the pie, but was tempted to mount upon a shelf to look what was put away so carefully in a covered earthen-ware dish. I found it was the pie, and I took it in the hope that it was not intended for early use, and would not be missed. I unlocked and unbolted the door into the Forge and got a file and ran for the misty marshes.

When I reached the churchyard, there was the man waiting for me. He was awfully cold. I half expected to see him drop down and die of deadly cold. His eyes looked so awfully hungry, too, that when I handed him the file and he laid it down upon the grass, it occurred to me he would have tried to eat it, if I had not opened the bundle and emptied my pockets. "What's in the bottle boy?" he said. "Brandy," said I. He was already handing mincemeat down his throat in a most curious manner—more like a man who was putting it somewhere in a violent hurry, but he left off to take some of the liquor. He shivered all the time that it was as much as he could do to keep the neck of the bottle between his teeth without biting it off. Like a large dog, he gobbled mincemeat, meat bone, bread, cheese and pork pie, all at once, staring round while he did so at the mist all round us, and even stopping his jaws to listen. Pitying his desolation I made so bold to say, "I am glad you enjoyed it." "Thank'ee, my boy," said the Convict, "I do."

Hans Christian Andersen's First Visit

Broadstairs, Early October 1847

WHEN Hans Andersen first visited England, one of the literary lions he was most anxious to meet was Charles Dickens. "How much I should like to shake the hand of Boz," he wrote. Dickens was just as eager for the meeting and wrote to Lady Blessington saying "I *must* see Andersen." Lady Blessington arranged it and the two writers, each famous in their own sphere, met at her home. They took to each other at once. "We shook hands," wrote Andersen, "looked into each other's eyes and when we spoke we understood." He thought Dickens was young-looking, and handsome with beautiful hair and a kind and wise expression on his face. On their second meeting at Gore House Dickens presented Andersen with a set of his books, each one inscribed, "To Hans Christian Andersen from his friend and admirer Charles Dickens."

Writing of his first impressions, Andersen gives an excellent description of the London of Dickens's day. "London is the city of cities," he said. "Here is Paris but with a mightier power; here is the life of Naples but without its bustle. . . . Omnibus after omnibus passes—they say there are four thousand teams; carts, cabs, hansoms, and elegant carriages are rattling, training, rolling and driving away. . . ."

The numbers of rich and highly cultured people he met made him giddy and the strict etiquette observed astonished him. "In this land of freedom," he wrote, "one almost dies of etiquette. Even the Queen, wanting to stay out in the park one glorious summer evening, was obliged to go home because the Palace dinner must be at 8 o'clock, 8 o'clock precisely."

On one end of the scale he noticed the fabulous furnishing and clothes of the rich, "only varying in gold, satin, lace and flowers," then on the other, the poor and hungry who "glide by like shadows and place themselves in front of a person and gaze at one with hungry sad expressions on their pale pinched faces".

There seems to be no record of a dinner for Andersen at Devonshire Terrace, but Dickens did invite him down to Broadstairs and we know that he stayed the night there before leaving for Denmark and home. He seemed surprised and very touched that his host took the trouble to see him off at Ramsgate and the last he saw of England was Dickens standing on the edge of the quay vigorously waving his hat. It was ten years before he visited England again, and then he stayed with Dickens and his family at Gad's Hill Place for five weeks.

A KATE DICKENS MENU	A MODERN MENU
(4–5 persons)	*(6 or more people)*
Broiled Mackerel	*Scallops Newburg*
	or
Stewed Rump Steak with Vegetables	*Scalloped Oysters*
Mashed and Brown Potatoes	
	Beef Goulash with Mushrooms and Tomatoes
Bread and Butter Pudding	*Creamed Potatoes. Green Vegetable*
Toasted Cheese (p. 40)	*Traditional English Summer Pudding*
	Biscuits and Cheeses

Scallops Newburg   *Serves 6*

1 pint scallops
3 tablesp. butter or margarine
2 level teasp. flour
2 teasp. lemon juice
$\frac{1}{4}$ pint ($\frac{1}{2}$ cup) milk or single cream
1 egg
2 tablesp. wine or sherry
Salt and pepper

(1) Cut scallops into quarters and cook for 4 minutes in 2 tablesp. of the butter or margarine.
(2) In another pan melt the other tablesp. butter and add the flour. Cook for 2 minutes. Whisk in the milk or cream.
(3) Add beaten egg and lemon and just bring to the boil. Season well with salt and pepper. Add the scallops.
(4) Either put into one ovenproof dish or into individual scallop shells or ramekins. Sprinkle with breadcrumbs and dot with butter. Put into a moderate oven for about 15 minutes, or grill until crumbs are a golden brown.

Broiled Mackerel

Have mackerel cleaned and split open
Oil or butter
Salt and pepper

(1) Heat griller for about 5 minutes.
(2) Brush mackerel with oil or butter and sprinkle with salt and pepper.
(3) Put a piece of foil on grilling rack. Lay fish on it, skin side down.
(4) Broil (or grill) until cooked through. Put a pat of butter on each half and garnish with lemon wedges.

Scalloped Oysters   *Serves 4*

Oyster Sauce (p. 63)
2 oz. (1 cup) soft breadcrumbs
1 tablesp. butter

(1) Have 6 scallop shells or small ramekins.
(2) Make the oyster sauce and fill the containers.
(3) Melt the butter and add breadcrumbs. Stir until well coated.
(4) Sprinkle on top of the oyster sauce. Grill until lightly browned. Garnish with parsley.

[147]

Beef Goulash with Mushrooms and Tomatoes   *Serves 8–10*

$2\frac{1}{2}$ lb. stewing beef
1 lb. onions, peeled and roughly
   chopped
2 tablesp. oil or butter
3 level tablesp. flour
$\frac{1}{4}$ pint ($\frac{1}{2}$ cup) water
$\frac{1}{2}$ lb. peeled tomatoes
$\frac{1}{4}$ pint ($\frac{1}{2}$ cup) red wine
1 teasp. dried basil
2 teasp. soy sauce, or 1 beef cube
2 teasp. sugar
1 teasp. salt and a little pepper
$\frac{1}{2}$ lb. mushrooms

(1) Preheat oven to 300° or No. $2\frac{1}{2}$.
(2) Cut meat into 1-inch cubes.
(3) Melt fat in pan. Add onions and cook for
   2 minutes.
(4) Add meat and continue frying until well
   seared. Add flour and cook for a little
   longer.
(5) Add water, tomatoes, wine, basil, soy
   sauce or cube, sugar, salt and pepper.
   Stir until thickened.
(6) Tip into deep casserole dish—a brown
   pottery one is excellent.
(7) Cook slowly for 3 or more hours.
Pressure cooking time: allow 35 minutes at
15 lb. pressure.

Traditional English Summer Pudding   *Serves 6*

Sliced white bread
1 cup raspberries
1 cup blackcurrants
$\frac{1}{4}$ cup water
8 oz. (1 cup) sugar
Cream

(1) Have a glass or china mould.
(2) Remove crusts from bread and cut into
   $\frac{1}{2}$-inch slices. Line the mould with the
   bread, leaving no spaces.
(3) Cook the fruit with water and sugar.
(4) Put half into mould, cover with more
   slices of bread then add the rest of the
   fruit and a topping of bread.
(5) Cover with a plate that will fit over the
   pudding. Put a weight on the plate and
   put away until chilled. Unmould and
   serve with cream.

Bread and Butter Pudding (Glorified)   *Serves 6*

3 large slices of bread $\frac{1}{4}$ inch thick
Butter
1 pint milk
3 eggs
4 level tablesp. sugar
1 teasp. vanilla
1 cup mixed fruits—cherries,
   sultanas, chopped dates
2 or more oz. chopped walnuts

(1) Spread slices with butter and cut into
   fingers.
(2) Place in deep pie dish.
(3) Beat eggs and add milk, sugar and
   vanilla.
(4) Tip fruit and nuts over bread, then pour
   in the egg and milk.
(5) Bake for about 40 minutes in oven at
   350° or No. 4.

Charles Dickens at age 47

Holiday House-Party

Broadstairs, August 1848

URING August and September at Broadstairs Dickens decided to forsake serious work and enjoy himself. Gaily writing to Forster he says, "When are you coming? Oh, what days and nights there have been here this week past!" When Forster did accept and set a date Dickens suggested that he should "Come down booked for Maidstone (I will meet you at Paddock Wood) and we will go thither in company over a most beautiful little line of railroad. The eight miles walk from Maidstone to Rochester and a visit to the Druidical Altar on the wayside, are charming. This could be accomplished on the Tuesday, and Wednesday we might look about us at Chatham, coming home by Cobham on Thursday. . . ."

Forster gives a list of some of the week-end guests he joined at Broadstairs. Some we have met before: the Mark Lemons, the John Leeches, Frank Stone and the Tom Beards. One also present and not mentioned yet in these pages was Augustus Egg, R.A., the artist responsible for the well-known picture of Georgina Hogarth busy at her needlework. He was four years younger than Dickens and died ten years before him at the age of 44. His death at such an early age was a sad loss to British art. He was known as "a subject painter" and created such tableaux as "Queen Elizabeth Discovers That She is No Longer Young". (Hardly a moment that many women would care to have recorded!)

After the two months of fun and relaxation Dickens and his family returned to Devonshire Terrace. He felt "all the better for my idleness" and immediately set to and completed his Christmas story *The Haunted Man*. Inspiration was also working on another long novel. It was a theme that would allow him to draw on some of his youthful experiences and so would benefit from being written in the first person. Forster was against this, but Dickens was already a slave to his idea and knew that it could only be told as it demanded. It was the title that refused to clarify itself. Today it would be unthinkable that the novel could be anything but *David Copperfield*, but before such perfection had been reached, Dickens had been considering such titles as "Mag's Diversions", "The Copperfield Records", and half a dozen others. At last the one and only title emerged from the confusion and Dickens was satisfied (and so are we).

A KATE DICKENS MENU	A MODERN COLD MEAL
(8 or 9 persons)	(6 or more people)
Cold Oysters	*Gazapacho, Spanish Chilled Soup*
Oxtail Soup (*p.* 51)	*Cold Saddle of Lamb Mint Sauce* (*p.* 64)
Turbot (*pp.* 55 and 163)	*or*
Saddle of Welsh Mutton Tomato Sauce. Vegetables	*Ham, Cheese and Tomato Triple-decker*
Cabinet Pudding (*p.* 72)	*Potato Salad* (*p.* 76). *Hawaiian Salad*
Savoury Omelette (*p.* 60)	*Cold Lemon Pudding Apple Tart* (*p.* 164)

Gazapacho, Spanish Chilled Soup   *Serves 6*

1½ lb. tomatoes
1 Spanish onion
1 peeled, sliced cucumber
Juice and grated rind of 1 large
   lemon
1 crushed clove of garlic
1 green pepper
1 cup soft bread cubes
2 teasp. sugar and salt and pepper
   to taste
3 or 4 tablesp. salad oil
Water

(1) Put into blender of electric mixer half the tomatoes, half the cucumber, all the onion, half the green pepper and the garlic. Blend until well mashed.
(2) Soak bread cubes in the lemon juice and add to the purée.
(3) Add seasoning. Put into a bowl and add sufficient water to make a fairly thin soup.
(4) Add the oil, drop by drop, beating well all the time.
(5) Put into refrigerator to chill.
(6) The rest of the vegetables should be cut up and either added to the soup just before serving, or put into small bowls and handed around. A bowl of ice is also usually included.

Hawaiian Salad   *Serves 4–6*

8 oz. cream cheese or cottage cheese
1 pineapple slice per serving and
   3 extra slices
2 oz. (½ cup) chopped walnuts
2 tablesp. mayonnaise
Lettuce

(1) Combine cream cheese with chopped walnuts.
(2) Chop the 3 extra pineapple slices and add. Add mayonnaise.
(3) Place cupped lettuce leaves on individual plates. Put a slice of pineapple on each and pile with some of the cheese mixture. Garnish with sprigs of mint.

Ham, Cheese and Tomato Triple Decker   *Serves 8–10*

Sliced stuffed olives
2 packets powdered gelatine
  (2 level tablesp.)
$\frac{3}{4}$ lb. minced cooked ham or bacon
3 tablesp. cream
$\frac{1}{2}$ pint (1 can) tomato purée, or
  peeled chopped tomatoes
2 teasp. sugar
Salt and pepper
6 oz. grated cheese
  (a good strong yellow colour)
2 teasp. celery salt
$\frac{1}{4}$ pint cream or evaporated milk
  and $\frac{1}{4}$ pint milk, or all milk
1 level tablesp. cornflour
Pepper

(1) Dissolve $\frac{1}{2}$ level teasp. of the gelatine in 2 tablesp. hot water and pour into a 2 pint mould. Arrange a ring of the olives on the bottom in the jelly. Put away until set.
(2) Dissolve 1 level dessertsp. of the gelatine in $\frac{1}{4}$ cup boiling water and when dissolved add the cream. Stir into minced ham. Add a little pepper and, if necessary a little salt. Tip into mould if bottom layer of jelly has set. Put away until firm.
(3) Heat half the tomato and stir in another 1 level dessertsp. of the gelatine. When dissolved add the rest of the tomato. Season with the sugar, salt and pepper. When ham layer is firm tip in the tomato. Let that layer set.
(4) Mix the rest of the gelatine with 4 tablesp. cold water.
(5) Heat together the cream and milk. Mix cornflour with 2 tablesp. water and stir in. Cook until thick. Add gelatine and allow to dissolve. Add cheese, celery salt and a little pepper. Cool to lukewarm then tip on to set tomato layer. When firm, dip mould into hot water and turn out. Very pretty.

Cold Lemon Pudding   *Serves 4–5*

2 large or 3 small lemons
1 pint water
8 oz. (1 cup) sugar
5 level tablesp. cornflour
2 eggs, separated
$\frac{1}{2}$ level teasp. salt

(1) Grate the rind of the lemons into a saucepan.
(2) Squeeze juice into $\frac{1}{2}$ pint cup and fill with water. Pour into pan. Add sugar and another $\frac{1}{2}$ pint water. Heat.
(3) Mix cornflour with 3 tablesp. cold water and stir in. Cook and stir until thick and transparent. Add salt. Remove from heat.
(4) Separate eggs, dropping whites into a bowl and yolks into lemon sauce. Whisk yolks in until well blended. Tip into large bowl and allow to cool.
(5) Whisk whites until very stiff and fold in. Tip into serving dish. May be topped with whipped cream.

Railway Food

The Uncommercial Traveller (1860)

DICKENS wrote, "I am always wandering here and there, seeing many little things and some great things, which because they interest me, I think may interest others."

I have seldom been blown by the late high winds to any English place where I could get anything to eat or drink in five minutes.

I am hungry, and to some extent exhausted when I arrive at the Refreshment Station where I am expected. Please to observe, expected. The apartment that is to restore me is a wind trap, cunningly set to inveigle all the draughts in that countryside as they rotate in two hurricanes; one about my wretched head; one about my wretched legs. The training of the young ladies behind the counter who are to restore me, has been from their infancy directed to a defiant, dramatic show that I am not expected and not wanted. The solitary man among the bottles would take pity on me if he dared, but he is powerless among the rights and might of Woman.

I find that I must either scald my throat by insanely ladling into it against time, brown hot water stiffened with flour; or I must make myself flaky and sticky with Banbury cakes; or I must stuff into my delicate constitution a currant pincushion; or I must extort from an iron-bound quarry, with a fork as if I were farming on unhospitable soil, some glutinous lumps of gristle and grease called Pork Pie.

I found the depressing banquet so like the banquet at the meanest and shabbiest of evening parties, that I began to think I must have "brought down" to supper the old lady, unknown, blue with cold, who is setting her teeth on edge with a cool orange at my elbow, that the pastry cook who has compounded for the company on the lowest possible terms per head, is a fraudulent bankrupt, and that the family giving the party have become my mortal foes and have given it on purpose to affront me.

Or I fancy that I am "breaking up" again at the evening conversazione at school, charged two and sixpence on the half year's bill. It is vain to represent by my humble and conciliatory manner that I wish to be liberal. Vain to represent to myself for the encouragement of my sinking soul that the young ladies behind the counter have a pecuniary interest in my arrival.

The Haunted Man is Christened

Devonshire Terrace, January 3rd, 1849

THE story, *The Haunted Man*, appeared for Christmas, 1848 and soon afterwards Dickens gave it a Christening dinner at his home. Kate's eighth confinement was imminent but this did not seem to interrupt the lavish entertaining.

Forster reports that amongst those present were: the Mark Lemons, Evanses, Bradburys, Leeches, Stanfields, John Tenniel, Francis Topham, Frank Stone, Robert Bell and the Thomas Beards. These, together with Georgina, Kate, Charles and possibly one of Charles's brothers, would make a dinner party of twenty, and judging from Kate's "Menu for Twenty Persons", the preparations must have been prodigious.

Bradbury & Evans were the publishers who were to deal with Dickens's work after the break with Chapman & Hall and Evans was to enter the life of Dickens in another role—that of his eldest son's father-in-law. Charley fell in love with Bessie Evans when he was only a child of 7 and from then was faithful until they married in 1861, and forever after.

Of the other guests not mentioned in previous pages, John Tenniel was a famous cartoonist and artist, known for his work for *Punch* and also for his illustrations for *Alice in Wonderland* and *Alice Through the Looking Glass*. He was knighted in 1893. Francis Topham was another artist friend. Two pictures of scenes from *Barnaby Rudge* and *The Old Curiosity Shop* were painted by him and later hung at Gad's Hill Place. Robert Bell was an Irishman and a writer. He sometimes joined Dickens and others in their play-acting jaunts.

Although Dickens loved to go off on these jaunts, his letters to Kate show that he was a most devoted and home-loving husband. Mamie endorses this when she wrote:

> . . . his nature was home-loving in every respect. When he became celebrated at a very early age, all his joys and sorrows were taken home; and he found there sympathy and companionship of his dear familiar friends. In his letters to my mother, to my Aunt Georgina and later to us children, he never forgot anything that he knew would be of interest about his work, his successes, his hopes or fears. And there was a sweet simplicity in his belief that such news would most certainly be acceptable to all, that is wonderfully touching and child-like coming from a man of genius.

Kate's baby, a sixth son, was born on January 16th, and named after the great 18th-century novelist, Henry Fielding.

A KATE DICKENS MENU

(14–20 persons)

White Soup.   Asparagus Soup (p. 27)

Boiled Salmon with Lobster Sauce (p. 55)
Fillet Soles with Shrimp Sauce (p. 7)

Mushroom Patties (p. 107)
Pork Cutlets
Oyster Curry.   Lamb's Fry
Grenadine of Veal (p. 120)
Forequarter of Lamb (p. 19)
Boiled Chicken and Tongue
New Potatoes.   Spinach.   Salad
Larded Capon.   Roast Pigeons
Asparagus

Clear Jelly.   Italian Cream (p. 120)
Prince Albert's Pudding
Ice Pudding

Brunswick Sausage with Small Salad
Anchovies.   Cheese

A MODERN MENU

(6 or more people)

White Soup (Cauliflower Cream Soup)

Cheese Soufflé

Japanese-style Chicken
Savoury Rice.   Two Vegetables
Side Salads (any green salad)

Apple Tart with Cream (p. 164)
Lemon Meringue Pie

Biscuits and Cheeses

White Soup (Cauliflower)   *Serves 6*

1 head of cauliflower (about $1\frac{1}{4}$ lb.)
1 packet chicken cream soup
$1\frac{1}{2}$ pints water
$\frac{1}{2}$ pint milk or cream
Grated cheese, about 3 oz.

(1) Break cauliflower into flowerettes, boil for 10 minutes in $\frac{3}{4}$ pint salted water.
(2) Add 1 pint of water to the packet soup. Add the cauliflower and water. Cook for 5 minutes, or the amount suggested on the packet.
(3) Add the milk or cream and season with a little salt and pepper.
(4) Serve topped with grated cheese.

Cheese Soufflé   *Serves 6*

1 pint (2 cups) thick white sauce
4 oz. grated cheese
Salt and pepper
3 eggs, separated

(1) Preheat oven to 350° or No. 4.
(2) Add cheese to hot white sauce. Cool.
(3) Beat in egg yolks, then fold in very stiffly beaten egg whites.
(4) Bake in greased soufflé dish for about 30 minutes. Serve at once.

Japanese-style Chicken

Serves 4

2 halved chicken breasts
3 tablesp. soy sauce
½ cup (¼ pint) Saki
2 teasp. ground ginger
3 level tablesp. sugar
2 finely chopped onions
2 teasp. horseradish sauce may be
   added if desired

(1) Preheat oven to 325° or No. 3.
(2) Combine all ingredients and pour over the breasts. Allow to marinate for an hour or longer, all night if it will be helpful.
(3) Tip into casserole dish, cover and bake for about 1½ hours.
(4) Half an hour before cooking time is up, remove lid and continue cooking uncovered.

Prince Albert's Pudding
(a Kate Dickens's Recipe and Charles's "Good Pud")

Put 1 lb. butter into a saucepan with ¾ lb. sugar, the yolks of 6 eggs and some candied orange. Beat to a fine paste. Line a dish with pastry. Fill with the butter mixture and cover with pastry.

Note. This is gorgeous and may be tried with one-quarter of the quantities for a start.

Lemon Meringue Pie (Quick)
(Dickens Fellowship Recipe)

Serves 6

Crumb Crust
4 oz. mixed digestive and other sweet
   wafers
2 oz. melted butter
1 level tablesp. brown sugar
¼ teasp. vanilla essence
8 oz. can of sweetened condensed
   milk
Grated rind and juice of 2 lemons
2 eggs, separated
4 level tablesp. sugar

(1) Crush the wafers either in electric blender or with rolling pin.
(2) Add sugar, melted butter and vanilla. Mix until damp and crumbly and tip into an 8-inch pie dish about 1½-2 inches deep. Press around neatly and neaten edge. If this is difficult, let the crust get firm then neaten afterwards.
(3) Combine lemon juice, rind and condensed milk.
(4) Separate yolks and whites, dropping whites into another bowl and the yolks into the lemon mixture. Beat well. Tip into firm crust.
(5) Whisk egg whites and the 4 level tablesp. sugar until very thick and pile on top of the pie. Bake in a slow oven, 250° or No. 1 or 1½ until meringue is crisp on the outside.

Sorry Food

David Copperfield

With his sweet young bride Dora and her little dog Jip, David Copperfield set up housekeeping in London's Kentish Town. But though he was happy to the point of ecstasy, he had to face the fact that a pretty face and good housekeeping did not necessarily go together.

Everybody we had anything to do with seemed to cheat us. Our appearance in shops was a signal for damaged goods to be brought out immediately. I myself referred to the Cookery Book and found it established as a quarter of an hour to every pound of meat and say a quarter over, but by a curious fatality we never hit on a medium between redness and cinders.

One of our first feats in the housekeeping way was a little dinner to Traddles. I began to think there was something disorderly in Jip walking about the table cloth and in his habit of putting his foot in the salt or melted butter. On this occasion he seemed to think he was introduced expressly to keep Traddles at bay; and he barked at my old friend, and made short runs at his plate, with undaunted pertinacity.

I could not help wondering in my own mind as I contemplated the boiled leg of mutton before me previous to carving it, how it came to pass that our joints of meat were such extraordinary shapes and whether our butcher contracted for all the deformed sheep that came into the world.

Dora said timidly, "I bought a beautiful little barrel of oysters Doady, but I'm afraid there is something wrong with them. They don't seem right." "Take the top shell off my love," I said. "But it won't come off," said Dora trying very hard. They had never been opened; we had no oyster knives—and could not have used them if we had; so we looked at the oysters and ate the mutton. At least as much of it as was done and made up with capers. I am satisfied that Traddles would have made a perfect savage of himself and eaten a plateful of raw meat to express enjoyment of the meal, but I would not hear of so much immolation of friendship; and we had a course of bacon instead; there happened by good fortune to be cold bacon in the larder.

The Polka Dance

Devonshire Terrace, January 6th, 1849

THIS was Charley's twelfth birthday and in writing to Miss Angela Burdett-Coutts thanking her for her gift of the huge birthday cake, Dickens said, "Charley had a very merry birthday—I had the honour of conjuring for the party, in a Chinese dress and very large mask—and his noble cake was the admiration and wonder of all beholders."

During the evening a demonstration of the new dance, the Polka, was given by Dickens and John Leech (six feet tall), with Mamie, (nearly ten) and Kate (eight and a half) as their partners. In later years Mamie wrote of her father's determination to perfect the steps of the dance and of how he had slipped out of bed in the night and in the bitter cold had, in readiness for the party, practised it by rushlight! The dance had been invented in 1830 by a Bohemian servant girl and had gradually spead across Europe. At this time it had reached England and was all the rage, even inspiring the fashion, still existing, for Polka Dot dresses and ties.

Dickens saw to it that his children learnt to dance at an early age. Mamie remembered lessons in Genoa in 1845 and wrote, "when we were at Genoa, though only babies, my father was determined that we should be taught to dance. He took pride in our success in the steps, exercises and dances which formed the lessons and when away wrote to my mother, saying, 'I hope the dancing lessons will be a success. Don't fail to let me know.' "

Apart from the children invited to this party, many "of larger growth" (as Dickens put it) were also present and stayed on after the younger ones had gone to bed. Many of the friends already mentioned in previous pages were there, including the Mark Lemons, Macreadys and John Leeches. Other people who belonged to the Dickens circle and who have since become celebrities were Captain Marryat whose great sea stories are still read today; John Delane, then Editor of *The Times* and responsible for bringing the paper up to such a high standard that it became one of the world's finest newspapers; Isambard Brunel, the famous engineer; Lord Carlisle, another great Victorian reformer, and Lord Mulgrave, a close friend ever since he and Dickens met on the voyage to America in 1842 and acted together in the amateur theatricals in Montreal. The novel *Dombey and Son* was dedicated to his mother, the Marchioness of Normanby.

CHILDREN'S BIRTHDAY PARTY MENU

Marbled Madeira Birthday Cake
Bread and Butter with Hundreds and Thousands
Cheese and Bacon Boats
Pear Sally Salads
Open Sandwiches
Frankfurter Rolls
Mixed Coloured Jellies with Ice Cream
Dishes of raw Vegetables such as Carrot Sticks, Celery, Lettuce
Chocolate Wholewheat Sticks or Animals

Marbled Madeira Birthday Cake

8 oz. (1 cup) butter or margarine
8 oz. (1 cup) sugar
12 oz. (2⅓ cups) S.R. flour
4 large eggs
½ teasp. salt
1 teasp. vanilla essence
¼ pint (½ cup) milk
2 level teasp. cocoa
A few drops of cochineal

(1) Preheat oven to 350° or No. 4.
(2) Cream together the butter and sugar. Two teasp. hot water could be added if the fat is hard.
(3) Put flour in sieve and add salt. Add 2 teasp. of this to the creamed mixture, then drop in 1 unbeaten egg. Beat well.
(4) Repeat with the other three eggs. Beat very well.
(5) Alternatively add flour and milk. Just stir, do not beat again. Add vanilla.
(6) Divide the mixture into three, putting one-third in each of two other bowls. To one part add cocoa mixed with 1 tablesp. water and to the other a few drops of cochineal to give a definite pink colour. Put the pink and chocolate parts back into main bowl and mix them with no more than three stirs with a wooden spoon. Just enough to "marble" them together.
(7) Well grease an 8½- or 9-inch cake pan about 3 inches deep. Put a piece of butter paper on the bottom. Tip in mixture and bake for about 1¼–1½ hours.
Ice in any gay way you wish.

Cheese and Bacon Boats
Makes 24

24 boat-shaped pastry cases
2 eggs
4 oz. grated cheese
3 bacon rashers
Seasoning
An extra ounce of cheese
White sails

(1) Remove rinds from bacon and cut into 1-inch pieces. Begin to fry.
(2) Beat eggs and add cheese. Season well.
(3) When bacon is sizzly, tip in egg and cook slowly, stirring constantly until thick.
(4) Place in the cases and sprinkle with a little more cheese. Grill or bake until top cheese is sizzling. Decorate with little white sails.

Pear Sally Salads

Pear halves
Lettuce
Cloves, cherries, cream and spring onion

(1) Arrange a cooked pear half, round side upwards, in a small rounded lettuce-heart leaf. One that would make a nice sunbonnet for Sally.
(2) Make a face with the cloves for eyes, and the nose and mouth with tiny pieces of cherry. The thinner end of the pear is the neck.
(3) With a fancy piping nozzle and bag, pipe whipped cream around the pear to look like a lot of curls. Finish the neck with a bow and ends made with the thin green ends of spring onions.

Open Sandwiches. Cut bread into rounds, ovals, squares or any fancy shapes. Spread with butter, then decorate with any sandwich fillings garnished with tomato slices, hard-boiled eggs, cucumber, parsley, ham, or anything that will make a gay platter.

Frankfurter rolls. Roll each Frankfurter in a square of fresh buttered bread. Secure each with a little flag.

Chocolate Wholewheat Sticks or Animals
Makes about 36

6 oz. ($\frac{3}{4}$ cup) butter or margarine
8 oz. (1 cup) brown sugar
1 egg
5 oz. (1 cup) S.R. flour
5 oz. (almost 1 cup) wholewheat flour
2 level tablesp. cocoa or chocolate powder
1 teasp. vanilla essence

(1) Preheat oven to 350° or No. 4.
(2) Cream butter and sugar, adding 2 teasp. of hot water if butter is hard.
(3) Add 2 teasp. of the flour, then the egg and beat well. Add the rest of the flour, wheatmeal and cocoa. Add vanilla.
(4) Mix to a dough.
(5) Either roll out and make into animals or other shapes with cutters, or press into a shallow pan about 8 × 11$\frac{1}{2}$ inches.
(6) Bake for about 20 minutes. If cooked in shallow pan, cut into fingers, then leave until cold before removing.

Food of Love

Our Mutual Friend

BEAUTIFUL Bella Wilfer runs away to marry John Rokesmith, but after all decides to divulge the secret to her loving little father and invite him to their wedding-day dinner.

The Dinner was put on under the auspices of a solemn gentleman in black clothes and a white cravat looking like an Archbishop of Greenwich. Conferring in secrecy with John Rokesmith on the subjects of punch and wines, he bent over his head as though stooping to the Papistical practice of receiving auricular confession. Likewise on John offering a suggestion which didn't meet his views, his face became reproachful and overcast, as enjoining penance.

What a dinner! Specimens of all the fishes that swim in the sea, had surely swum their way to it and if not to be recognized, it was only because of being cooked in batter among the whitebait. And the dishes being seasoned with Bliss were of perfect flavour and the golden drinks had been bottled in the golden age and hoarding up their sparkles ever since.

The three diners had made a covenant that they would not reveal to mortal eyes any appearance whatever of being a wedding party, but a slender young waiter, as yet unversed in the wiles of waiter-hood, decrying the position of affairs which even his innocence could not mistake, languished admiringly when Bella did not want anything, swooping to her side when she did.

Him the Archbishop perpetually obstructed, cutting him out with his elbow, dispatching him in degrading quests of melted butter, and when by chance he got hold of a dish worth having, bereaved him of it and ordered him to stand back. With his own hands the dignatory put the dessert on the table and would have retired but for the young waiter finding by ill fortune a piece of orange flower somewhere in the lobby, now approached undetected with the same in a finger glass. The Archbishop instantly ejected and excommunicated him; but the thing was done.

All burst into loud and merry laughter; "Disguise is no use," said Bella. "They all find me out; I think it must be because I look so happy." Her Father proposed a toast to, "many, many happy returns of this most happy day." "Here, ten thousand times," cried John. "I fill my glass and my most precious wife's."

"And O there are days in this life worth life and worth death. O 'tis love, 'tis love that makes the world go round."

Dinner for an American Visitor

Devonshire Terrace, April 19th, 1849

WHILE Dickens was in America in 1842, one of the eminent writers who had been generous with his welcome and friendship was George Bancroft (1800–91), historian from Harvard and author of *The History of the United States*. But by the time he visited England in 1848 to begin a lecture tour, *Martin Chuzzlewit* had been published and read in America and Bancroft was one of those patriots hurt by it. So angered were the Americans by the book's frankness about some of the less attractive aspects of their new country that during a burlesque of *Macbeth* at a New York theatre, copies were flung with fury into the witches' cauldron! Carlyle, over there at the time, said that "All Yankee-doodledum fizzed like one universal soda-water bottle!"

Dickens, defending his motives, said: "In the American portion of this book, if I have ridiculed absurdities it was not with any animosity. I would have done the same thing if the same opportunity had arisen in reference to London or Dublin or Paris or Devonshire." It was probably the realization of this trait in Dickens's character that finally mollified Bancroft because we know that he accepted an invitation to dine at Devonshire Terrace on April 19th and also that a few weeks later he had returned the invitation by inviting Dickens to a breakfast party at which the guests were the Duke of Argyll, Macaulay the historian, Hallam, Bunsen, and Milman, Dean of St. Paul's. On another occasion Bancroft and Dickens had met at Forster's Lincoln's Inn Fields rooms when fellow American Emerson, the philosopher and essayist, and Thomas Carlyle were present. So it is likely that by the time he returned to Boston, any coolness caused by *Martin Chuzzlewit* had disappeared.

Forster gives the list of guests at the April dinner as Mrs. Proctor, wife of the poet, Mrs. Macready whose actor husband was away in America, Lady Graham, wife of Sir James Graham and Catherine Hayes the actress whose "homely and good-natured mother had startled them all very much by complimenting Mrs. Dickens on her having had for her father so clever a painter as Mr. Hogarth"! The confusion was of course with William Hogarth, famous English painter and chronicler who was born 1697 and was in his grave by 1764.

A KATE DICKENS MENU	A MODERN MENU
(8–10 persons)	*(4 or more people)*
Turbot with Shrimp Sauce (p. 7)	*Turbot with Cucumber Sauce*
Roast Loin of Mutton (p. 31)	*Ham and Celery Vol-au-Vents*
Pigeon Pie	*with Lettuce*
Broccoli. Mashed Potatoes	
Salad	*Roasted Spring Chicken*
	New Potatoes. Peas
College Puddings	
Macaroni (p. 104)	*Apple Tart with Cream*
	Biscuits and Cheeses

Turbot with Cucumber Sauce   *Serves 4*

1 lb. turbot, skinned and filleted
Salt and pepper
2 tablesp. water
2 tablesp. white wine or pale sherry
1 bay leaf
Cucumber sauce (p. 119)

(1) Poach the fish in the water and wine, adding seasoning and bay leaf. Cook, covered, either in oven or on hob.
(2) Make the sauce.
(3) Lift out fish and pour liquor into sauce. Serve on individual plates and pour sauce over.
(4) Garnish with parsley.

Ham and Celery Vol-au-Vents   *Serves 4*

4 large puff pastry vol-au-vent
   cases
6 oz. ham
2 level tablesp. celery soup powder
¾ cup milk
1 teasp. sugar

(1) Mince ham.
(2) Cook together for 5 minutes or longer the packet soup and the milk. Add sugar.
(3) Add ham, and fill the cases. Re-heat before serving.

Roasted Spring Chicken

Buy forcemeat stuffing or make your
   own, or
Use a rice stuffing with parsley and
   grated onion
1 spring chicken
Bacon rashers
Foil
2 tablesp. fat.

(1) Preheat oven to 400° or No. 6 or heat the spit oven.
(2) Fill chicken with stuffing. If you use bought stuffing, it is usually rather strong in herbs, so if you prefer it milder add an extra ½ cup or so of breadcrumbs and some fresh parsley. Secure cavity with thread, then truss bird again.
(3) Put a few rashers of streaky bacon on the breast and wrap chicken in foil. Put fat in roasting pan.
(4) Roast for about 1¼ hours, then remove foil and finish until nicely browned. Of course foil is not used for spit roasting.

Apple Tart, Crunchy Topped

Serves 4–6

8 oz. short pastry, or the shortcake
   pastry shown in the Mince Pie
   recipe on p. 111.
1 lb. apples
½ cup sultanas
6 level tablesp. sugar
2 tablesp. lemon juice
1 tablesp. butter
1 cup crushed cornflakes
2 oz. (2 tablesp.) chopped walnuts
3 tablesp. coconut
½ teasp. vanilla essence
2 tablesp. brown sugar

Apple and Orange Tart
Add ½ cup orange segments

(1) Preheat oven to 350° or No. 4.
(2) Roll out pastry and line an 8- or 8½-inch
    pie plate, first wetting the edge. Put a
    1-inch strip around and decorate.
(3) Fill with peeled, sliced apples.
(4) Sprinkle with the sultanas, sugar and
    lemon juice.
(5) Melt butter and stir in the cornflakes,
    walnuts, coconut, vanilla and brown
    sugar.
(6) Spread on top of the apples, and bake
    for ¾ hour. Reduce heat a little if edges
    are browning too quickly.
(7) Serve with cream, or whipped cream
    laced with brandy.

College Puddings (Victorian Recipe)

Serves 6

4 oz. (2 cups) breadcrumbs
4 oz. (½ cup) chopped suet
2 oz. (2 tablesp.) each of currants
   and sultanas
3 oz. (4 level tablesp.) sugar
Pinch of nutmeg, and cinnamon
1 level teasp. baking powder
1 egg
4 tablesp. milk

(1) Butter 6 dariole moulds (oven proof).
(2) Preheat oven to 350° or No. 4.
(3) Combine in a mixing bowl the crumbs,
    suet, dried fruit, sugar, baking powder
    and spices.
(4) Beat egg and add milk.
(5) Stir into the dry mixture and mix well.
(6) Put into moulds. Place on baking tray
    and bake for about 20–25 minutes. Turn
    out and serve with custard or cream.

Pigeon Pie

Serves 6

Ingredients as for Casserole of
   Pigeons on p. 91
6 oz. short or puff pastry

(1) Follow the recipe for the Casserole and
    tip into a deep pie dish.
(2) Roll out pastry. Put pie funnel in and
    wet edge of dish.
(3) Fit pastry over and neaten and decorate
    edge. Brush over either with top milk or
    beaten egg. Cut two slits in pastry.
(4) Bake in a hot oven for about 35 minutes.

Charles Dickens the Younger, 1852, 15 years old

A Dinner and a Toy

Devonshire Terrace, May 12th, 1849

THE first number of *David Copperfield* had been launched at the beginning of this month, and one of the guests at this dinner, the great Thomas Carlyle, delighted Dickens by replying to an inquiry after his health, that he was "a lorn lone creatur' and everything went contrary with him"! This set the tone for some gay and clever banter during the meal, though at one stage Dickens showed a little irritation when the Rev. Tagert began to talk "shop"—evidently feeling it his duty to remind them not to forget to nourish their souls as well as their bodies.

The others present were Thackeray, Sam Rogers, Mrs. Gaskell, wife of a Unitarian Minister and well-known author whose best-known work *Cranford* was a few years later serialized in Dickens's *Household Words*, Douglas Jerrold, and Halbot Browne (Phiz).

In the nursery the children were enjoying different sorts of fun. Dickens had bought them a toy theatre. Charley, remembering it, wrote later:

> I well remember the first spectacle produced in my toy theatre, called *The Elephant of Siam*. Its production necessitated the designing and painting of new scenes which resulted in a competition between my father and Stanfield. You would have thought their very existence depended on the mounting of this same elephant! Even after Stanfield had had enough, my father was still hard at work and pegged away at the landscapes and architecture of Siam with an amount of energy which in any other man would have been something prodigious, but which I soon learned to look upon as quite natural. This energy of my father was well expressed by the character of Captain Swosser in *Bleak House* whose maxim was that "if you only have to swab a plank you should swab it as if Davy Jones were after you and if you have to make pitch hot, you cannot make it too hot!"

All through the books written by Charley and Mamie, we find tributes to the kindness and consideration of their father to his children. Mamie wrote: ". . . we never had a snub from him or a cross word under any circumstances. He was always glad to give us 'treats' as he called them and used to conceive all manner of these 'treats' for us, and if any favour had to be asked we were sure of a favourable answer."

The children were growing up as children will. Charley was now 12 and soon to be a pupil at Eton College, Mamie was 11, Katie 10, Walter 8, Francis 5, Alfred 3, Sydney 2 and Henry a baby of 4 months. (And there were yet more to come!)

NURSERY SPECIALS

Fresh Tomato Soup

———

Stuffed Potatoes
Tossed Salad (p. 75). Kate Dickens's Dressing
or
Spaghetti Surprise

———

Rice Moulds or Lime Jelly Ring
Fresh Fruit Compote

Fresh Tomato Soup   *Serves 6*

1 lb. tomatoes
1 large onion
1½ pints (3 cups) water
2 rashers of bacon, or a handful of
   left-over bacon rinds
1 chicken cube
1 teasp. sweet basil
2 good teasp. sugar
2 level teasp. salt and a little pepper
2 level tablesp. small sago

(1) Peel and halve the tomatoes and chop the onions.
(2) Put into large pan and add water, bacon, cube, basil, sugar, seasoning and sago.
(3) Simmer for about 35 minutes.
(4) Lift out rinds and check for seasoning before serving.

———

Stuffed Potatoes   *Serves 6*

6 large floury potatoes
3 oz. grated cheese
2 oz. (2 tablesp.) butter
1 egg
Salt and pepper

(1) Scrub potatoes, brush with oil or butter and bake in a moderate oven until cooked through—about 1½–2 hours, depending on size.
(2) Cut in halves lengthwise. Scoop out the potato into a bowl.
(3) Add cheese, butter and beaten egg.
(4) Re-fill the potatoes, top with more grated cheese and re-heat before serving. Serve with any green salad.

Kate Dickens's Dressing. 1 teasp. water, ½ teasp. salt and pepper, 2 wineglasses of oil, one dessertsp. vinegar and some sweet herbs chopped fine.

Spaghetti Surprise

Serves 4–6

2 cans of spaghetti in tomato sauce
1 egg per serving
Grated cheese or fine dry
  breadcrumbs
Salt and pepper

(1) Preheat oven to 350° or No. 4.
(2) Open cans. Tip contents of one into deep pie dish.
(3) Break whole eggs in on top of spaghetti. Try not to break the yolks. Sprinkle with salt and pepper.
(4) Carefully spoon the contents of the other can over the eggs. Sprinkle with grated cheese or breadcrumbs and bake for about 25 minutes.

Rice Moulds

Serves 4–6

2 cups cooked rice
2 oz. (2 tablesp.) sugar
2 eggs
½ pint (1 cup) milk

(1) Preheat oven to 350° or No. 4.
(2) Beat eggs and add to rice with milk and sugar.
(3) Grease 6 dariole moulds and fill with mixture.
(4) Bake for about 20 minutes or until set. Carefully turn out on to a serving dish.

Lime Jelly Ring

Serves 4

2 packets of lime jellies, with almost the quantity of water necessary as given on packets (usually 1 pint each)

(1) Have a 2-pint ring mould.
(2) Measure the water necessary for the two packets, but remove 2 tablesp. of it. The mould needs to be fairly stiff to turn out and keep its ring shape.
(3) Bring half the water to the boil and dissolve the two jellies. When completely dissolved add the rest of the water. Tip into mould and allow to set.
(4) Dip into hot water and turn out. Put some of the following fruit compote in the hole and the rest around the ring.

Fresh Fruit Compote

Serves 4

About 3 or more cups of fresh fruit in season
Sugar

(1) Use any fresh ripe fruit. Pears, apples, strawberries, peaches, apricots, nectarines, raspberries, etc. Choose 2 or more types.
(2) Sprinkle with one-third the amount of sugar—that is for 3 cups fruit, use 1 cup sugar. If the fruit is very sweet such as pears, less sugar could be used.
(3) Allow to stand until sugar has melted and a lovely syrup has formed.

British Food

Household Words

SHORT articles on every variety of subject appeared in the weekly magazine *Household Words*. In this extract Dickens's imaginary American visitor speaks of Dinner in a Stately Home.

The soup is various; in Scotland it is usually what they call Hodgepodge, a mixture of vegetable and some meat. After soup the fish cover is removed and this is generally served round without any vegetables, but certainly not more of one kind. After the fish, come the plain joints, roast or boiled with potatoes, peas or beans and cauliflower. Then sherry wine is handed by the servants to everyone. German wine is offered to those who prefer it; this is always drunk in green glasses; then champagne is offered; after this remove, come ducks or partridge or other game; after this the bon bons, puddings, tarts, sweetmeats, blancmange; then cheese and bread and a glass of strong ale is handed round; then the removal of the upper cloth, and often times the most delicious fruit and confectionery follow, such as grapes, peaches, melons, apples and dried fruits etc. etc. After this is put upon the table a small bottle of Constantia wine, which is deemed very precious and handed round in small wine glasses, or noyau, or other cordial.

Finger glasses are always furnished, though in some cases I have seen a deep silver plate filled with rose water, presented to each guest in which he dips the corner of his napkin to wipe his lips or his fingers.

No cigars or pipes are ever offered and soon after the removal of the cloth, the ladies retire to the withdrawing room and have coffee or tea. I have never heard any discussion of the wines on the table. Port, sherry, claret, seldom madeira, all of the most expensive quality, excepting that I have been repeatedly asked what wine we usually drink in America.

It is noticeable that the guests do not dash at the dishes and contend with one another for the "fixings" they contain, but put their trust in providence and the servants and in a good time coming if they wait a little longer.

Pastures New

Bonchurch, Isle of Wight, Midsummer 1849

THE decision to forsake Broadstairs for the summer and go instead to the Isle of Wight was taken after Dickens had become friendly with the Rev. James White, clergyman and writer. He had offered his house, Winterbourne, at Bonchurch and Dickens had gladly accepted.

At first he was wild with enthusiasm about his choice and at the end of July wrote to Forster, saying: "There are views which are only to be equalled on the Genoese shore of the Mediterranean; the variety of walks is extraordinary; things are cheap, and everybody is civil. The waterfall acts wonderfully and the sea bathing is delicious. . . ." The reference to the waterfall concerns the showerbath he had made from it as it dropped into the stream. According to his eldest son, a shower-bath was a necessity to his father and at their next home, Tavistock House, "there was one of such severity as to earn for itself the name of The Demon".

Besides the walks and bathing, they seem to have had a particularly gay social round. Charley writes:

> the society of a number of friends both old and new made the time pass in the liveliest manner, and although the climate did not suit him, my father was full of energy and go. There seems to have been continual excursions and picnics during the day; constant impromptu dances and games and forfeits, performances of conjuring tricks with my father as the magician and John Leech as his attendant.

Added to this, Dickens himself, writing to Forster, says: "we have been sufficiently rollicking since I finished the number (the first of *David Copperfield*) and have great games of Rounders on the sand with all Bonchurch looking on." Only the weather was caddish enough not to lend a hand to the fun. Of the garden tea at Lady Swinburn's Dickens says: "The rain came in with the first teapot and has been active ever since." The picnic weather is not mentioned, but as Dickens on one occasion insisted that they "must find materials for a fire" and take a "great iron pot to boil potatoes in", that must have been one fine day at any rate.

Unfortunately the Isle of Wight climate eventually defeated Dickens. In glorious exaggeration he writes to Forster, blaming Bonchurch for "extreme depression of mind", "great prostration of strength, so that my legs tremble under me", "ten miles an insupportable distance", "an extraordinary disposition to sleep (except at night)" and many other such phrases. No wonder he was glad to get back to bracing Broadstairs!

A VICTORIAN PICNIC HAMPER FOR TWENTY

Four Lobsters
Forequarter of Lamb with Cold Mint Sauce
A Small Ham
A Galantine of Veal
A Chicken Pie
Four Roasted Chickens
Salad Dressing
Two Large Apple Tarts
Two Large Cheese Pies (p. 124)
Two Dozen Balmoral Tarts
Two Jellies
2 lb. of Biscuits
Four Loaves of Bread
1½ lb. of Cheese and 1 lb. Butter
6 lb. Strawberries and 5 pints of Cream

MODERN PICNIC BASKET FOR TEN

Thermos of Chilled Soup (see below)
Two Chickens, Cooked and Disjointed
Two Bacon and Egg Pies
Two large Jars of Tossed Salad
Jar of Mayonnaise
Two Dozen Bread Rolls
½ lb. Butter
Two Jars of Fruit Salad
Jar of Cream
Maori Kisses
Biscuits and Cheeses

Tomato Chicken Chilled Soup   *Serves 8*

2 large cans of chicken consommé,
  or 1½ pints of the liquid in which
  chickens were boiled
1 pint tomato purée
3 tablesp. sherry or brandy
2 teasp. sugar

(1) Combine chicken consommé and tomato purée or tomato soup.
(2) Add ¼ pint water, the sugar and the sherry or brandy.
(3) Chill thoroughly in refrigerator, add two or three lumps of ice and put into thermos flask or flasks.

The sherry or brandy may be omitted—or increased.

Ham, Boiled then Baked

1 ham, any size
Cloves and bay leaf
Cider or fruit juice
Brown sugar and breadcrumbs

(1) Soak ham for several hours or overnight. If it is a sugar-cured ham this will not be necessary.
(2) Cover with fresh water and simmer for about 3–4 hours or until the rind will slip off easily. Remove rind.
(3) Place in oven dish and pour over some cider or fruit juice. Pineapple is popular. Bake for about half an hour, basting once. Rub fat with brown sugar and breadcrumbs.

Bacon and Egg Pie

½ lb. bacon rashers (not too fat)
6 eggs
4 tomatoes
¾ lb. short pastry
2 teasp. sugar
Salt and pepper

(1) Preheat oven to 375° or No. 5.
(2) Divide pastry into two pieces and roll out thinly. Put one half into an 8½- or 9-inch shallow cake tin or oven-proof pie dish.
(3) Remove rinds from bacon, arrange half of it over the bottom of the lined dish.
(4) Break in the eggs, trying not to break the yolks. Cover with sliced tomatoes and sprinkle them with sugar, salt and pepper.
(5) Cover with the rest of the bacon, then the top layer of pastry. Neaten and decorate the edge and prick surface with a fork.
(6) Bake for about 40 minutes. Reduce heat if pastry is browning too quickly.

Fruit Salad   *Serves 12*

1 lb. can of pears
1 lb. can of peaches, sliced
1 lb. can of pineapple
1 lb. can of apricots
2 oranges
2 lemons
6 oz. sugar
1 lb. bananas, peeled and sliced
12 passion fruit (optional)

(1) Open cans. Drain syrup into salad bowl and add sugar and lemon juice.
(2) Cut up the fruit and add.
(3) Peel oranges, remove pith and put segments into salad bowl.
(4) Add bananas. Taste and add more sugar if necessary.
Firewater in the shape of brandy, sherry or champagne may replace some of the syrup.

Maori Kisses   *About 16 pairs*

3 oz. chopped dates
2 tablesp. lemon juice
4 oz. (4 tablesp.) butter
4 oz. (½ cup) brown sugar
5 oz. (1 cup) flour
2 level tablesp. cocoa
½ teasp. vanilla essence
Chocolate filling

(1) Preheat oven to 350° or No. 4.
(2) Put dates and lemon juice into small pan and bring to the boil. Remove from heat and mash to a mush.
(3) Tip into mixing bowl. Add butter and sugar and beat well.
(4) Add flour and cocoa, then vanilla. Form into a soft dough.
(5) Break off pieces about the size of a walnut and make into balls with floury hands. Place on ungreased oven trays. Flatten each ball with a fork. Bake for 18–20 minutes.
(6) When cold, put together in pairs with the filling.

Picnic Food

Pickwick Papers

MEDICAL science has often been surprised at the way Dickens was able to diagnose illness by observing and recording the symptoms. In this book "The Fat Boy" is continually falling asleep, no matter where he might be, and students of medicine, noting the symptoms, have decided that it was the first case of "narcolepsy associated with obesity" ever recorded.

A grand Field Day and Bivouac was in noisy progress on the Lines at Rochester. There was a fine gentle wind and Mr. Pickwick's hat rolled sportively before it. The wind puffed, and Mr. Pickwick puffed and the hat rolled over and over as merrily as a lively porpoise in a strong tide until it was blown with some violence against the wheels of an open barouche occupied by six cheerful souls. Mr. Tupman called, "Pickwick —Pickwick, come up here, make haste" and a stout gentleman in a blue coat and bright buttons, cordery breeches and top boots said, "Come along Sir, Pray come up. Joe! Damn the boy, he's gone to sleep again. Joe, let down the steps."

Fastened up behind the barouche was a hamper of spacious dimensions and on the box sat a fat, red faced boy whom no speculative observer could regard for an instant without setting down as the official dispenser of the contents of the afore mentioned hamper. Joe rolled slowly off the box and when his task was done, waddled back and fell asleep instantly. He remained asleep during the rest of the Review as soundly as if the roaring cannon were his ordinary lullaby. "Damn that boy," cried Mr. Wardle again, "He's gone to sleep as usual! Be good enough to pinch him in the leg sir, nothing else wakes him." "Joe, look sharp, undo the hamper." The fat boy rolled off the box again and proceeded to unpack the hamper with more expedition than could have been expected from his previous inactivity. The leaden eyes which twinkled behind his mountainous cheeks leered horribly upon the food, keeping awake because of the glorious sight of capons and veal patties.

"Now Joe, the tongue," cried Mr. Wardle. "Now the pigeon pie. Take care of that veal and ham. Mind the lobsters. Take the salad out of the cloth; give me the dressing." Dishes were placed in everybody's hands and on everybody's knees, after which the Fat Boy fell asleep again. Mr. Wardle said, "He's always asleep. Goes on errands fast asleep and snores as he waits at table. I'm proud of that boy, wouldn't part with him. He's a natural curiosity."

For the Eight-and-Thirtieth Time

Devonshire Terrace, February 7th, 1850

Answering the Rev. James White's letter declining the invitation to his birthday dinner, Dickens wrote: "Am I born (for the eight-and-thirtieth time) next Thursday, at half past five and do you mean to say you are *not* coming to dinner? Well, well, I can always go over to Puseyism to spite my friends, and that is some comfort."

The word "Puseyism" is interesting. It stemmed from the Rev. Edward Bouverie Pusey of Oriel College, Oxford, who began a movement intended to restore some of the old ceremonial parts of religious services. It was established in 1833 and became known as the Oxford Movement.

For some months Dickens had been toying with an idea. The expenses of keeping up a large house and educating and clothing a growing family were increasing yearly and even though his novels were selling in enormous numbers, he knew that he would have to find some further source of revenue. He had in mind a weekly paper—one that would not only bring in extra income, but would also be a vehicle for his radical ideas and those of his equally dedicated associates. He further hoped that such a paper should help young hopefuls who needed a platform from which to make their first steps towards a career in writing.

To Forster he had said of the idea: "My notion is a weekly journal, price three-half-pence or twopence, matter in part original and in part selected and always having, if possible a little good poetry. . . ." The title bothered him and he tried many before making the final decision. He worked his way through such concoctions as "The Microscope", "The Rolling Years", "Weekly Bells", "The Household Face" and others, then at last (as always) hit on perfection and *Household Words*.

It was launched in March of this year and was a tremendous success, fulfilling its purpose and adding helpfully to Dickens's income. It continued right through the years to 1859, when it gave way to *All the Year Round*, a paper run on similar lines.

For several years running, Dickens had taken Kate for short spells to Brighton. He found the air there bracing and the peace and quiet of Sussex relaxing and helpful to his work. They stayed sometimes at the Old Ship, still an attractive Georgian inn looking out to sea, and sometimes at the Bedford Hotel, destroyed by fire in 1964 and now rebuilt into a new hotel and luxury skyscraper block. The hotel commemorates the visits by calling the bar the Dickens Bar.

A KATE DICKENS MENU	BIRTHDAY BUFFET SUPPER

A KATE DICKENS MENU

(8–10 persons)

Pea Soup (p. 143)

Filleted Soles with Shrimp Sauce (p. 7)

Roast Turkey (p. 56).   Sausages
Cold Ham (p. 171)
Mashed and Brown Potatoes
Broccoli

Jam Roll Pudding
Open Damson Tart
Macaroni

BIRTHDAY BUFFET SUPPER

Hors d'œuvres (p. 127 and below)
or
Cocktail Snacks (p. 107)

Greek Moussaka.   Rice
Salad Niçoise

Fruit Salad (p. 172).   Meringues (p. 180)
Nesselrode Pies

Cheese Straws (p. 108)

Hors d'œuvres (see also p. 127)

Stuffed Eggs. Hard-cook the eggs, shell and cut in halves lengthwise. Remove yolks into a bowl. Add a little mayonnaise, then anything savoury such as grated cheese and capers, mashed sardines, and cheese–tomato purée and chopped gherkins. Many other ideas will occur to you. Refill halves and garnish.

Prosciutto: Italian Parma ham, cut into slices.

Mexican Sweetcorn. In cans.

Raw Mushrooms. Scrub mushrooms and slice. Marinate in vinegar, then drain and shine with a little oil. Place in hors d'œuvre dish and sprinkle with chopped parsley.

Smoked Salmon Squares. Have 2-inch-square slices of buttered bread, place a square of thin smoked salmon on each.

Smoked Salmon Rolls. As for the squares, but a slightly larger square. Roll up and secure with picks.

Moussaka   *Serves 8*

2 lb. cooked leg of lamb, diced
   small
2 Spanish onions
2 tablesp. oil
1 crushed or chopped clove of garlic
$\frac{1}{2}$ lb. mushrooms
3 aubergines
$\frac{1}{2}$ pint can of peeled tomatoes
2 good teasp. sugar
Salt and freshly ground black pepper
Flour, butter, cheese

(1) Peel and chop onions and fry in the oil adding the garlic.

(2) Add washed sliced mushrooms and meat and continue frying for a few minutes.

(3) In another pan, heat another tablesp. oil. Slice aubergines and fry them on both sides.

(4) Sprinkle $1\frac{1}{2}$ level tablesp. flour on to meat mixture, then add tomatoes and sugar. Stir well and bring just to boil. Thin with a little water, and season well.

(5) Put half into a deep casserole, cover with half the aubergines, then repeat the two layers. Sprinkle heavily with grated cheese and bake in a moderate oven until cheese is sizzling.

Salad Niçoise

Serves 8–10

1 small or half a large Spanish onion
6 tomatoes, peeled and quartered
1 green pepper
1 cucumber
A few sticks of celery, chopped
1 can tuna fish
1 can anchovies
8 ripe olives
3 hard-boiled eggs
French dressing

(1) Slice the onion into thin rings and drop into a large wooden salad bowl.
(2) Add tomatoes, then de-seeded and finely sliced green pepper.
(3) Peel cucumber and halve. Scoop out seeds and chop into dice. Add to salad.
(4) Add celery, tuna, anchovies, olives and hard-boiled eggs, shelled and quartered.
(5) Serve with the dressing.

Note. The salad bowl may be lined with lettuce-heart leaves.

Nesselrode Pie

Serves 6

Shortcake pastry,
  see Apple Shortcake Pastry
  on p. 136
½ pint (1 cup) milk
4 oz. (½ cup) sugar
1 packet (1 level tablesp.) powdered gelatine
6 tablesp. sherry
2 eggs, separated
2 tablesp. each chopped Maraschino cherries, and sliced blanched almonds
Whipped cream with or without brandy

Note. The Crumb Crust given with the Lemon Meringue Pie on p. 156 is sometimes used with this pie.

(1) Preheat oven to 350° or No. 4.
(2) Line an 8- or 8½-inch pie dish about 1½–2 inches deep with the pastry, first wetting the edge. Put an extra 1-inch strip around, then neaten and decorate.
(3) Cover the bottom with stale crusts then bake for about 20–25 minutes or until crisp. Remove crusts.
(4) Heat milk and sugar. Beat yolks and stir in. Cook until mixture will coat the spoon. Do not boil.
(5) Mix gelatine with 2 tablesp. cold water. Stir into hot custard. Allow to dissolve.
(6) Add sherry, then tip into a bowl and put away until beginning to thicken. Add cherries and almonds.
(7) Beat egg whites until as stiff as possible and fold in. Pour into prepared dish. Allow to become firm. Cover with whipped cream, with or without brandy.

Jam Roll Pudding (Baked)

Serves 6

1 lb. puff pastry
Jam
Top milk or beaten egg for brushing

(1) Preheat oven to 400° or No. 6.
(2) Roll pastry out to a piece about 7 by 11 inches.
(3) Spread with jam and roll up into a long roly-poly.
(4) Seal seam and lift on to baking dish. Have seam underneath. Brush with top milk or beaten egg.
(5) Bake for about 35–40 minutes, reducing heat a little after 20 minutes.

Birthday Food

The Uncommercial Traveller

DICKENS said that, while working on a paper for his magazine, he had to leave off to wish the owner of a certain bright face that looked in at his door, "Many happy returns of the day", which incident diverted his mind to Birthdays.

When shall I disconnect the combined smells of oranges, brown paper and straw from birthdays at school, when the coming hamper cast its shadow before, and when a week of social harmony—shall I add of admiring affectionate popularity—led up to that institution? What noble sentiments were expressed to me in the days before the hamper, what vows of friendship were sworn to me, what exceedingly old knives were given me, what generous avowals of having been in the wrong emanated from else obstinate spirits once enrolled among my enemies! The birthday of the potted game and guava jelly, is still made special to me by the noble conduct of Bully Globson. Letters from home had mysteriously enquired whether I should be much surprised and disappointed if, among the treasures in the coming hamper, I discovered potted game and guava jelly from the West Indies.

I had mentioned these hints, in confidence, to a few friends and had promised to give away, as I now see reason to believe, a handsome covey of partridges potted, and about a hundred weight of guava jelly. It was now that Globson, Bully, no more sought me out in the play ground. He was a big fat boy, with a big fat head, and a big fat fist and at the beginning of that half had raised such bumps on my forehead that I couldn't get my hat of state on to go to Church. He said that after an interval of cool reflection (four months), he now felt this blow to have been an error of judgement, and that he wished to apologise. Not only that, but holding down his big head between his big hands, in order that I might reach it, he requested me to raise a retributive bump upon it in the presence of witnesses.

This handsome proposal I modestly declined and he embraced me, and we walked away conversing, respecting the West Indian Islands and in the pursuit of knowledge he asked me with much interest whether, in the course of my reading, I had met with any reliable description of the mode of manufacturing guava jelly; or whether I had happened to taste that conserve which he had been given to understand was of rare excellence.

A Bottle of the "Twenty", Expressly for You

Devonshire Terrace, July 21st, 1850

Tʜɪs time the Rev. James White was able to dine with Kate and Charles. The invitation, dated July 13th, 1850 read: "Tomorrow week I shall expect you. You shall have a bottle of the 'Twenty'. I have kept a few lingering caskets with a gem enshrined therein, expressly for you." Judging from the rest of the letter, the topics of conversation at dinner could have been the progress of the journal *Household Words* and the delights of Broadstairs where White and his family had decided to go for their summer holiday. In the letter Dickens had said: "You will find it the healthiest and freshest of places; and there are Canterbury, and all varieties of what Leigh Hunt calls 'greenery' within a few minutes' railroad ride. . . ."

In another part of the letter he had said, "*Household Words* goes on *thoroughly well* . . . and I have no doubt yields a good round profit." Two of the other guests at this dinner began their careers as contributors to this paper. One was Mrs. Elizabeth Gaskell, mentioned on p. 166 and the other Wilkie Collins, then a young man of 26. He contributed his great novels *The Woman in White, No Name*, and *The Moonstone*, all in weekly instalments. Other writers considered by Dickens as worthy of space were Augustus Henry Sala, Percy Fitzgerald, author of *Fatal Zero*, Edmund Yates, author of *Kissing the Road*, Adelaide Proctor, who contributed poems under the pen-name of Mary Berwick, and Mrs. Jane Louden, the first "Lady Gardener". She also ran the *Ladies Gardening Companion*.

Kate was expecting her ninth child the following month and was ill again, so Charles took the children down to Broadstairs and left her in peace until after the confinement. The baby, a girl, was born on August 16th and christened Dora Annie, after Dickens's fictional Dora, David Copperfield's pretty little child wife who was to die soon afterwards. When Kate was well enough she joined the rest of the family at Broadstairs and they remained there until the end of October.

Every day Dickens worked for long hours on *David Copperfield*. He knew that he was producing a good story. "There seems to be a bright unanimity about Copperfield," he had written to a friend, "I am very much interested in it and pleased with myself." But was he aware that out of his intensity of concentration he was creating a masterpiece that was to be claimed by generations far into the future as one of the greatest novels ever written?

A KATE DICKENS MENU	A MODERN MENU

A KATE DICKENS MENU

(8–10 persons)

Salmon with Shrimp Sauce (p. 7)
and Cucumbers

Veal and Ham Patties
Lamb's Fry
Roast Saddle of Mutton
Boiled Fowl and Tongue
New Potatoes.   Salad

Gooseberry Tart, Devonshire Cream
Cabinet Pudding (p. 72)
Macaroni (p. 104)

A MODERN MENU

(6 or more people)

Melon with Parma Ham

Veal and Ham Vol-au-Vents.   Lettuce
Baked Crumbed Giggots of Lamb
Scalloped Potatoes (p. 16).   Peas
Stuffed Tomatoes

Gooseberry Marmalade Tart
Meringues

Biscuits and Cheeses

Melon with Parma Ham. Either serve the melon in wedges with a slice of ham on the plate, or cut the melon into small cubes and make ham rolls by putting cubes on slices of ham and rolling up. Secure with picks.

Veal and Ham Vol-au-Vents   *Serves 6*

6 oz. minced cooked veal
6 oz. minced cooked ham
2 level tablesp. packet asparagus
  soup
$\frac{1}{4}$ pint ($\frac{1}{2}$ cup) milk
2 teasp. sugar
6 very large vol-au-vent cases

(1) Combine veal and ham.
(2) Mix soup with milk and cook until thick. Add a little water if necessary to make a thick white sauce. Add the sugar.
(3) Stir in the veal and ham.
(4) Fill the cases and heat.

Lamb's Fry   *Serves 6*

$1\frac{1}{2}$ lb. lamb's fry
12 rashers of bacon
2 teasp. butter
Flour

(1) Remove skin from fry and cut into slices, or ask the butcher to do it.
(2) Remove rinds from bacon and fry with the butter until cooked and fat has run out. Remove and keep hot on a plate.
(3) Coat fry with flour and fry for only a few minutes on either side. Add more butter or, if you have it, bacon fat, as the fry takes it up. Serve with the bacon.

Baked Crumbed Giggots of Lamb

Serves 6–8

3 tablesp. fat
6 giggots, or leg chops
Milk, seasoned breadcrumbs

(1) Preheat oven to 400° or No. 6.
(2) Put fat in baking pan and put into oven to get hot.
(3) Add 1 teasp. salt and a little pepper to the milk. Dip chops in this, then in breadcrumbs.
(4) Place in hot fat, then turn over so that both sides are coated.
(5) Bake for about 1 hour, reducing heat to 300° or No. 2½ or 3 after 15 minutes. Do not allow to overcook or dry. They are delicious.

Stuffed Tomatoes. Wash tomatoes and cut the skin around the circumference in a zig-zag pattern with a sharp pointed knife. Pull apart giving two halves with pinked edges. Scoop out some of the flesh and fill with cooked green peas. Arrange around the meat.

Gooseberry Marmalade Tart

6 oz. short pastry
½ lb. gooseberries
4 oz. (½ cup) sugar
3 or 4 tablesp. marmalade
Cream
Meringues if desired, see recipe below

(1) Preheat oven to 350° or No. 4.
(2) Roll out pastry and line an 8½- or 9-inch pie dish, first wetting the edge. Cut a 1 inch strip and fit around the edge. Neaten and decorate.
(3) Cover the bottom with stale crusts and bake for 20–25 minutes or until crisp.
(4) Meanwhile top and tail the gooseberries and put into a pan with the sugar and 3 tablesp. water. Cover and cook for a few minutes, just until berries are soft without breaking.
(5) When crust is cooked, remove crusts. Spread with marmalade, then add the gooseberries. When cold, spread with whipped cream.
(6) Small meringues arranged on the cream will make an attractive finish.

Meringues

Makes about 24

3 egg whites
6 oz. sugar
Whipped cream

(1) Preheat oven to 225° or No. 1.
(2) On electric mixer, beat eggs and sugar until so stiff that the mixture will stand alone in stiff peaks.
(3) Put into small piles on greased oven trays. Bake until the outside is crisp but the inside soft—about 40 minutes.
(4) If not used on top of Gooseberry Tart put two together with whipped cream.

Tavistock House

A Stag Dinner—and Tears

Devonshire Terrace, March 12th, 1851

MACREADY's entry in his Diary gives us the date of this dinner and the guests present. They were listed as Edward Bulwer Lytton, Mark Lemon, Douglas Jerrold, Augustus Egg and John Forster. No wives were mentioned.

Bulwer Lytton had by now become one of the family's closest friends but there was a time, back in the early 1830s, when this might have seemed unlikely. While Bulwer was a Member of Parliament and son of a family of rank, Dickens was a mere Gallery reporter. But Dickens's social rise was relative to his rise in fame and eventually the two men met on an equal plane. They had a great deal in common. Both were successful authors (Bulwer a brilliant historian), both were keen amateur actors and both were interested in helping the less fortunate. It was while Charles, Kate and Georgy were staying at the Lytton family seat, Knebworth in Hertfordshire, that their Guild of Literature and Art was planned. Its aim was to help the less successful in the two spheres, but soon fizzled out for want of grateful patrons. (Who wants to admit defeat?)

Kate had been both physically and nervously ill ever since the birth of her baby, Dora and the hectic life of Devonshire Terrace with a demanding social life and nine children clamouring for attention, gave her no chance to recover. So Charles decided to take her, with Georgy, to Malvern Spa and leave her there to enjoy a complete rest.

Had his hopes been realized and Kate recovered her health and vitality, perhaps she should have been able to deal effectively with her sister's encroachment on her rightful domain. But alas, Fate had her destiny in its grip. On April 14th, while Charles was presiding at a dinner in London, their frail little baby died suddenly. He had just returned from Malvern and was knee deep in commitments, so Forster offered to make the journey and bring Kate and Georgy back. Charles, obviously worried about the effect on Kate of the tragic news, tried to postpone the truth until he could be with her. His poor pathetic letter, carried by Forster, read, "Mind, I will not deceive you. I think her very ill and I cannot encourage myself with much hope of her recovery. I do not— why should I say I do, to my dear!—I do not think her recovery at all likely." And so on. Poor Charles! Did he really think a mother would not guess the truth? Surely there could have been no doubt in Kate's mind during that long journey home that sorrow and tears awaited her?

A KATE DICKENS MENU

(6 or 7 persons)

Fresh Herrings

*Roast Leg of Mutton stuffed
with Oysters (p. 31)
Stewed Kidneys (p. 48)
Mashed Turnips
Mashed and Brown Potatoes*

*Greengage Tart
Macaroni with Bacon (p. 104)*

A MODERN MENU

(6 or more people)

*Chicken Liver Pâté
Spinach Soup*

*Roasted Duck with Cherries
Roasted Potatoes.   Creamed Celery
Side Salads (p. 201)*

Lemon Cream Russe

Biscuits and Cheeses

Chicken Liver Pâté   *Serves 6–8*

3 oz. butter
1 lb. chicken livers
¼ lb. sliced ham
1 large Spanish onion
Salt and pepper
3 tablesp. sherry
2 tablesp. brandy

(1) Melt butter then add livers, peeled and chopped onion, and chopped ham.
(2) Fry gently without browning for 10 minutes.
(3) Add sherry and continue cooking for another 10 minutes, still gently.
(4) Remove from heat and add brandy. Set alight at once, while the mixture is still hot. Season well.
(5) Put into electric blender and blend until deliciously smooth.
(6) Put into a dish or individual ramekins and chill until firm.

Spinach Soup   *Serves 6–8*

A few sticks of celery
2 large potatoes
1 large onion
2 lbs. spinach
Handful of parsley sprigs
Salt and pepper, sugar
½ pint (1 cup) milk (optional)

Note. The bowls may be topped with whipped cream with or without brandy.

(1) Wash and chop celery. Peel and slice potatoes and onions.
(2) Put all into a large pan with 1½ pints water and simmer, covered, for 25 minutes, or until potatoes have cooked.
(3) Add well-washed roughly chopped spinach and the parsley.
(4) Season with 2 or more teasp. salt, a little pepper and 1 teasp. sugar.
(5) Continue simmering for another 15 minutes.
(6) Either blend together in electric blender or push through a colander.
(7) Add milk or, if preferred, more water. Reheat and serve hot.

Roasted Duck with Cherries

Serves 6

3 tablesp. fat
1 duck, about 5–6 lb.
1 bottle of cherries in Maraschino
  syrup (any size)
3 tablesp. sherry
½ lb. streaky bacon rashers
Salt and pepper

Bacon Rolls. Remove rinds from rashers, cut into 5-inch lengths and roll up. Put on an enamel plate or other oven-proof plate and cook for about the last 15 minutes with the duck

(1) Preheat oven to 400° or No. 6.
(2) Stuff duck with sage and onion stuffing, or see *Stuffings* in Index. Retruss.
(3) Drain liquid from cherries into a cup or jug. Pour a little of the liquid over the duck and place in roasting pan. Add fat, putting some on the breast. Cover breast with 3 of the rashers.
(4) Roast duck at the high heat for 10 minutes, then reduce to 325° or No. 3. Allow about 2 hours, or longer if necessary.
(5) If potatoes are to be roasted, peel and boil them in salted water for 3 minutes, then drain and place around the duck. Baste with the fat.
(6) Make a sauce with the Maraschino syrup thus: melt 2 level tablesp. butter then stir in 2 level tablesp. flour and cook without browning for 2 minutes. Mix the syrup with enough water to make $\frac{3}{4}$ pint (1½ cups) and stir in. Cook and stir until thick and smooth. Add the cherries and sherry. Serve in a sauceboat. To serve, arrange the bacon rolls around the bird with bunches of watercress.

Lemon Cream Russe

Serves 6

2 large or 3 small lemons
6 oz. castor sugar
3 eggs, separated
½ pint double cream
Sponge fingers
White wine or pale sherry
Crystallized violets if desired

(1) Zest the rind of the lemons into a pan. Add juice and sugar. Begin to cook.
(2) When boiling, remove from heat. Separate yolks and whites, dropping whites into a bowl and the yolks into the lemon, which must be off the boil. Whisk well.
(3) Beat the whites with a pinch of salt until very stiff. Beat the cream until thick.
(4) Dip sponge fingers quickly into wine or sherry and place around a glass serving dish.
(5) Add cream to lemon, then egg whites. Pour into serving dish. Chill before serving. May be decorated with crystallized violets.

Citizen's Food

A Tale of Two Cities

In the St. Antoine suburb of Paris in the year 1775, a large cask of wine bumbled out of a cart and spilt its contents out on to the uneven stones of the street. It then lay, shattered like a walnut shell, at the door of the wine shop of Citizen and Citizeness Defarge.

All the people within reach had run to the spot; some men kneeled down, made scoops of their hands joined, and sipped, or tried to help women who bent over their shoulders to sip the red wine before it had run out between their fingers. Men and women, dipped in the puddles with little mugs of mutilated earthenware, or even with handkerchiefs from women's heads, which were squeezed dry into infants' mouths; others devoted themselves to the sodden and lee-dyed pieces of the cask, licking and even champing the moister wine-rotted fragments with eager relish.

There was an inclination on the part of everyone to join some other one which led to frolicsome embraces, drinking of healths, shaking of hands and even joining of hands and dancing. When all the wine was gone a gloom gathered on the scene that appeared more natural to it than the sunshine. One tall joker, besmirched with wine, his head more out of a squalid bag of a nightcap than in it, scrawled upon the wall with his finger in the muddy wine-lees . . . BLOOD.

Cold, dirt, sickness, ignorance and want settled back into gloom upon St. Antoine. The children had ancient faces and grave voices. The sign Hunger was prevalent everywhere. Hunger was pushed out of the tall houses in the wretched clothing that hung upon poles and lines. Hunger was patched into them with straw and rag and wood and paper. Hunger stared down from the smokeless chimneys; and started up from the filthy street that had no offal among its refuse, of anything to eat. Hunger was the inscription on the baker's shelves, written on every small loaf of his scanty stock of bad bread; at the sausage shop in every dead dog preparation that was offered for sale. Hunger rattled its dry bones among the roasting chestnuts in the turned cylinder. Hunger was shred into atoms in every farthing porringer of husky chips of potato, fried with some reluctant drops of oil. Nothing was in a flourishing condition save tools and weapons; the cutler's knives and axes were sharpened bright, the smiths' hammers were heavy, and the gunmakers' stock was murderous.

"A Gipsy Sort of Cold Dinner"

Office of *Household Words*, July 22nd, 1851

DICKENS was again indulging in his precious theatricals and the dinner was a half-past-three affair to be held at his office. The invitation was to Frank Stone and it read: "Lemon and his wife are coming here, after rehearsal, to a gipsy sort of cold dinner. Time, half past three. Viands, pickled salmon and cold pigeon pie. Occupation afterwards, lying on the carpet as a preparation for histrionic strength"! Did Dickens nip out and buy the "viands" himself?

The rehearsal was for another performance of Bulwer Lytton's play, *Not So Bad As We Seem*, written first for a theatrical evening in aid of the Guild of Literature. It was performed in the presence of Queen Victoria and the Prince Consort in the Piccadilly home of the Duke of Devonshire, the Patron of the Guild. Dickens produced it and played an important part, and his friends Lemon, Augustus Egg, Frank Stone, Wilkie Collins, John Forster and others were also in the cast. The women's parts were played by professional actresses, notably Mrs. Henry Compton. The play was repeated several times during the year, both in London and in other parts of the country and the fund benefited to the tune of £4000.

While Dickens was thus engaged in London, his family were at Broadstairs. Devonshire Terrace had become such a house of sorrow after the death of little Dora that Dickens had moved Kate, Georgina and the children down for the whole summer. Here Kate gradually picked up after her serious illness, though she was never again able to regain complete physical and nervous health.

Often she was forced to allow Georgina to act as hostess and chatelaine in her home. It must have been galling for her to see her sister, strong and calm, not only playing the part that should have been hers, but also replacing her at her husband's side on his evening outings. For Georgina, worshipping her famous brother-in-law, it must have been even more galling to realize that his affection for her was never to go beyond the brotherly sort. One day when they were out walking together, Charles felt it his duty to reveal this fact. Had she accepted it and moved to an establishment of her own, things might have been very different for the future of Charles and Kate. But she knew that there was another satisfactory role to play and she made up her mind to play it. (It proved to be equally mischievous.)

COLD "VIANDS"

Galantine of Veal
Radiance Salad
Shrimp and Avocado in Tomato Ring
Chicken Salad Mould
Decorative Tomato Cubes
Chilled Wine Punch

Galantine of Veal   *Serves 8–10*

1 knuckle of veal
2 lb. stewing veal
¼ lb. ham
2 large onions
1 pint water
1 tablesp. lemon juice
1 bay leaf
2 teasp. sugar
1½ teasp. salt and a little pepper
½ teasp. thyme

(1) Put knuckle into large pan with water. Boil, covered, for half an hour.
(2) Trim stewing veal and cut into 1-inch cubes. Peel and chop onions. Add these to the knuckle after the half hour.
(3) Cut up ham and add. Add also the lemon juice, sugar, seasoning, thyme, and bay leaf.
(4) Simmer, still covered, for 1½ hours.
(5) Lift out knuckle and remove any meat still clinging. Add to the rest. Take out bay leaf. Taste and check seasoning.
(6) Tip into a mould or tin, any shape. When set, turn out. The top could be decorated with sliced hard-boiled eggs.

Radiance Salad

1 large lettuce
2 handfuls of watercress
Chopped raw spinach (any amount you fancy)
3 tablesp. chopped chives
2 grated carrots
1 cup grated cheese
1 cup cooked green peas
Tomato cubes for decoration (see next page)
Mayonnaise or French dressing

(1) The bowl may be rubbed with a cut clove of garlic, and lined with lettuce leaves (or be left unlined).
(2) Tear lettuce into penny-sized pieces and drop into salad bowl.
(3) Add chopped watercress, spinach, chives, carrot, cheese and peas. Sprinkle with salt and pepper and a little sugar.
(4) Mix gently, then decorate with the cubes. Serve mayonnaise or dressing separately.

Shrimp and Avocado in Tomato Ring

Serves 10

1¼ pints (2½ cups) tomato purée or peeled mashed tomatoes
½ pint water
2 tablesp. lemon juice
2 level tablesp. sugar
1 level teasp. salt and a little pepper
Bouquet garni
2 packets (2 level tablesp.) powdered gelatine
3 avocado pears
8 oz. cooked shrimps
2 tablesp. lemon juice
¼ pint whipping cream
1 level tablesp. sugar
Parsley

(1) Heat 1 cup of the tomato with the lemon, sugar and bouquet garni.
(2) Mix gelatine with 4 tablesp. cold water and stir in. Allow to dissolve thoroughly. Remove from heat. Lift out bouquet.
(3) Add the rest of the tomato and the water. Tip into a ring mould (about 2 pint size). Put away until firm, then dip into hot water for a few seconds and turn out.
(4) Peel and cut up the avocados. Sprinkle with the lemon juice and sugar. Allow sugar to dissolve.
(5) Whip the cream until stiff and fold in to the avocado.
(6) Spoon this into the centre and around the ring. Decorate with the shrimps and parsley.

Chicken Salad Mould

Serves 6–8

½ pint (1 cup) water
1 lb. cooked chicken, minced or cut small
1 packet aspic jelly (enough to set ½ pint)
2 oz. sliced blanched almonds
1 or more cups finely chopped celery
1 packet (small) frozen green beans, or fresh green beans
1 grated carrot
Salt and pepper

(1) Heat the water and add the celery, beans and carrot. Boil for no more than 6–8 minutes.
(2) Add the aspic and allow to dissolve. Remove from heat.
(3) Add the chicken and almonds. Season well. A little garlic salt, onion salt or celery salt (or all three) may be added.
(4) Allow to cool to lukewarm, then tip into mould.
(5) When firm, dip into hot water for a few seconds, then turn out.

Decorative Tomato Cubes. Use all the ingredients for the Tomato Ring down to the powdered gelatine. Half quantity might be sufficient, but if you make the whole quantity, it could be stored in the refrigerator and used for many salads. Combine the ingredients then pour into a square or oblong shallow cake pan. When set, cut into ½-inch cubes and use to decorate a salad.

Wine Punch, chilled. Combine 1 bottle white wine with half the quantity of soda, the juice of 2 or 3 oranges, or canned frozen orange juice, the juice of 1 lemon and 2 or 3 tablesp. sugar. Add several sprigs of mint and chill before serving.

Worker's Food

The Uncommercial Traveller

THE American Civil War advanced the comfort of the British workers first in Glasgow, then Manchester and in Whitechapel, London. Dickens made a point of investigating the arrangements for food for the workers in America.

Within a little window, like a pay box at a theatre, a neat and brisk young woman presided to take money and issue tickets. Everyone must take a ticket. Either the fourpence halfpenny ticket for the upper room, or a penny ticket for a bowl of soup, or as many penny tickets as he or she chose to buy. For three penny tickets one had a plate of cold boiled beef and potatoes; or a plate of cold ham and potatoes; or a plate of hot minced beef and potatoes; or a bowl of soup, bread and cheese, and a plate of plum pudding. Some postponed decision, but the choice of the boys was as rapid as their execution, and always included pudding.

Nothing to eat was touched by hand. As soon as a waitress saw a new customer at her own table in the upper room, she took all his dinner, soup, potatoes, meat, pudding piled up dexterously and set it before him and took his ticket. This method greatly simplified the business of attendance and enabled the customers to vary the routine of dishes; beginning with soup today, putting soup in the middle tomorrow, putting soup at the end the day after tomorrow, and ringing similar changes on meat and pudding.

The rapidity with which the waitresses discharged their duties was as agreeable to see, as the neat smartness with which they wore their dress and had dressed their hair. If I seldom saw better waiting, so I certainly never ate better meat, potatoes and pudding. The soup was an honest, stout soup with rice and barley in it. The dinner service too was neither conspicuously hideous for High Art, nor for Low Art, but was of a pleasant, pure appearance.

There is an absence of beer, showing some distrust of the working man, because anyone at all experienced in such things knows that the drunken workman does not get drunk where he goes to eat and drink, but where he goes to drink, expressly to drink.

I dined at my Pall Mall Club a few days afterwards for exactly twelve times the money, and not half as well.

"*Dinner at $\frac{1}{2}$ past 5*"

Fort House, Broadstairs, September 12th, 1851

WITH the lease of Devonshire Terrace falling due in the autumn, Charles had earlier in the year decided to take a house in Tavistock Square, Bloomsbury, occupied by their friends Mr. and Mrs. Frank Stone. He had been in London for several days attending to his periodical *Household Words* and arranging for alterations to the new house, and from his office at 16 Wellington Street, Strand, he wrote reassuringly to Kate about their choice. "Of the bow window in the drawing room, and of the general air of the room, I cannot speak in terms of sufficient praise," he said. "I almost begin to doubt whether the back room on the second floor which we once intended for Mamey and Katey will not be the best room for us. . . . I think it will be best for you in a week or so to come up with me for a few hours and choose the paperings."

Apparently the Stones had just moved out and had left rather a mess. Towards the end of the same letter Charles wrote: "Think of all the broken birdcages in the world, sticking in all the broken chairs, with their legs uppermost—and you will have a faint idea of their 'moving'—not including the dust." He ended the letter by letting her know that Sir Thomas Talfourd was coming down with him and asking her to "bring the little carriage to meet the cheap express. Dinner at $\frac{1}{2}$ past 5."

It is to be hoped that the learned Talfourd was an enthusiastic walker. Dickens expected his guests to leap up after lunch and step out with him on a brisk twenty-mile walk (even though one of Kate's menus may have induced a preference for a lazy post-prandial snooze). This completed, they would then have to be ready for games, bathing, and in the evening, strenuous dancing!

Later this year, in early October, Dickens was the guest for a few days of the Duke of Devonshire at his magnificent seat, Chatsworth. As usual he kept Kate well posted with all his doings. Indeed many wives would envy the devotion of a husband who when away began writing the first night of his arrival, no matter how late the hour, and went on, sometimes daily, until he was able, joyfully, to announce his return to her and the children. Writing from Chatsworth before going to bed he had to tell her of the grandeur of the accommodation. "I am now in a state bedchamber of enormous dimensions with a bedstead like a brocaded and golden Temple," he wrote, "without the slightest idea of anything beyond me but corridors and staircases innumerable."

Then in a postscript added the next day he said, ". . . this place is the most wonderful thing in the world. . . ."

A KATE DICKENS MENU	A MODERN MENU
(4–5 persons)	(4 or more people)
Fried Oysters (p. 79)	*White Soup*
Rump Steak à la Soyer	*Hot Calves Tongue with Cumberland Sauce*
French Beans. Potato Balls	*Potato Balls. Green Vegetable*
Salad	*Side Salads (p. 201)*
Pound Pudding (p. 200)	*Strawberry or Peach Flan*
	Chartreuse
Toasted Cheese (p. 40)	*Biscuits and Cheeses*

White Soup (Victorian Recipe)

Serves 6–8

2 level tablesp. butter
2 large onions
2 or 3 leeks
6 or more sticks of celery
1 lb. potatoes
Several sprigs of parsley
1 bay leaf
3 pints (6 cups) water
½ pint milk or cream or half and half
Salt and pepper

(1) Melt butter. Add peeled chopped onions and cook for 2 minutes without browning.
(2) Add washed sliced leeks, washed chopped celery and fry for another 2 minutes.
(3) Add water, then peeled halved potatoes, parsley and bay leaf.
(4) Cover and simmer for about ¾ hour or until all the vegetables are soft. Season well with salt and pepper.
(5) Strain through a colander, mashing as much vegetable through as possible.
(6) Return to pan and add milk or cream. Check for seasoning and serve hot.

Rump Steak à la Soyer
(a Kate Dickens's Recipe)

Rump to be boiled, dressed with seasoned flour (pepper, salt, cayenne). Chop a shallot and put into stewpan with a little ketchup. When steak is sufficiently done add a little butter to it. Strain sauce.

Potato Balls
(a Kate Dickens's Recipe)

Mash potatoes, make into balls, brush with yolk of egg and put in oven or before fire to brown. Grated ham or tongue may be added.

Calves Tongue with Cumberland Sauce

1 or 2 calves tongues
Water
1 tablesp. vinegar
3 cloves
Bay leaf
1 onion, any size
½ teasp. dried or 1 teasp. fresh sage
1 level tablesp. sugar
Cumberland sauce, below
For ox tongue allow about 4–4½ hrs.

(1) Soak tongue for a few hours or overnight and throw off the water.
(2) Add 3 cups fresh water, also the vinegar, cloves, bay leaf, onion, peeled and quartered, the sage and sugar.
(3) Cover and simmer for about 3 hours, or until skin will come off easily.
(4) To serve slip off skin and remove the little bones. Either pour the sauce over, or serve it separately.
The tongue may be pressed and served cold.

Cumberland Sauce

1 tablesp. marmalade
1 tablesp. redcurrant jelly
¼ pint cream or evaporated milk
1 beef cube or 2 teasp. soy sauce
3 or 4 tablesp. red wine or sherry

(1) Stir the marmalade, jelly, and beef cube or soy sauce into the cream or milk.
(2) Heat, beating well.
Delicious also with ham or bacon.

Strawberry or Peach Flan Chartreuse   *Serves 4–6*

1 sponge flan
½ lb. or more strawberries or the same of sliced peaches
2 level tablesp. sugar for ½ lb. strawberries. For the peaches add less if canned
3 tablesp. Chartreuse
¼ pint or more whipping cream

(1) If it is to be strawberries, hull and halve them and place in a bowl. Add sugar and 2 tablesp. of the Chartreuse. Allow to stand until sugar has melted and a syrup has formed. Do the same if it is to be peaches.
(2) Pour the syrup over the sponge to soak it slightly.
(3) Pile the fruit in the flan.
(4) Beat the cream until stiff, then stir in the rest of the Chartreuse. Place on top of the fruit.

Food Afloat

Sketches by Boz

To Londoners a day out on the River Thames has always held a great attraction. Such an occasion forms the basis of the sketch, "A Steam Excursion".

Mr. Percy Noakes, a Law student, was generally termed, "a devilish good fellow" and twenty of his acquaintances gladly agreed to join in a day's excursion under his direction.

"The boat will start from the Customs House in Lower Thames Street, go down to the Nore lightship at the mouth of the river, round it and return," said Mr. Noakes. "We shall have a capital cold dinner laid out in the cabin before we start and we shall have lunch laid out on deck by the paddle boxes. We shall hire a steamer expressly for our party and a Bard and have the deck chalked and dance quadrilles all day."

These predictions duly took place, but when they put about to return, the wind which had been with them the whole day, was now directly in their teeth. The rain began pouring in good earnest, the wind was freshening fast and the waterman at the wheel expressed his opinion that there would shortly be a squall. The party repaired to the cabin and sat down to dinner, but the storm was violent. A substantial cold boiled leg of mutton shaking like a blancmange; a previously hearty sirloin of beef suddenly seized with the palsy; and some tongues darting from side to side and end to end of too large plates. The sweets shook and trembled; and the pigeon pie looked as if the birds, whose legs were stuck outside, were trying to get them in. Ominous demands were made for small glasses of brandy; the countenances of the company underwent most extraordinary changes; one gentleman rushed suddenly from the table without the slightest ostensible reason. The rest soon gave up all disguise and staggered on deck, muffled in shawls and cloaks and lay about on the seats and under the seats in the most wretched condition.

Never was such a blowing and raining and pitching and tossing endured by any pleasure party before, and they arrived off the Custom House at about two o'clock in the morning, dispirited and worn out. All save Mr. Percy Noakes who was as lighthearted and careless as ever.

A New Year's Eve Dinner

Tavistock House, December 31st, 1851

ICKENS and his family moved into Tavistock House at the end of October. As usual Dickens found the upheaval distracting and in a letter to Miss Burdett-Coutts he let off steam. "I have no news," he wrote, "except that I am three parts' distracted and the fourth part wretched in the agonies of getting into a new house—pending which desirable consummation of my troubles, I *can not* work at my new book— having all my notions of order turned completely topsy-turvy." The next letter, written on November 17th, indicated that the move had been made. "We are beginning to settle in to our new house," he said, "and I am beginning to find my papers and to know where the pen and ink are."

His exclusive use of a pen is mentioned by Charley, "My father always wrote with a quill pen and blue ink", he wrote, "and never with a lead pencil. His manuscripts were written upon white 'slips', though sometimes on blue paper. On the shelf of his writing table were many dainty and useful ornaments; gifts from his friends or members of the family, and always a vase of bright fresh flowers." (See picture on p. 81.)

This New Year's Eve dinner was held at 6.15 p.m. and afterwards the evening passed gaily with games, acting and dancing. We know that amongst the guests was a clever and charming amateur actress called Mary Boyle. Kate and Charles had met her at Rockingham Castle, the palatial home of their friends Mr. and Mrs. Watson. She had acted there with Charles, and his help and encouragement made her his slave for ever afterwards. In later years when he began his public readings, Mary always made sure that a buttonhole would be sent to him before every performance.

Theatricals for children and grown-ups were continually being held at Tavistock House and for the rehearsals as well as the performances Kate was faced with the task of feeding hoards of people on numerous occasions. Indeed the butcher was so astonished at the size and number of joints he was continually delivering that he thought it his duty to mention it to her in case there had been some mistake. Confirming the need for so much food, Charley wrote: "We played to an audience of ninety for three nights at home. At the first supper for the performers and guests, Lord Campbell declared that he would rather have written *Pickwick* than be Lord Chief Justice of England." Lord Campbell was, in fact, Lord Chief Justice of England! He was also a famous law re- former and author of many important works on questions of law.

A KATE DICKENS MENU
(18–20 persons)

Pea Soup (p. 143)

Broiled Salmon.   Turbot
Lobster Sauce (p. 55)
Cucumbers

Mushroom Patties (p. 107)
Lamb's Fry (p. 179)
Lobster Curry (see Salmon Curry, p. 28)
Rissoles
Roast Saddle of Mutton
(see Roast Lamb, p. 19)
Mayonnaise of Chicken
Broccoli. New Potatoes.   Peas
Roast Duck (p. 116)

Pudding.   Clear Jelly   Italian Cream

Macaroni Cheese (p. 104)
Brunswick Sausage

A MODERN NEW YEAR'S EVE BUFFET SUPPER
(Any number)

Oyster Patties
Lobster Cutlets with a Green Salad (see Index)
Turbot with Asparagus Sauce and
Garnished with Smelts
Peas.   Scalloped Potatoes (p. 16)
Curry and Rice

English Apple Pie with Ice-cream
Strawberries Romanoff (p. 68)

Cheese Straws (p. 108)

Oyster Patties
Makes 12

1 doz. 1½-inch puff pastry vol-au-vent cases (may be ordered from the pastrycook)
24 oysters
1 pint white sauce flavoured with 1 tablesp. anchovy sauce and chopped parsley

(1) Beard and halve the oysters.
(2) Add to the hot sauce. Do not reheat at this stage.
(3) Fill cases. Reheat just before serving.

Lobster Cutlets (Victorian Recipe)
Makes 12 or more

1 hen lobster
2 level tablesp. butter
3 level tablesp. flour
½ pint (1 cup) milk
Salt and a little cayenne pepper
¼ cup oil for frying
1 beaten egg
Fine dry breadcrumbs

(1) Remove flesh from lobster and cut into small pieces. Pound spawn (if any) with 1 tablesp. butter.
(2) Make sauce by melting butter, then adding flour. Cook for 2 minutes then whisk in the milk. Add salt and a few grains of cayenne pepper.
(3) Add lobster and spawn. Mix well then spread on a large plate and leave until cold. Heat oil.
(4) Form into flat patties, dip in the beaten egg, then in breadcrumbs and fry in the hot oil.

Turbot with Asparagus Sauce and Smelts   *Serves 6*

2–3 lb. turbot (depending on size
  of helpings)
Water and wine
Bay leaf
Salt and pepper, sugar
Packet asparagus soup
Smelts (below)

Asparagus Sauce
See Step 2

(1) Have turbot skinned and boned. Cut
into serving portions and poach in about
$\frac{1}{4}$ cup water or water and wine. Add a
bay leaf and salt and pepper. Cook
covered.
(2) Make a sauce by mixing $2\frac{1}{2}$ tablesp.
asparagus soup powder with 1 cup milk
or milk and cream. Boil until a good
thick consistency. Add 2 level teasp.
sugar.
(3) Tip liquid from turbot into sauce. Serve
turbot with sauce poured over. Garnish
with lemon wedges and parsley, and
surround with fried smelts.

Fried Smelts. Wash and dry smelts. Heat oil. Dip smelts first in flour, then in
beaten egg, then in fine dry breadcrumbs. Fry in the hot oil. It should be quite still
with a faint white mist rising (375° F).

Curry and Rice   *Serves 6–7*

2 lb. stewing steak
4 rashers of streaky bacon
2 level tablesp. flour
3 large onions, peeled and chopped
1 level tablesp. curry powder or
  paste, or more if you wish
$\frac{3}{4}$ pint ($1\frac{1}{2}$ cups) water
2 peeled chopped eating apples
1 cup sultanas
Salt and pepper

(1) Cut meat into $\frac{1}{2}$-inch cubes.
(2) Remove rinds from bacon. Cut into
1-inch pieces and fry in a large pan.
(3) Add chopped onions, then meat coated
in flour. Fry together for about 5 minutes,
browning well. Add curry powder.
(4) Add water, then apples and sultanas.
Season well with salt and pepper.
(5) Simmer, covered, for 2 or more hours,
or put into ovenware dish and allow $2\frac{1}{2}$
hours slow cooking. Cook longer if shin
meat is used. *Pressure cooking time:* 30
minutes.
Add more water during cooking if necessary.

Boiled Rice. Allow 4 times as much water as rice. Cook for about 15 minutes or
until just soft, but not too soft. Rinse through a strainer. Add salt.

English Apple Pie

$\frac{1}{2}$ lb. short or puff pastry
$1\frac{1}{2}$–2 lb. apples
3 tablesp. sugar per pound of apples
Lemon juice and water

(1) Peel and slice apples and drop into a
deep pie dish.
(2) Preheat oven to 375° or No. 5.
(3) To the apples add the sugar, 2 tablesp.
lemon juice and $\frac{1}{2}$ cup ($\frac{1}{4}$ pint) water.
(4) Wet edge of pie dish. Roll out pastry.
Put pie funnel or funnels in pie dish. Fit
pastry over loosely. Do not stretch. Neaten
edge. Put a 1-inch strip around rim. Decorate. Make 2 slits in pastry. Bake for
$\frac{3}{4}$–1 hour. Pastry may be brushed with
beaten egg or top milk before baking.

Three of Dickens's cheques

A Cookbook—and the Last Christening

Tavistock House, Late March, 1852

NOT until it was almost finished did Charles discover the secret of the cookbook. When Kate bravely made her confession he was delighted and astonished at her initiative and teased her for stealing his thunder and becoming a rival author! No one could doubt that it was he who had thought up the nom de plume, Lady Maria Clutterbuck, wife of Sir Jonas Clutterbuck. Could anything be more Dickensian?

During the months of inactivity forced upon her by two difficult pregnancies, Kate had been diligently copying from her "Commonplace Book" all the Menus she had used since she began giving dinner parties at Furnival's Inn, together with some of the recipes. The book, *What Shall We Have for Dinner?* was published by Bradbury and Evans and had good notices, but it was many years before it was universally known that it was a gastronomic revelation of the Dickens dinner table.

When in her introduction, Kate explained that "Sir Jonas" was not a gourmand, although a man of great gastronomical knowledge, she was doubtless thinking of Charles. His descriptions of the meals eaten by his characters might lead one to believe that he was himself a large eater. But this was not so. His son Charley wrote of his father's food habits and said, "I wonder for how many years his breakfast consisted of a rasher of broiled ham; how many dinners were begun with a glass of Chichester milk punch; how many were finished with a dish of toasted cheese; for he was conservative in his personal arrangements." Mamie, too, writing on the same subject said, "I think that no more abstemious man ever lived."

Kate's tenth and last baby was born on March 13th and at the Christening acquired the names of another of their close friends, Edward Bulwer Lytton. Neither Charles nor Kate had been pleased when the pregnancy began, but as so often happens, the little boy wound his way into their hearts and became the favourite of them all.

The record of the Menus had ended, but the entertaining went on. Their circle continued to widen and included many more famous Victorians, many still well known today. Tavistock House rang with the fun of amateur theatricals and dancing, with Dickens still the gayest and most dedicated of them all. For the next eighteen years his life was packed with change, events and triumphs and when he died on June 9th, 1870 all the world mourned its loss. In his will he had asked to be buried in a Kentish country churchyard, but the Nation decided that so great an Englishman should be given a fitting burial in Westminster Abbey. He lies there in Poet's Corner.

A KATE DICKENS MENU

(8–10 persons)

Spring Soup
Oxtail Soup (p. 51)

Salmon with Lobster Sauce (p. 55)
Mackerel à la Maître d'Hôtel
Soles.   Potatoes

Two Boiled Spring Chickens
Asparagus Sauce (p. 196)
Lobster Curry.   Sweetbreads (p. 52)
Forequarter of Lamb (p. 19)
Tongue.   Veal Olives
Oyster Patties (p. 195)
Two Ducklings (p. 116)
Peas.   New Potatoes.   Asparagus

Lemon Jelly
Strawberry Cream.   Marble Cream

Toasted Cheese (p. 40)

A MODERN MENU

(6 or more people)

Spring Vegetable Soup (Packet)

Baked Stuffed Haddock

Roasted Pheasants with Trimmings
or
Veal Olives
Potatoes.   Green Vegetables
Celery and Beetroot Side Salads (p. 201)

Pound Pudding
Orange or Apple Fritters with Cream
or
Baked Alaska

Biscuits and Cheeses

Baked Stuffed Haddock   *Serves 6*

2 haddocks
Thyme and parsley stuffing
1 beaten egg
Butter or margarine
Salt and pepper

(1) Have fish cleaned and scaled. Wash.
(2) Make stuffing and fill fish. Secure with thread.
(3) Brush with the egg, then coat with the breadcrumbs. Sprinkle with salt and pepper.
(4) Put into baking dish with 2 tablesp. butter or margarine. Bake in oven at 350° or No. 4, for 30–40 minutes.

Veal Olives   *Serves 6*

12 very thin slices of veal
12 thin slices of ham
Thyme and parsley stuffing
2 tablesp. oil or butter
1 medium-sized onion
2 level tablesp. flour
¾ pint (1½ cups) water with
  1 chicken cube
Wine or sherry may replace some of
  the water
Seasoning

(1) Preheat oven to 300° or No. 2½.
(2) Place ham on slices of veal and add about 1 tablesp. of the stuffing. Roll up and secure with thread or tiny skewers.
(3) Heat oil or butter and fry the rolls until lightly browned. Remove to a plate.
(4) Add another tablesp. oil or butter to the pan. Peel and chop the onions and add. Fry for 2 minutes then add flour and continue frying for another minute. Add water and chicken cube and season well. Cook until thick. Add wine if desired.
(5) Put rolls and gravy into casserole dish. Cover and cook for about 1½ hours.

Roasted Pheasant

1 plucked and drawn pheasant
$\frac{1}{4}$ lb. beef
3 bacon rashers (fat)
2 tablesp. fat

(1) Preheat oven to 350° or No. 4.
(2) Put the piece of steak inside the bird. Cover breast with the bacon. Truss.
(3) Put into roasting dish with fat. Allow about 1 hour. Baste once. Remove bacon and allow to brown for the last 20 minutes.

Serve with game chips, buttered breadcrumbs, Bread Sauce (p. 55) and gravy. Bacon Rolls (p. 184) may also be arranged around the dish.

Pound Pudding (Victorian Recipe)   *Serves 10–12*

1 lb. shredded suet
1 lb. each of currants and sultanas, or raisins
$\frac{1}{2}$ lb. each of breadcrumbs and S.R. flour
1 teasp. ground ginger and $\frac{1}{2}$ teasp. nutmeg
$\frac{1}{2}$ teasp. salt
$\frac{1}{2}$ pint (1 cup) milk
4 eggs

(1) Have a large pan one-third filled with water. Bring to the boil.
(2) In a mixing bowl combine the suet, fruit, breadcrumbs, flour, ginger and nutmeg. Add $\frac{1}{2}$ teasp. salt.
(3) Beat eggs and add, with the milk. Mix well.
(4) Put into greased pudding bowl, or bowls and cover with a cloth. Today we might as well use our trusty foil. See that it is sealed well. Allow room for rising.
(5) Boil for about $3\frac{1}{2}$–4 hours.

Orange or Apple Fritters

Packet pancake-mix, or make your own with your usual pancake recipe.
Orange slices, or apple rings
$\frac{1}{2}$ cup oil, or $\frac{1}{4}$ lb. lard

(1) When making the pancake batter, do not have it quite as thin as for pancakes. Add a little sugar.
(2) Peel oranges and cut into pith-free slices. Core, peel, and slice apple into rings.
(3) Have oil or lard very hot—until it is very still and a faint haze is rising (about 375°F).
(4) Dip fruit into batter and fry until golden brown. Dust with icing sugar.

[200]

Baked Alaska

1 oblong piece of sponge cake
Fruit and syrup
Sherry
Ice-cream
White of 3 eggs and 4 good tablesp.
   sugar

(1) Preheat oven to 450° or No. 9.
(2) Put cake on to flat dish. Pour a little fruit syrup and sherry over it.
(3) Put a block of ice cream on top, slightly smaller in size. Arrange some fresh or canned sliced fruit on top.
(4) Beat whites and sugar until stiff and cover ice-cream and cake thoroughly. Bake for 4 minutes only in the hot oven. Serve at once with cream.

Marble Cream (Victorian Recipe)   *Serves 4–6*

2 oz. (4 level tablesp.) cornflour
1 pint (2 cups) milk
4 level tablesp. sugar
1 bay leaf
1 teasp. coffee essence
A little green, yellow and red
   colouring

(1) Heat milk with sugar and bay leaf. Mix cornflour with 2 tablesp. milk and stir in. Cook and stir until thick. Lower heat and continue cooking and stirring for another 4 minutes.
(2) Put into 4 bowls. Colour one light brown with the coffee and the others with the other colourings.
(3) Put all three coloured mixtures into a mould and stir once or twice to give a marbled effect. Put away until cold. Turn out.

Strawberry Cream (Victorian Recipe)   *Serves 6*

1 lb. strawberries
½ pint (1 cup) cream
5 oz. (5 rounded tablesp.) castor
   sugar
1 packet of powdered gelatine
   (1 level tablesp.)
2 egg whites

(1) Hull and mash strawberries, or squash in electric blender.
(2) Add sugar and allow to dissolve.
(3) Dissolve gelatine in 2 tablesp. boiling water and when every grain has disappeared, stir into the strawberry purée. Leave until showing signs of setting.
(4) Whip cream until thick and stir in.
(5) Lastly, whip eggs until as stiff as possible and fold in.
(6) Pour into serving dish and allow to set.

Side Salads

These are individual salads on small individual dishes put at the side of each placing and eaten either with or just after the main course.

Celery and Beetroot Salad

Combine equal quantities of finely chopped celery and sliced beetroot. Sprinkle with equal quantities of vinegar and sugar. Chopped mint or parsley may be added.

Mock Turtle Soup (**Victorian Recipe**) *Serves 8*

2 rounded tablesp. butter
1 large onion, chopped
3 oz. chopped bacon
2 rounded tablesp. flour
½ tin calf's head
4 sticks of celery, cut up
Bouquet garni
5 pints of stock or water with
  2 meat cubes
salt and pepper
3 glasses of sherry
Forcemeat Balls
Use Forcemeat Stuffing (page
  131), form into balls, roll in
  flour and fry until lightly
  browned.

(1) Melt butter in large saucepan, and add onion and bacon. Cook for 5 minutes, then add flour. Cook until browned.
(2) Drain liquid from tin and add to water. Pour into pan and cook and stir until lightly thickened. Add celery.
(3) Season well, then cover and simmer until vegetables are soft.
(4) Meanwhile cut meat into tiny pieces.
(5) Skim, then pass through a sieve, mashing through the vegetable.
(6) Tip back into pan and lastly add sherry and pieces of meat. Reheat. Serve with Forcemeat Balls

Caramel Custards *Serves 6*

2 oz. cube sugar
2 tablesp. water
2 large eggs
¾ pint (1½ cups) milk
1 teasp. vanilla essence
½ teasp. salt
3 teasp. castor sugar

(1) Preheat oven to 350° or No. 4.
(2) Cook cube sugar and water until browned in a heavy-bottomed pan.
(3) Grease 6 small oven proof moulds and pour a little of the caramel into each, using it all up.
(4) Heat milk with vanilla and salt. Remove from heat.
(5) Beat eggs with castor sugar and stir in. Pour into moulds.
(6) Cover each with foil. Put 1 cup water into baking dish. Place moulds in dish and bake for about 15–20 minutes.

Lobster Salad (**Victorian Recipe**) *Serves 6*

1 hen lobster
1 large lettuce
2 hard-boiled eggs
2 sticks finely chopped celery
4 tablesp. mayonnaise
2 teasp. anchovy sauce
3 inches of cucumber peeled and
  sliced
Chopped parsley

(1) Remove flesh from lobster body and claws. Cut into pieces.
(2) Remove outer leaves from lettuce and tear the heart into small pieces.
(3) Place torn lettuce in salad bowl and add eggs, celery and mayonnaise mixed with the anchovy. Mix then add the lobster.
(4) Put whole leaves on to individual plate. Pile some of the salad into each. Garnish around with the cucumber and sprinkle with parsley.

Charitable Food

DICKENS set the scene for these stories in a Charitable Shelter for six homeless souls, paying fourpence each for a night's poor lodging. As the seventh traveller, he provided a Christmas Eve dinner, after which each person told a tale of his own choosing.

I went back to my Inn from Watt's Charity to give directions for the Turkey and Beef, and could settle to nothing for thinking of the poor travellers advancing on their resting place along various cold roads. Upon the stroke of nine I set out for the Charity, carrying my brown pitcher of Wassail in my arms. Following me in procession came;

Ben with the Beer
Inattentive Boy with hot plates
Second inattentive Boy with hot plates
The Turkey
Female carrying sauces to be heated on the spot
The Beef
Man with tray on his head, containing Vegetables and sundries.
Volunteer Hostler from the Hotel, grinning and
rendering no assistance.

We passed along the High street comet-like, and left a trail of fragrance behind us which caused the public to stop, sniffing in wonder. So soon as the wall-eyed young man we had left in the yard should hear the railway whistle, always carried by Ben, he was to dash into the Inn kitchen seize the hot plum-pudding and mince pies, and speed with them to Watts Charity, where they would be received by the sauce female, who would be provided with brandy in a blue state of combustion.

All these arrangements were executed in the most exact and punctual manner. I never saw a finer turkey, finer beef, or greater prodigality of sauce and gravy; and my Travellers did wonderful justice to everything set before them. It made my heart rejoice to observe how their wind and frost hardened faces softened in the clatter of plates and knives and forks, and mellowed in the fire and supper heat. While their hats and capes and wrappers, hanging up, a few small bundles on the ground in a corner, and in another corner three or four old walking sticks, worn down at the end to a mere fringe, linked this snug interior with the bleak outside in a golden chain.

Index

[205]